Dec 2022

Louise
ADVENTURE

To Colin,

Great to meet you at Staffordshire University last month.

Hope you enjoy these pages!

Best wishes,

Louise
ADVENTURE

A Round-the-World Sailing Odyssey

Grant Gordon

Front and back cover:
Cape Renard, Antarctic Peninsula

Published by New Generation Publishing in 2021
Copyright © Grant Gordon 2021

First Edition

The author asserts the moral right under the Copyright, Designs and Patents Act 1988 to be identified as the author of this work.

All rights reserved. No part of this publication may be reproduced, stored in a retrieval system or transmitted, in any form or by any means without the prior consent of the author, nor be otherwise circulated in any form of binding or cover other than that which it is published and without a similar condition being imposed on the subsequent purchaser.

Hardback ISBN: 978-1-80031-326-2
Paperback ISBN: 978-1-80031-327-9

www.newgeneration-publishing.com

To Brigitte

For she is the true captain and mate of the *Louise* Adventure

'I am a voyager and a seaman; that is, a liar and a stupid fellow, in the eyes of that class of indolent haughty writers, who in their closets reason in *infinitum* on the world and its inhabitants.'

Louis-Antoine de Bougainville
A Voyage Round the World

Louise Adventure route

Contents

Foreword	xiii
Prologue	xvii
Chapter 1 – In the Trades: Jersey, Channel Islands to Rio de Janeiro, Brazil	1
Chapter 2 – Pampero Country: Angra dos Reis, Brazil to the River Plate and Stanley, Falkland Islands	16
Chapter 3 – The Big South: Stanley, Falkland Islands to South Georgia, Antarctica and Ushuaia, Argentina	36
Chapter 4 – Land of Fire: Ushuaia, Argentina to Puerto Montt, Chile	62
Chapter 5 – The Horse Latitudes: Puerto Montt, Chile to the Marquesas Islands, French Polynesia	87
Chapter 6 – Islands of Paradise: The Marquesas Islands to the Society Islands, French Polynesia and Auckland, New Zealand	112
Chapter 7 – The Race: Sydney to Hobart, Australia	136
Chapter 8 – The South Pacific: Auckland, New Zealand to Fiji and Cairns, Australia	143

Chapter 9 – The Spice Islands: Cairns, Australia to Indonesia and Phuket, Thailand	177
Chapter 10 – Monsoon Run: Phuket, Thailand to Sri Lanka and the Seychelles	208
Chapter 11 – African Shores: The Seychelles to Madagascar and Cape Town, South Africa	231
Chapter 12 – South Atlantic High: Cape Town, South Africa to St Helena and Grenada, Lesser Antilles	260
Chapter 13 – Treasure Islands: Grenada, Lesser Antilles to Bermuda and Halifax, Canada	276
Chapter 14 – Home Waters: Nova Scotia, Canada to St Pierre & Miquelon and Jersey, Channel Islands	296
Acknowledgements	319

Foreword

A voyage begins in the imagination and this one, about an adventure by sea, is no different. I found inspiration from my heroes, the sailors who have made it their goal to navigate the world.

As a boy, my bookshelf at home was full of tales of those who pioneered long voyages across the oceans, including Joshua Slocum, Sir Francis Chichester, Bernard Moitessier and Sir Robin Knox-Johnston. The modern equivalents of these single-handed sailing legends, such as Dame Ellen MacArthur and Michel Desjoyeaux, have used their skill and tenacity to excel in the Vendée Globe Race, the yachting equivalent of a solo trek to the top of Mount Everest.

Other daring ocean sailors have made their names in the Whitbread Round the World Race and its successor, the Volvo Ocean Race. Sir Peter Blake was prominent among this group of adventurers, along with Lawrie Smith and others. These fearless skippers led their crews across the southern oceans, inspiring so many through their courage and determination. Following in their wake, a new generation of intrepid sailors are now able to charge around the world in modern ultra-light racing boats in well under the eighty days described in Jules Verne's famous novel.

My imagination as a young man was also captured by the stories of the great mariners of the Age of Discovery. In 1518, Portuguese explorer Ferdinand Magellan received the backing of the King of Spain to command an expedition to the East Indies, sailing through the Atlantic Ocean to South America and beyond. The voyage, which lasted from

1519 to 1522, became the world's first circumnavigation, though Magellan would not live to bask in the glory of this extraordinary achievement, as in 1521 he was killed in a battle with locals on the island of Mactan in the Philippines. A few years earlier, another Portuguese navigator, Vasco da Gama, discovered the maritime route to India and the East in the name of the Portuguese crown during a 1497–98 expedition, while in 1492 the Genoese explorer Christopher Columbus had reached the shores of islands in the Caribbean.

These trailblazing adventurers all sought their personal fortune and glory. The rival royal courts of Spain and Portugal similarly chased after enrichment, but their leaders were also motivated by religious fervour, wishing to convert the indigenous inhabitants of these newly discovered places to Christianity. The sailors who accompanied these expeditions took their lives in their hands. Many met their graves in the sea or on land, never seeing their loved ones again. The men may have feared what lay undiscovered over the horizon, but the voyages that they embarked upon helped to dispel myths about the Earth and reveal the mysteries of life in distant countries.

In the wake of these early maritime pioneers, other legends followed, such as Sir Francis Drake, whose circumnavigation between 1577 and 1580 revealed the existence of a stretch of ocean off the tip of South America, now named the Drake Passage. While sailing the southern Indian Ocean in 1642, Dutch seafarer Abel Tasman discovered an island off the south-east of mainland Australia, later named Tasmania in his honour. In 1616, fellow Dutchman Willem Schouten gave the name of his home port, Hoorn, to the most feared of headlands located on the southern end of Chile, Cape Horn. Step by step, charts began to show how the continents were shaped, as new shorelines were explored and mapped by keen adventurers who were skilled in cartography.

Expedition leaders who had a military focus such as Afonso de Albuquerque, the Governor of India, emerged, which enabled Portugal to become the first European nation to succeed in achieving its imperial ambitions. But it was not long before the court in Lisbon lost its lead to the Dutch. Established in 1602, the Dutch East India Company, or VOC, would secure a tight grip on the spice trade in the Moluccas of eastern Indonesia. In the quest for riches, the European invaders plundered their way forward and had little time for compromise or leniency with anyone who stood in their way.

During the eighteenth century, the unfolding of the Age of Enlightenment in Europe heralded a time of change when, in addition to colonial powers conquering new territories, seafaring expeditions also started to pursue scientific objectives. This era is epitomised by the much-revered Captain James Cook, a former merchant navy apprentice from Yorkshire, whose three voyages to the Pacific between 1768 and 1780 ended up crowning him in posthumous glory. As an expedition leader, Cook arguably stands above his contemporaries, both in terms of his command of men and navigational skills. French naval officer and explorer the Comte de La Pérouse would continue Cook's pursuits in the Pacific. He conducted wide-ranging explorations from August 1785 until his disappearance in March 1788, when the two French expedition ships in Pérouse's small fleet were wrecked near the island of Vanikoro in the South Pacific's Solomon Islands. By the eighteenth century, England had emerged as ruler of the seas, with France as its main rival.

Of all the great navigators from across the ages, the sailor who most stoked my imagination was Louis-Antoine de Bougainville. A latecomer to the ranks of the trailblazers of oceanic discovery during the Age of Enlightenment, this artful Frenchman was revered by his royal masters, sailors and rivals who were greatly impressed by him. His round-the-world passage from 1766 to 1769 captured the hearts and minds of a whole nation, and his book *Voyage Autour du Monde* (*A Voyage Round the World*), published in 1771, was an instant bestseller. Commissioned by Louis XV, he was the first Frenchman to circumnavigate the globe. His legacy lives on in many of the places he visited, including Papua New Guinea's Bougainville Island, but perhaps most memorably in the species of tropical flower, Bougainvillea.

Bougainville's voyage was the main inspiration for the seafaring exploits described in *Louise Adventure*. Although this quest is carried out under very different circumstances and without the huge risks that early expeditions faced, I hope that readers will enjoy the story that follows, even if I am unable to rise to the literary standards of my hero's epic book.

Prologue

Landing in Düsseldorf after an early-morning flight from Heathrow, my wife Brigitte and I were surprised to bump into Jim Walker, an old friend from the north-east of Scotland. We started chatting and soon discovered that Jim was on his way back home after attending a trade fair at the Düsseldorf Messe, where he had been promoting his family's wonderful Walkers shortbread, Scotland's very own biscuit. Naturally, Jim was interested to know where we were going, and so we explained that we were heading to the first day of the Düsseldorf Boat Show. Wishing Jim well, we parted company and left the airport.

Germany, the economic powerhouse of Europe, boasts huge exhibition centres in most of its major cities. Düsseldorf Messe hosts an annual boat show, which has become pre-eminent in Europe for showcasing boats, yachts and related sailing services for pleasure-seekers. That morning, in January 2011, we passed through its doors, ready to browse and marvel at the amazing boats and designs on view.

Huddled together in one of the large halls were a number of French boating companies. In their midst, we met a short, stocky gentleman with a pleasant smile who had a small stand displaying some designs that had caught our attention. He introduced himself as Olivier Racoupeau, and over coffee we leafed through pictures of boats that he had built and sketches of concepts under development. We also met his wife Isabelle. Taking a liking to each other, we agreed to stay in touch and thanked the Racoupeaus for their time. The rest of the day was spent wandering round the massive boat show, before we caught our return flight home in the afternoon.

The idea of sailing around the world had first been mooted a few years earlier, but to this point it had been just a pipe dream. The twelve years I had spent working at the Institute for Family Business had been among the most satisfying of my professional life, and during this time I had met many great people, but now I was about to retire from that role and gain the freedom to explore new horizons.

Sitting together on the plane bound for London, Brigitte and I chatted about the future and the possibility of a round-the-world adventure by sea. As we flew back over northern Europe, I took a sheet of paper and drafted the specifications of the ideal boat that could enable us to achieve this goal.

In the weeks after our trip to Düsseldorf, we scoured the Internet looking at pre-owned yachts that were for sale. After failing to find what we wanted, a few months later we arranged a rendezvous with Olivier Racoupeau near the Gare du Nord railway station in Paris. Our agenda was the content of the one-page document that I had titled 'Project Bougainville – World Cruising Programme', which I handed over to Olivier. The sheet of paper outlined the aims of the planned east-to-west global cruise and the main parameters and requirements for a 'high-performance bluewater cruising yacht'. During the brief meeting, we discussed 'Project Bougainville' and clarified a few details. Brigitte and I left Paris that day with a positive feeling that we could work together with Olivier in building the boat of our dreams.

It was a sunny day and as we strolled through one of the parks in the centre of Paris, we passed some stalls selling collectable postage stamps. On one of the stands in the section on explorers, we discovered a stamp commemorating Louis-Antoine de Bougainville, which we bought. Printed on the stamp was the route that he had taken during his circumnavigation around the world. My curiosity was piqued and over the course of our Adventure I would learn a lot more about the life of this great French admiral and explorer.

* * * * *

In the months that followed, Brigitte and I enjoyed further conversations and meetings with the team that would shape the ideas for a new-build boat. Once a contract had been agreed, the Racoupeau design office sprang into action and a draft set of plans for a new 65–68-foot vessel soon emerged. A boat of this size would be large enough to incorporate accommodation for Brigitte and me, up to four guests and a professional crew of two. With performance in mind, the designers would have to keep the boat's weight within sensible limits to enable her to sail well. The deck layout and rig plan would also ensure that she could be easily handled with four to six people on board during a long passage. Taking the project one step further, we were introduced to Mark Hampton, a youthful and amiable Scot who helped to develop the vessel's detailed specification. Mark went on to be the project manager, working with the design and build teams to achieve a successful outcome. With an eye on the end result, he pushed everyone forward when it was needed.

One of the first jobs was identifying where to build the boat, which led to the choice of Claasen Shipyards, located on the banks of the River Zaan near Zaandijk, north of Amsterdam. The values of the company had been deeply ingrained from the time of its founding by Nico Claasen, who still lived next to the yard. The Dutch craftsmen shared a sense of pride and attention to detail. One of the yard's most memorable features was a dog that would sit in the boatshed while his master, one of the shipbuilders, was busy with his work.

Rounding out the project team was Dick Young, of Rhoades Young Design, an affable Englishman with a sense of humour combined with stubbornness, who helped the project immeasurably. Others who gave their input at different stages included Bouwe Bekking, Simon Fry, Neil Macleay, Richard Haworth, Wouter Verbraak and René Villefrance, and many more made invaluable contributions to building a boat fit for sailing the oceans. With English, Dutch, Danish, French, Scots and other nationalities working together, this was a European project team formed by people with a shared passion for the sea.

Once the decision to construct the new boat had been made in 2011, Brigitte and I started our monthly commute to Holland. The short trips to Amsterdam and the yard brought with them a sense of excitement and expectation. Driving a rental car around the Amsterdam ring road, we would pass by smart office buildings, busy docks and wind generators. Whether in the cities or the villages of the Netherlands, the country is neat and tidy. People go about their work quietly and there is an aura of civilisation. The Dutch commute equally by bike, on foot or by car, waiting without fuss at railway crossings or when a canal bridge is opened. Being patient seems to come second nature to the citizens of this flattest of countries.

When staying overnight, we found the lodgings would serve breakfast with cold hams and cheese, which wasn't to my personal taste. But no wonder the Dutch are the tallest nationality in Europe with their high-protein diet. On the occasions that we stopped over on a weekend, there were opportunities to go to the Rijksmuseum in Amsterdam and marvel at the imagination of the nation's great artists. Many of the masterpieces record the country's colonial past, a reminder of earlier conquests in the Age of Discovery.

One day, we drove north along the dyke that forms the barrier to the Ijsselmeer, a vast, man-made lake which faces the tidal waters that lead into the North Sea. The village of Makkum in Friesland, on the banks of the Ijsselmeer, is where some of the finest aluminium hulls have been built at Bloemsma, which formed part of the Claasen group. On this visit, I was invited to make the first weld on the boat. We could see the hull taking shape, sitting upside down with her longitudinal stringers and crossbeams spaced out every half metre, like the skeleton of a huge whale. A few weeks later, a shiny aluminium body emerged, ready to be turned over. Gleaming in the bright winter sun, the hull looked elegant and sleek.

* * * * *

Building projects frequently encounter bottlenecks and ours was no exception. The plan was to build the boat to Lloyd's Register shipping standards, which are reputed to be the world's highest in terms of safety, and so a considerable amount of extra work would be undertaken throughout the construction period to meet the strict criteria involved. Despite the additional pressure, the team's focus never wavered and when we later received official confirmation that the exacting regulatory standards had been met, it was acknowledged as a great accomplishment for all concerned.

As soon as the building of the deck was completed and it had been fixed onto the hull – not dissimilar to putting the roof onto a house – final installations of equipment and interior furnishings could be carried out. We started to think of the day when the boat would be ready to be launched. Once she was in the water, her mast and rigging would be fitted. The yard's manager, Victor Weerens, exuded quiet confidence, and even when there were challenges he was positive about finding solutions to any issues that arose.

There was an air of excitement at the yard, with craftsmen quietly going about their business, installing everything from furniture and flooring to machinery with the utmost care. In the carpentry shop, the joiners patiently manufactured pieces of woodwork with great skill. Indispensable accessories such as the boat's set of sails and her dinghy, which would be essential for getting ashore when anchored, had also been delivered. A sense of purpose and attention to detail in the technical area was very much apparent, and the small team at Jongkind, led by Carl Grootjes, managed their contribution to the project with determination.

On 14th June 2013, with the yacht launched and final touches largely completed, we invited friends to the yard for the traditional christening ceremony. As the guests arrived on the bright and breezy day, flags flew from the shiny new mast. With everyone gathered on the dock next to the boat, our daughters Juliette, Valerie and Claire cracked the traditional bottle of champagne on the hull. They had prepared a short speech, which they read out to everyone's applause. I then thanked all those who had worked on the project for their contributions, after which a band struck up and we enjoyed a barbecue with the yard's employees and others involved in the venture. In the evening, accompanied by our friends, we took a brief canal cruise through Amsterdam, followed by a memorable dinner at the Ship Chandlers Warehouse on the Geldersekade.

However, the biggest surprise of the day concerned the boat's name. This had been a secret kept hidden until the launch ceremony. The idea of naming the boat after my mother was sparked by my long-standing Belgian friend Guy de Poorter. At a dinner one evening early in 2013, Guy reminded me of how she had always looked after us when we went sailing on our family's boat, *Cinderella*, as teenagers. In good weather or bad, she kept everyone well fed and happy. My mother was always good company at sea, and encouraged a sense of friendship and camaraderie on board. Our family summer cruises were filled with great memories, and so it was fitting that the new boat should be named in memory of Louise Gordon.

Chapter I – In the Trades
Jersey, Channel Islands to Rio de Janeiro, Brazil

Caleta Hornos, Chubut, Argentina

Following *Louise*'s launch, we sailed her to St Helier on Jersey where she was officially registered, thereby establishing the island as her home port. Because she had become a British-registered yacht, we could proudly fly the red ensign from her stern. To join *Louise*, who was tied to the floating pontoon dock adjacent to the large sea wall in Jersey's Elizabeth Marina, Brigitte and I took the forty-five-minute flight from London Gatwick, which afforded us a good view of the Isle of Wight before we crossed the English Channel, where vessels were plying the busy shipping lanes.

The Channel Islands are notorious for the magnitude of the tides caused by vast volumes of water flowing in and out of the bay formed by the Normandy Peninsula on one side and the northern shore of Brittany on the other. With this in mind, we had planned our exit from the harbour to coincide with high water, in order to clear a weir at the entrance to the marina that stops it from drying out at low tide. My brother Glenn came down to wish us farewell. I had the feeling that perhaps he too would have liked to have been setting off on such an adventure.

At 5.30 p.m. on Friday 30th August 2013, we let go our lines to leave the harbour. Joining us on board for the first leg to Lanzarote in the Canary Islands were our two friends, Ian Reid and Jean-Louis Peyreyre. Ian's parents were my surrogate family for much of the time that I attended boarding school at Rugby, kindly inviting me to their home near Nottingham for weekends. As teenagers, Ian and I discovered that we shared a passion for sailing. I had come to know Jean-Louis much later, through my professional career working with the family firm Laurent-Perrier, and we had become good friends. A Basque from Biarritz, Jean-Louis' passion for the sea extends to both sailing and marine archaeology. His work in underwater explorations searching for antiquities had happily led him to meeting Morgan Morice and Cheryl Herne, who were engaged as *Louise*'s trusted crew for the quest. This introduction was to prove invaluable and we owe a huge debt of gratitude to both Morgan and Cheryl, who together helped to turn our pipe dream into reality.

Our immediate aim was to pass the French island of Ushant, gateway to the Bay of Biscay and the Atlantic Ocean. The sea was calm, which made progress smooth, notwithstanding a modest westerly breeze. A large inflatable motorboat approached us at speed and we recognised that my brother was at the wheel. He had come to say one last goodbye and wish us well. Speeding past our stern, the boat kicked up a wave that splashed seawater all over me. There was laughter all around at this fraternal prank. Soon after, we settled down to our first evening at sea.

For our first dinner, Cheryl served a tasty lamb tagine and we made a toast to *Louise*, praying for a safe passage. During the night, those who were not on watch retreated to their bunks to sleep. Brigitte and I shared the small cabin to port amidships, which has two pilot berths. The cabin is rather snug, especially if you are sleeping in the top bunk as you can bang your head if you sit up in bed.

On Saturday morning, under a cloudy sky, we passed by the north-west tip of France at Ushant. Two tall and slender lighthouses stand on the low-lying island, helping to guide ships in and out of the Channel. In his younger days, Ian had contributed an article to *Yachting Monthly* about cruising Ushant, and he recalled some interesting facts about the iconic island which points into the Atlantic and marks the westerly limit of France. The surrounding rocks in particular have caused the demise of many unfortunate vessels.

With phone signal finally lost as land was out of sight, *Louise* slipped out into the Atlantic under full mainsail and reacher, also known as a Code Zero sail. Then we changed course to the south-west to cross the Bay of Biscay. During the night we were joined by a seagull that successfully landed on our cockpit dodger. The bird seemed happy to stay put on his perch, oblivious to the fact that every minute it remained on board took it further away from land. By the time our winged passenger decided to leave the boat, he had travelled another 50 miles or so out to sea. On inspecting the dodger, we found that it was covered with bird droppings, which Ian kindly cleaned up. Nature still had more to keep us entertained, as a school of pilot whales appeared on Sunday 1st September, coming very close to the boat.

Fortunately, the summer was not yet over and the Bay of Biscay offered us some enjoyable days downwind, sailing in a steady north-easterly. As a teenager, I had cruised on our family yacht *Cinderella*, passing the north-west coast of Spain to reach Baiona in southern Galicia, a town which Portuguese pilgrims would have gone through on their way to Santiago de Compostela. In the summer months, sailors have to contend with strong north-easterly winds that usually blow off Spain's Cape Finisterre. Once autumn arrives, Atlantic depressions become more frequent and the Bay of Biscay too often becomes an unwelcome place for seafarers. Our passage was made easy by the following winds that carried the boat at speed past Cape Finisterre, which we passed on Monday morning.

The excellent conditions allowed us to achieve our first daily run of over 250 nautical miles or an average speed of nearly 10 knots. The start of the week was also marked by our first catch of fish. A small, long-tailed tuna took our bait and Morgan filleted it, ready for eating the following day. Early on Monday morning the wind died and we motored through foggy but calm conditions, parallel to the coast of Portugal. As a precaution we slowed down a little, hoisting our radar reflector to ensure that we would be 'seen' by other vessels. Poor visibility is common here, as a consequence of the cold Atlantic current from the north meeting warmer air. Later that day, Morgan surprised us with an unannounced safety drill; we all rushed on deck to our stations where we practised a 'man overboard' situation.

On Tuesday, we ate our fresh tuna pan-seared and also tasted it raw as carpaccio. During the afternoon, the wind reappeared from behind and we were able to fly our spinnaker for the first time, which we carried for the next twenty-four hours, helping *Louise* to make good progress south. The sail's bright red-and-white striped pattern, which had been chosen by Brigitte, made *Louise* distinguishable to passing vessels.

One way of putting my time on board to good use was to contribute to our collective nourishment. After experimenting at home making bread using the 'Cleo recipe', which I had discovered through a food charity in London, I started to produce a sourdough loaf using a live starter as mother dough for the bread. My first loaf accompanied a lunch of salad, cheese and cold meats on our fifth day at sea. Laziness later caught up with me, though, and I quietly abandoned this short-lived hobby.

On Wednesday 4th September, our sixth night at sea, far to our east we passed the Strait of Gibraltar, which forms the entrance to the Mediterranean Sea. Inside the strait lies the vast expanse of water that is the cradle of ancient civilisation and now highly popular with Europeans seeking sun, sea and relaxation during the holiday season. For now, *Louise* would bypass the Mediterranean and continue on our way south.

Over to starboard, slightly further out west in the Atlantic we passed Madeira, a much-loved island that has long been a stopping place for vessels travelling outbound from Europe. Man's thirst for a fine drink attracted ships to this beautiful location, famed for its fortified sweet wines.

From here, their letters could also be sent home, which was usually no longer possible once an expedition had reached far-flung places.

To cap our last full day at sea before arriving in Lanzarote, all afternoon and into the evening we continued to sail under spinnaker. Unfortunately, the spinnaker became twisted around the forestay during the evening, but with patience we managed to sort out the mess and took the sail down.

The north-west African coast loomed ever closer, as well as our destination in the Canary Islands. The following afternoon, land was sighted and just before dusk on Friday 6th September we docked in the tidy Rubicon Marina on the southern end of Lanzarote. *Louise* had come through the test of her first passage with flying colours, covering the distance from Jersey to the Canaries comfortably, at an average speed of 9 knots. The Adventure was now no longer just a dream and finally beginning to unfold.

With phone contact re-established now we were back on land, Jean-Louis was able to reassure his wife Alexandra that *Louise* had safely found port and he was alive and well. That evening we enjoyed a celebratory dinner ashore, and the next day Jean-Louis and Ian took their leave of *Louise* to head home.

Louise remained at the marina in Lanzarote, sitting at her berth with the look of a newly born thoroughbred. The boat is equipped with a complex web of modern systems and technology that is designed to help with her safety, performance and the comfort of on-board living. Getting all these systems to function as designed and sorting out any teething problems was a task that fell in the main to Morgan, the boat's captain, but after our arrival in the Canaries, a small group of technicians from Claasen Shipyards also came to carry out warranty work on *Louise* and resolve various issues.

With all this essential maintenance being undertaken, Brigitte and I returned home to London for a short spell.

* * * * *

The Canary Islands are arid, but the lack of rain is made up for in good measure by the wind. The archipelago is a favoured destination for kite surfers as well as for sailors seeking waters that offer warm weather conditions during the winter with plenty of breeze. And so, on returning to the boat almost a fortnight later, we were keenly anticipating our first ocean crossing.

A signpost in the marina highlighted multiple directions; one of the signs pointed west, indicating 'America 6,500 km'. Morgan and Cheryl had made many similar passages before, but for Brigitte and me this was our first such trip. I felt uncertain about what lay ahead, how we would adapt to the daily routine, the potential weather conditions we might face and so on. After washing the dishes following dinner on Wednesday 18th September, we prepared to let go the mooring lines, bound for Brazil on the other side of the Atlantic. As we motored away from the pontoon, we were given a send-off by a friendly barking dog.

Heading out as the harbour lights dimmed, the heavens seemingly lit up above us, revealing a clear and starry sky. The wind backed nicely towards the east and by the middle of the night the engine had been switched off with the boat under full sail. The sound of the sea was audible and we began to feel that our maiden Atlantic crossing was truly underway. We passed Fuerteventura, the second largest of the Canary Islands, skirting its westerly side. Fuerteventura is the closest island on the archipelago to Africa, renowned for its beaches and pleasant year-round climate.

Just before lunch the next day, the fishing line went taut and we jumped into action hauling it in. It wasn't too long before a marlin leapt out of the water. Morgan continued to wrestle with the catch, but eventually it disappeared under our hull and the line snapped. It was disappointing to lose the fish, but it had certainly given our fishing tackle a good test.

Our plan was to head south, almost hugging the west coast of Africa. The route took us into Mauritanian waters where we encountered many fishing boats. Judging by the considerable number of vessels we saw, it seemed that this country was not a committed supporter of sustainable fishing. Under spinnaker on Friday, towards the end of the afternoon we came within 15 nautical miles of the Mauritanian coast at Cap Blanc. At this point in West Africa the land is low-lying, and although close by it wasn't discernible through the haze. The poor visibility was probably caused by dust accumulating in the air above Western Sahara. Here we gybed, with the wind now on our starboard quarter, and started to make our way out into the Atlantic. Entertainment was on hand with appearances from some dolphins and a pair of killer whales.

Lying approximately two days' sailing south-west were the Cape Verde Islands. There was a clear sense of disappointment from Brigitte that, in our rush to get into the Southern Atlantic in time for the southern hemisphere's summer, we weren't able to visit this destination. The islands are renowned for their laid-back culture and natural beauty, and I realised I would need to make amends in the future for having to bypass them on this occasion.

The next day, the continuing on-board silence was interrupted by the sound of a loud bang, perhaps caused by a floating pallet or another large object. Sadly, our oceans are all too often dumping grounds which, when combined with items of freight accidentally falling off ships, create a real hazard for vessels underway. Sailing on, we inspected the boat's hull and rudders as best we could and were relieved to find that no damage had been caused.

Approaching the tropics, we began to perceive a rise in the temperature. At night, we only needed a T-shirt and shorts while on deck. During the day it was best to keep out of the sun, although Brigitte enjoyed some sunbathing.

Flying fish became a new distraction. Both Cheryl and Brigitte were hit in the face by some during the hours of darkness. Collecting a few after they'd landed on deck, we cooked them and were pleasantly surprised to find that they were rather tasty. Now I understood why Sir Francis Chichester, one of my boyhood heroes, was glad to eat them during his epic round-the-world voyage in 1966–67 on *Gipsy Moth*. His expedition, stopping only once in Sydney, was the first west-to-east single-handed circumnavigation of the world via the great Capes.

Five days after leaving the Canaries, the Cape Verde Islands were abeam of *Louise*, but too far west to be visible.

* * * * *

Navigators aiming to reach the South Atlantic have to pay particular attention in planning a route to cross the doldrums. This area of weak winds, which is generally disliked by sailors partly because of the oppressive heat, is officially known as the Intertropical Convergence Zone (ITCZ). Modern communications provide seafarers with a range of weather-forecasting tools and applications. A former chairman of the UK Met Office, whom I had encountered a few years earlier, told me that the mainframe computer that ran the UK's official weather modelling was one of the largest calculators built to date. Using sophisticated algorithms, weather can be predicted anywhere on Earth. All that one needs to obtain these forecasts is access to the Internet. Happily, satellite communications are available across most of our planet and its oceans.

When on board, we download meteorological information in the form of GRIB files, which only cost the price of the Internet connection. After uploading a file, we can overlay the forecast onto the boat's computer navigation software. Arguably the greatest advance in sailing in recent decades has been the propagation of weather forecasts, which are now accessible globally.

Nothing regulates life aboard a sailing boat more than the wind, in terms of its strength and direction. Many a time, especially in the morning, we huddled around the chart table in anticipation of Morgan giving us his daily commentary on the weather. Decisions then had to be made about the course we should sail, whether action was needed to avoid any weather, which sails we should be setting, and so on.

Although the doldrums are generally less extensive further west, our aim was to reach the south-east trade winds as early as possible. Therefore, we continued to sail directly south from Cape Verde at around 20 degrees west of the Greenwich meridian. We found the doldrums at about 13 degrees north, at which point we motored over a mainly flat, calm sea for three days. Brigitte described the conditions as *lémanique*, a Swiss expression familiar to people living on the shores of Lake Geneva, where the winds are usually very light. During the day, the temperature was really warm.

Taking advantage of the absence of any wind, one day we took a swim in the 30°C tropical water. Before plunging into the sea, for safety we ran out a line from the stern to hold onto, as well as lowering a ladder over the side. Fishing was also the order of the day and we landed in succession a wahoo and a 60-pound sailfish. By the time our various catches were filleted and vacuum-packed, the freezer was stuffed full.

We were kept on our toes by rain showers that we periodically passed, which usually brought strong gusts of wind and torrential downpours. The showers were tricky to spot at night, but by keeping a watch on the radar we could detect oncoming rain. By crossing the ITCZ this far east, the advantage was that when we encountered the south-east trade winds, we had a good wind angle for the remainder of the passage towards Brazil. Vessels heading south that enter the trade winds too far west can struggle to make it on one tack past the north-east tip of Brazil. In olden times, square-rigged boats were sometimes forced to sail all the way back into the North Atlantic, a detour that could cost months of additional time at sea and consequently put expeditions at risk, because victuals were limited and sailors had to be fed.

The first sign of the pending wind was the appearance of a long ocean swell coming from the south-east. No sooner had we become a little frustrated by the oppressive heat than a band of clouds appeared, moving north-west, which signalled a change in the weather. We unfurled our headsails and set off, carried along by the heaven-sent winds commonly known as the trade winds. The boat came alive in the fresh breeze; we could feel that our first landfall in Latin America would not be long in coming.

✵ ✵ ✵ ✵ ✵

The next milestone was the invisible line running around the Earth's circumference – the equator. For first-timers, which included Brigitte and me, the age-old tradition required that we be initiated as 'Scallywags'. We crossed the line in the middle of the night, so a simple ceremony was held below deck, sparing us a dunking. Morgan proposed a toast, wishing us many safe crossings, and he presented us with certificates marking the event. Meanwhile, *Louise* was making light of the miles and, within a day and a half of crossing the equator, on Monday 30th September the Brazilian archipelago of Fernando de Noronha came in to view, first sighted by Cheryl. It's easy to spot from a distance thanks to a huge rock, the Morro do Pico, that overlooks the anchorage.

Almost twelve days after leaving the Canaries and travelling nearly 2,500 nautical miles, we dropped anchor in the bay at Fernando de Noronha, also the main island in the archipelago, and went ashore on Monday afternoon. Fernando lies 220 miles off the north-east corner of Brazil and has a small population of just under 3,000. Tourist flights are available from the mainland, but there are no major resorts so the place has a laid-back feeling. Many of the locals make their living from the sea. Morgan had been here before and he met up with an old friend and fisherman who had sadly lost his fishing boat the year before, when it got smashed onto the island by a large ocean swell.

A highlight of our visit was diving off the very eastern end of the island, where the underwater visibility was spectacular with plenty of sea life, including reef sharks, nurse sharks, barracuda and a variety of tropical fish. Back onshore, we enjoyed our first caipirinha cocktails at sunset on a terrace overlooking the sea. With the first sip we could really taste the tropics.

During the stopover, Morgan made some checks to the boat. Diving under *Louise* and looking into the keel trunk, he discovered an adjustable spanner that had been left by one of the workmen. The boat's upright stability derives from its ballasted keel that protrudes underneath the hull, which on *Louise* weighs 9 tonnes. For convenience, she is equipped with a lifting keel powered by two hydraulic rams, which enables us to reduce our draught from 13 feet to 8 feet (4 metres to 2.5 metres). With the keel in a lifted position, this opens up many more opportunities to enter marinas or anchorages closer to the shore.

* * * * *

On Thursday 3rd October, we set off again after our three-day break in Fernando de Noronha. We soon picked up our routine and made good progress heading south-west, taking full advantage of the push that the trade winds had given us since the doldrums.

We set a course that would lead us gradually closer to the mainland, passing the famous north-eastern city of Recife, and continued our way south towards Salvador, capital of the state of Bahia. Fortunately, the trade winds held up for a few more days until we reached the latitude of Bahia State. Looking back to the start of the *Louise* Adventure, we had travelled approximately 4,500 nautical miles since leaving Jersey with the wind in our back. *Louise* had enjoyed an excellent run so far, and I hoped this was a positive sign.

All good things come to an end, however, and conditions over the next few days were not as favourable, with the wind shifting to the south. We experienced our first extended period of sailing to windward, when sheets are tightened and the boat consequently leans over, heeling to one side. This was our first encounter with a low-pressure weather front, but *Louise* took it in her stride. The wind picked up to Force 6 on the Beaufort scale, but the seas weren't steep so the sailing wasn't notably uncomfortable thanks to warm air temperatures. Steadily making our way further south, our track drew closer to the coast.

Reaching the shallower waters north of Rio de Janeiro, we passed huge offshore oil and gas platforms. Brazil has considerable reserves of fossil fuels under the seabed. The sheer scale of the natural resources under the Atlantic Ocean resulted in the development of one of the world's largest offshore investment programmes. Billions of dollars were invested every year, which led to a national corruption crisis known in the country as the Car Wash scandal. Easily visible at night, the oil platforms are brightly lit industrial units, usually with a few support vessels located nearby. Closing in on Cabo Frio, the headland east of Rio that sticks out into the South Atlantic, gradually we encountered more traffic, including fishing boats and other ships.

At 6 a.m. on Thursday 10th October, as the sun was rising, the Corcovado mountain emerged to our west. The wind dropped as we approached, so we lowered the sails and motored the last few miles. Within a couple of hours, we had arrived in Guanabara Bay, passing north of the iconic Sugar Loaf Mountain. We tied up on one of the pontoons in Marina da Glória in downtown Rio and were surprised to find the Clipper Race yachts moored in the same harbour. Only one of the crews had yet to finish the first leg, having got stuck in the doldrums for over a week. The rest of the fleet were busy making their preparations to leave for Cape Town, which was the following leg on their round-the-world yacht race.

Once *Louise* was secure, we met a local agent who helped us to navigate through the government bureaucracy that subjects visiting sailors to constant checks as they move around the country. However, we didn't let red tape affect the positive feeling of completing our first ocean crossing and arriving in this most spectacular of waterfront cities. That afternoon, I put on some smarter clothes and set off to register for the

Family Business Network's world conference that was being hosted in Rio.

A couple of days later, after the conference had closed, we invited aboard some friends who had attended the same event to watch the yachts depart in the next stage of the Clipper Race on Saturday afternoon. There was a steady wind for the start, which helped the boats to get going. Motoring behind the fleet with *Louise*, we followed the leaders for a while before turning back to the marina.

Early on Sunday morning, we left Rio to move to Angra dos Reis, where we would be leaving the boat during the stopover in Brazil. Motoring the 70-mile trip down the coast on a calm day, we were moored up by mid-afternoon in the large marina complex. Once again, a small group of workmen was going to join *Louise* to deal with some of her teething problems. While the work was taking place, our plan was to return home to the UK, and by early evening we were in a taxi making our way to Rio Airport to catch our plane. We left behind Morgan and Cheryl, who had planned a short break on Ilha Grande, a beautiful island that was only a brief ferry ride away from Angra.

Taking off for London that night, while slumped in my seat on the plane, I cast my mind back over the first 5,500 nautical miles we had travelled, including our first Atlantic crossing. So far we had been very fortunate, as the weather had been good and we had enjoyed some great sailing. We had also managed to achieve our goal of reaching Rio in good time to enable us to explore the South Atlantic during the summer.

Chapter 2 – Pampero Country
Angra dos Reis, Brazil to the River Plate and Stanley, Falkland Islands

Carcass Island, Falklands

After leaving Rio, the next three weeks included a trip to the US to Harvard Business School, where I attended a three-day programme on the governance of non-profit organisations. Charged with new concepts and strategies, I left Boston to drive over to New York City and visit my father Charles. Recently discharged from hospital he looked weak, but as usual he made light of his frail health and was excited to hear all about our Atlantic crossing and future cruising plans. Of course, he was also happy to be back home in his apartment with my stepmother Francesca.

On Sunday 3rd November 2013, Brigitte and I were back on board *Louise* at Angra dos Reis and, thanks mainly to Morgan and Cheryl's efforts, the boat was shipshape and ready for the resumption of the Adventure. Joined by our old friends Marijke de Milliano and Tobias and Caroline Straessle, we had planned a mini-cruise down the coast from Angra to Ilhabela, making some stops on the way. This stretch of Brazil's coastline is dotted with beautiful, unspoilt islands.

Leaving for Ilha Grande on the Monday morning, by the afternoon we were enjoying a walk on the deserted Lopes Mendes beach that faces the South Atlantic. Strolling on the sand with our friends, the only other visible company were sand crabs scurrying in and out of the water. A lone vulture circled above looking for some prey. It was close to dusk by the time we had returned to *Louise*, who was moored at the quiet anchorage at Praia do Pouso in the lee of the island.

On Tuesday morning, we awoke to the patter of rain on the deck and looking outside we saw the skies were an unfortunate shade of grey. Not letting the weather dampen our spirits, we set off further south and settled later in the day at Enseada do Sítio Forte, a tranquil bay on Ilha Grande facing Angra. Late in the afternoon we dropped in at Tapera Bar, where a few sailors from other boats were also enjoying a drink. We met a solo French yachtsman on his way from the Caribbean towards Ushuaia, at the tip of Argentina, and two friendly Argentinian couples who were on holiday on a charter boat.

To comply with Brazilian administrative by-laws, yachts must check in and out each time they pass any state boundaries. Not only does this require time, but also a good dose of patience. To complete the mandatory paperwork, we backtracked under engine to the mainland and returned to the bustling seaside town of Angra on Wednesday morning. Morgan visited the authorities and obtained official clearance to proceed to our next destination. The goal that day was to reach the historical port of Paraty, which began to build up from the late seventeenth century when gold was discovered in the interior. This waterfront location on Brazil's Costa Verde was dedicated to loading the precious cargo for export to Europe.

With the rain still falling three hours later, we motored into the anchorage at Paraty, which was flat calm. We passed a beautiful sailing schooner, *Tocorimé*, lying at anchor, one of whose owners happened to be Marijke's brother Jacques de Milliano. His vision was to build a vessel for cruising, as well as making it available to local charities for chartering. A traditional design, *Tocorimé* was constructed using indigenous woods from the Amazon. As teenagers, Jacques and I had sailed many miles together during our summer holidays, on trips far from our home port of Breskens in the southern Netherlands where his family originate. During his successful and diverse career, Jacques has been everything from local GP doctor and elected national politician to inspirational change-maker, responsible for establishing a series of successful non-governmental organisations.

We spent the afternoon exploring Paraty's old cobbled streets, sheltering in the small shops and cafes to avoid the constant downpours. In one establishment, we treated ourselves to a tasting of cachaça, Brazil's native distilled spirit. There were over a hundred varieties to choose from and we were pleasantly surprised by the quality of the products we sampled.

Our next stop on Thursday 7th November was further south at Praia Tabatinga in the state of São Paulo, where our Brazilian friends Peter and Marcia Graber have a holiday home by the beach. We were fortunate to catch a mahi-mahi during the brief passage, which Brigitte and I brought with us that evening. Marcia made use of the fish as she prepared a delicious meal comprising several local dishes. Before that, Peter taught us how to make a proper caipirinha, which we enjoyed before dinner was served. We were kindly invited to stay overnight at the Grabers' house and, after breakfast the following morning, all four of us went aboard *Louise* to motor the short distance to the marina at Ilhabela Yacht Club, where we had agreed to rendezvous with some other friends.

Arriving there, we were greeted by the Alexanders, Jacobsbergs, Hilueys and Galvãos. Dario and Gina Galvão had co-ordinated the weekend, bringing us all together. During a Scottish Series regatta on the west coast of Scotland a few years earlier, Dario and I had sailed together on our previous boat, a Swan 45 named *Fever*. The weather had been so miserable that he had bought an entire set of warm-layered clothing to wear under his oilskins. This weekend in Ilhabela, the programme of activities included a two-boat match-racing competition on identical one-design keelboats. The breeze was fairly light and, with the help of three of my friends as crew, we managed to beat Dario's team while everyone had a great time.

The morning of Saturday 9th November was warm and sunny, so we went out with our Brazilian friends for a sail. We gave everyone who wanted to the chance to steer *Louise*, but didn't venture too far from the marina before returning to harbour. The afternoon was spent having a pleasant lunch at one of the local beach restaurants in Ilhabela. Our Brazilian hosts were very welcoming and we made the most of the laid-back atmosphere. For anyone who lives and works in fast-paced and heavily polluted São Paulo, the largest metropolis in South America and the nearest major city to Ilhabela, getting down to the sea on a weekend must provide a much-needed escape.

Early the next morning, the Straessles, who had been our wonderful companions for the past week, left for Rio to do some sightseeing there before flying home to the UK. The wind had picked up and we had some more fun sailing Dario's keelboat. My friend Alberto Jacobsberg, who had not sailed before, came along for the ride and enjoyed steering the boat. That afternoon we said our farewells to our Brazilian hosts, and spent a quiet evening on *Louise* together with Marijke.

Taking the foot ferry over to São Sebastião on the mainland on Monday morning, there were numerous people on board, many of whom were doubtless travelling to their place of work. Our main destination was the Port Authority building, where we had to obtain our official clearance to leave Brazil, and then we needed to pick up enough fresh food to see us through to our arrival in Argentina. Marijke also bid us goodbye at the bus station before starting her own journey back to Holland. By lunchtime, Brigitte and I were back aboard *Louise*, along with Morgan and Cheryl, and ready to cast off to begin our journey south.

* * * * *

The next leg to Buenos Aires saw our first encounter with waters south of the tropic of Capricorn. It was expected that we might experience variable weather conditions and would have to watch out for a pampero wind heading our way and blocking our path. The famous pampero is a frontal weather system that comes off treeless plains in Argentina and Uruguay known as the pampas. When it eventually reaches coastal waters, seas can become rough, with strong headwinds for any vessels travelling south. We were fortunate enough to have favourable conditions, but on the second night of the passage the wind rose briefly over 30 knots. After midnight, with the sea also building, we reduced sail, carrying two reefs in the mainsail as well as setting the storm jib.

By Wednesday 13th November, our weather forecast predicted a strong southerly blow coming up from Uruguay. To avoid the pampero we decided to stop off in Rio Grande, the most southerly harbour in Brazil. Beyond this port there is a 250-mile stretch of coast with no suitable shelter available before the River Plate estuary. So, late on Thursday afternoon, we motored up the 12-mile long channel from the sea, passing the commercial and fishing docks, before we reached the Rio Grande Yacht Club. The shallow depth of water in the club's marina provided insufficient draught for *Louise* to moor, but fortunately there was a small pier extending out into the channel that was sitting empty. Seeing that we were about to dock the boat, some locals rushed along the pier to take our mooring lines. Once we were safely tied up, we switched off the engine and settled down to wait patiently for the storm to pass.

Getting up the following morning, the place seemed very quiet. We soon discovered it was a public holiday, which explained why the town appeared deserted. Luckily, the yacht club was open at all times and later that day we would enjoy the buffet lunch that it served. The club also had a decent-sized outdoor swimming pool and so I was able to do some lengths.

A bonus of our stopover was the opportunity to visit the Oceanographic Museum near to the yacht club, which told the story of the Brazilian Antarctica base. I also found the Harbour Museum to be of interest, housed in a building erected in 1905 with the support of French investors. North of the town, a waterway extends into the Lagoa dos Patos, a huge expanse of water that leads up to Porto Alegre, the main city in southern Brazil.

* * * * *

For planning our arrival in Argentina, we had been in touch with our good friends Hugo and Patricia Fescina. Patricia is a keen yachtswoman and a member of Yacht Club Argentino (YCA), and through her we were able to find out more information about Mar del Plata as a possible stopover in Argentina. The YCA has a clubhouse in this provincial seaside resort, which lies south of the River Plate estuary, but we received news from Patricia that the marina was too shallow to accommodate *Louise*. So we made up our minds to travel up the estuary towards Buenos Aires.

With the weather having settled, at dusk on Saturday evening we cast off our moorings at the Rio Grande Yacht Club to set off south again. *Louise* passed quietly down the channel alongside the docks, with their silent cranes and conveyors. The silhouettes of the moored ships stood out against the lights on the quayside. Back out in the open sea, we motored into a light southerly wind. Local fishing boats were back at work after the pampero and we passed through some small fleets that were grafting through the night to find their catch.

At dawn on Sunday 17th November, we saw our first seals swimming near the boat and the air felt a bit cooler. By the afternoon we had drawn parallel to the coast of Uruguay, which we were tracking to the west. The Uruguayan Control Marítimo service was quite active and we reported in to them at regular intervals on our way south. The sunset over the Uruguayan coastline was one of the most beautiful that we had experienced so far.

After a day back at sea, we were able to switch off the engine and set the sails. Under the light of the full moon, we had an excellent following wind that carried *Louise* nicely towards the River Plate estuary. As we sailed into the estuary on Monday 18th November, we passed Punta del Este, the popular Uruguayan seaside town where, years ago, my father had arranged for my grandmother to visit to take a break from the Scottish winter.

Gradually, we altered course westerly, making our approach in the middle of the estuary and leaving the capital of Montevideo out of sight about 25 miles north. In the afternoon the wind faded and we motored along the lengthy buoyed channel that led towards Buenos Aires, the River Plate Delta and destinations beyond. We could tell we were in the estuary by the brownness of the water, whose discoloration is caused by sediment being carried down the massive river system from deep inland before spilling out into the sea. There was a steady procession of freighters travelling in each direction. Most ships were small bulk carriers, mainly loaded with grains such as wheat, which were on their way to feed people all over the world.

Later that afternoon, further inside the River Plate estuary, a ship hailed us and passed on a message that the Argentine maritime control was trying to contact us. After an exchange on the radio, we were asked to stand by at La Plata until a pilot became available. This instruction didn't come as a surprise, as we had previously checked the Internet and learnt that vessels of over 50 gross tons are required to have pilotage to enter or leave Argentinian ports. A yachting website indicated that a fee of around 500 US dollars might be payable.

The anchorage at La Plata was already crowded with cargo ships waiting their turn to proceed. There was no wind and we drifted while we awaited further news. As we were eating dinner, an official launch drew up alongside *Louise* and the pilot greeted us before stepping on board. In the brief conversation that followed, we discovered that it would cost over 3,000 US dollars for the pilotage services. With a gentle smile, the man suggested that we consider other options. 'There is a very nice harbour opposite here called Montevideo,' he said. We laughed, thanking him for his tip and shaking his hand before he jumped back onto the launch and sped off to another client.

In the meantime, our friend Patricia had been busy at the Yacht Club Argentino in Buenos Aires making enquiries on our behalf, but had finally reached the conclusion that there was little we could do to get around the unfortunate pilotage regulation. We therefore decided to moor nearby, off the entrance to the small port of Ensenada, 50 miles south-east of Buenos Aires, where we would make a plan.

Unfortunately, the wind got up during the night, accompanied by a swell from the south-east, which made the anchorage quite uncomfortable. Rising early, Morgan proposed that we chance our luck entering Ensenada in the hope that the authorities would not question our arrival. Radioing in to announce our approach, when the duty officer told us to proceed into the harbour we breathed a huge sigh of relief.

It was a quiet Tuesday morning as we gently motored past the Club de Regatas La Plata at breakfast time. To our surprise we discovered that *Mollymauk*, a boat owned by Nick and Jill Schinas, old friends of Morgan's family, was moored there. We hailed the bright-yellow boat, whose name was written in large type on each side of the hull, and a head popped out of the hatch, immediately recognising Morgan. After we had dropped anchor close to the yacht moorings, we were invited on board *Mollymauk* and Jill offered us some freshly baked cake. After catching up on news, Nick and their son Cesar helped us to get ashore, which proved rather challenging. The rising sea level had raised the marina pontoons to such an extent that they were floating higher than the car park, which was mostly flooded.

Flood defences are very limited and probably an expense that the state cannot afford. Buenos Aires and the nearby coastal towns are among the areas in the world that are most vulnerable to rising sea levels. By all accounts, much of the low-lying coastal land will have to be given up to the sea by the end of this century. Who knows how the Argentinians who live close to the ocean will manage to avoid being engulfed by flooding when global warming sends sea levels even higher?

After finding transport, Morgan, Cheryl, Brigitte and I headed into the town of Ensenada, passing along streets lined with abandoned cars. We managed to locate the official building where the authorities stamped our papers, clearing us into Argentina. This marked the end of the leg for Brigitte and me, even though we had not been able to reach Buenos Aires by boat as hoped. But with flights booked for that afternoon, we ordered a taxi to take us to Buenos Aires Airport for the journey home.

It wasn't very practical for the crew to be based in Ensenada during the stopover in Argentina, as there were few services at hand. Therefore, on Wednesday afternoon, *Louise* continued onwards to the YCA's San Fernando Marina, 60 miles to the west in the Paraná River Delta. Around the delta, the waters are generally shallow and access is via a series of channels. With the keel raised, however, the boat was able to make it into the marina, touching the soft mud on the bottom before reaching her berth. The yacht club was to be *Louise*'s base for the next few weeks and a lot of preparatory work had to be carried out to ensure that she was ready for the upcoming trip to the Big South and Antarctica. Cheryl and Morgan worked tirelessly through the jobs list during this period.

* * * * *

The trip home lasted a fortnight, and included a visit to New York City to see my father who had returned to hospital. My two brothers also made the journey, so that we were all able to spend time together. When he was not too tired we could chat with him. My stepmother Francesca was constantly at his side, and just being there with my brothers meant that we could give her some support. Before I left, he wished me well for my future adventure. This was the last conversation we shared. My father Charles passed away a few weeks later on 21st December 2013.

* * * * *

Brigitte flew back to Buenos Aires with our friend Ian Reid on Sunday 1st December, in anticipation of resuming the expedition around the middle of that week. Work was still being finished on the boat, and Morgan and Cheryl were busy with some last-minute jobs. I returned to Argentina on Wednesday morning, and we stayed in the downtown area of Buenos Aires that evening, having been invited to dinner by our friends Patricia and Hugo Cebrowski. Known as the Paris of the southern hemisphere, Buenos Aires is an enchanting city that we have enjoyed on each of our visits. Palermo is one of our favourite neighbourhoods, with its low buildings, good restaurants, boutiques and relaxing cafes. During our short stay, the Cebrowskis went out of their way to be helpful and made us feel most welcome in their country.

By Thursday afternoon, it was time to drive to the marina to put our gear on board and complete the departure formalities. In the evening we were invited to a farewell meal with our friends the Kemenys, who live on the south bank of the delta. Andres and Marcela treated us to a copious 'asado-style' dinner prepared on their barbecue. The meats, including the traditional lomo, were all really tasty and accompanied by some amazing reds produced by the now familiar Bianchi Wines, where Andres worked for years heading up their exports. Before leaving Buenos Aires, Andres most generously delivered a few cases of the winery's finest to *Louise*, for us to sample on our travels.

With 1,500 nautical miles to sail to reach our final destination for the year, it was time to press on. Accompanying us on our journey was Cesar Schinas, who had kindly offered to help us on the passage south to the Falklands. While Brigitte and I were out of the country, Cesar had been assisting Morgan in prepping *Louise* for the extreme conditions that we would encounter in Antarctica. One of the main tasks had been to make a temporary Perspex double-glazing seal for every window and most of the hatches to prevent condensation from forming inside the cabin. And so, before breakfast on Friday 6th December 2013, we left the marina at San Fernando.

For the first few miles on this warm summer's day, we weaved our way along waterways with densely wooded islands on all sides. We passed numerous houses that had been flooded, with water rising well above ground-floor level. It was hard to imagine that this area was formerly dry land. The rest of the day we motored eastwards out into the estuary, passing north of the city of Buenos Aires, before gradually turning south-east towards the open sea.

The plan was to make our way down the coast of Argentina to the northern Patagonian town of Puerto Madryn. Leaving the River Plate estuary behind, we continued to head south-east to clear Punta Médanos, the most easterly land in Argentina, before moving south past Mar del Plata. In the afternoon we were able to hoist the spinnaker, sailing for a while until a dark cloud appeared to our south. Not wishing to tempt fate we reduced sail, dropping the spinnaker, and with the sun shining brightly we waited for the rain.

Due to the cloud cover, the wind picked up sharply while still blowing from the east, so *Louise* made good headway. Happily, the forecast remained settled and high pressure assisted us with some useful easterly winds. We progressed nicely in a southerly direction and on Sunday crossed the 40th parallel south, a circle of latitude 40 degrees south of the equator. The temperature was gradually dropping, but most noticeable at this point was the appearance of seals, puffins and other seabirds, which was a sign of cooling waters.

During the evening, we received the happy news that our daughter Valerie had accepted a proposal of marriage from her boyfriend Luka, and so they were now officially engaged.

* * * * *

At 3.30 p.m. on Monday 9th December, we sighted Península Valdés, a large promontory sticking out into the South Atlantic Ocean. The peninsula is a World Heritage Site and forms the eastern side of the Golfo Nuevo. During the spring, this vast bay is home to one of the biggest populations of breeding southern right whales. Our arrival, however, was rather late in the season, but while we were at anchor, Cheryl spotted two whales that must have been stragglers.

Passing the lighthouse at Punta Delgada, which marks the south-east corner of the peninsula, we were swept into the gulf on the flood tide. We reached the quiet city of Puerto Madryn a little after midnight, dropping anchor close to the pier. Welsh settlers had founded the township in 1865, arriving in this sparsely populated coastal region where conditions were harsh and irrigation ditches had to be dug in order to yield the first crops. Their descendants still uphold many old traditions, including singing in the town's Welsh choir.

The next morning, Ian, Brigitte and I set off to do some exploring. Our first stop was at the inland city of Trelew, on the banks of the River Chubut, which we reached by bus. While there we visited the Palaeontology Museum, where we learnt how Patagonia had been a habitat for dinosaurs. Close by in the desert near La Flecha, about 155 miles west of Trelew, fossilised bones were found belonging to a 130-foot-long titanosaur, believed to have been the largest dinosaur that wandered the Earth.

On Wednesday, we were taken on a 250-mile round trip of Península Valdés, during which we discovered its flora and fauna, and explored the main sights. Our guide was a man named Richard Williams, who revealed himself to be a third-generation descendant of Welsh immigrants. While surveying the beaches that faced the ocean, we saw sea lions, elephant seals and penguins. Inland, there were guanacos, armadillos, merino sheep and various other species wandering around.

The town of Puerto Pirámides presented itself as a small frontier-style tourist destination. In season, the place is popular with people going on whale-spotting day trips. Sadly, we found the tourist shops a little tacky.

By lunchtime we had reached Punta Delgada, where we climbed up the lighthouse that we had seen when passing the point on *Louise*. In the simply appointed restaurant we ate some delicious salty lamb, which was cooked on an open wood fire and served with French fries.

Driving back across the open and dry expanse of eastern Patagonia, the views gave us a real sense of the sheer scale of this sparsely populated corner of Latin America. We discovered even more seals, which we dodged past on the steps down from the harbour pier, when Morgan collected us with the dinghy after our excursion.

On Thursday morning, we all went ashore for the final time in Madryn to complete our check-out formalities for leaving Argentina. We had already informed the authorities that we were planning to stop at the Falkland Islands, but regulations required that we obtained an official permit to visit them. We had previously been advised that British-registered yachts bound for Port Stanley should avoid going via Argentina in case the vessel was refused permission to go to the Falklands. But we had chosen to ignore these voices and found the local authorities to be most reasonable. This was further proven a few weeks later, when we received a call to the on-board satellite phone from the Argentinian coastguard requesting confirmation of our position and asking when we would be arriving in Ushuaia. Morgan passed on the details and the caller thanked him and wished everyone a Happy Christmas before hanging up.

With all our papers in order, we lifted anchor and had a gentle sail towards the exit of Golfo Nuevo. During the night we made good progress south, but a minor front passed through and we had to make a few sail changes. Before dawn we were able to make out the Punta Lobos lighthouse, and we continued paralleling the coast over a very smooth sea. By Friday lunchtime the wind had died and we dropped our sails while making our way around the point adjacent to Punta Lobos, which sticks out into the South Atlantic, to our anchorage. Well concealed, the inlet of Caleta Hornos is a spectacular hidey-hole for any yacht, and a good stopping place for boats sailing south towards the Magellan Strait or heading to the Falklands.

Located at 45 degrees south, we found the entrance to the inlet just around the corner from Cabo Dos Bahías. Gently motoring in, we were surprised to discover another boat already secured there. With *Louise*'s keel lifted, we moored her in a good spot held at the bow by our anchor with two stern lines run ashore. Taking the dinghy, we rowed over to the other boat, which was named *Leava*, and introduced ourselves to the owners. Alain and Bernadette were a retired French couple who had been sailing two-handed for over a decade and had completed the North-West Passage two years previously. At the time of our meeting they were on their way to Antarctica.

When we woke up on the morning of Saturday 14th December, the other boat had already moved on, leaving us alone in the Caleta. We decided to go for a walk, climbing a small hill that overlooked the anchorage. Passing over a ridge we were confronted by a number of guanacos that were quietly grazing. This long-necked animal roams over much of Patagonia and has a similar appearance to the llama.

After a relaxed lunch sitting in the warm sunshine, it was time to move on. Thanks to a good forecast predicted for the coming days, we had decided not to delay our departure any longer. We cast off our moorings and motored slowly out of the inlet to start the passage to the Falklands, which were 500 nautical miles distant in the South Atlantic.

For the first twenty-four hours, we experienced a fast reach across the Gulf of San Jorge heading south, courtesy of the strong westerly that was blowing offshore from the Patagonian coast. Passing Cabo Blanco about 50 miles offshore, it was here that we changed course, pointing *Louise* south-east, straight at the Falkland Islands. The forecast was holding well and, although we had to motor a little, the rest of our passage was very smooth.

The following day, we enjoyed our first encounter with an albatross, arguably the most majestic of all seabirds and revered by sailors. During the early hours of Tuesday morning, we approached the coast of East Falkland, passing Cape Bougainville during the night, a reminder that my seafaring hero had previously sailed these waters. In 1764, the French named the islands the 'Malouines' after the settlers from St Malo, known as the Acadians, who had been expelled from Nova Scotia when France lost possession of Quebec to England. Thanks to Louis-Antoine de Bougainville, a number of Acadians became the first incomers to inhabit the remote archipelago in the South Atlantic, establishing a settlement at Port Louis on East Falkland. During Bougainville's subsequent visit in 1767, at the start of his round-the-world voyage of exploration, he handed over the islands to Spain to fulfil the orders of the French king, Louis XV.

During the passage, Ian gave us an erudite lecture on the history of the Falkland Islands and the 1982 war with Argentina. We learnt that, in turn, Britain, France, Spain, the United States and, not least of all, Argentina have each had a claim to or occupied the islands at some stage. Perhaps this helps to explain why these remote and sparsely populated islands have been the source of so much friction over the centuries.

The day before reaching the Falklands we passed 50 degrees

south, which marks the entrance to the Southern Ocean. A telling sign when you stepped into the cockpit was the chill in the air. Although strong winds associated with these waters were absent during our journey south from Argentina, the wind-chill factor was already noticeable. While on watch, you needed three layers of clothes covered with your oilskins, woolly hat and gloves to stay warm. Inside *Louise*, the boat's heating created a pleasant fug in the cabin.

On the morning of Tuesday 17th December, with dolphins escorting us as we ate breakfast, we motored the last few miles to Port Stanley. The well-sheltered natural harbour, located on East Falkland, came into view surrounded on all sides by gentle slopes coming down to the shore. Neat and tidy houses were covered with brightly coloured tin roofs. We moored alongside the dock in time for Brigitte and me to celebrate our thirty-first wedding anniversary with a cup of refreshing morning tea.

We had booked flights home towards the end of the week in order to celebrate Christmas with family, which gave us some time to explore East Falkland. One full day was spent visiting the battlegrounds from the 1982 Falklands War in the company of a guide. Then the following day, we hired a car and drove to the two principal war cemeteries. Sadly, we would discover that most of those who had lost their lives, particularly among the Argentinians, were very young indeed.

While Brigitte, Ian and I were heading home, Morgan and Cheryl would be spending Christmas and New Year on board *Louise* in Port Stanley, and Cesar Schinas, who had been extremely helpful throughout our passage to the Falklands, was flying back to Buenos Aires. The boat would stay tied up for the duration of the stopover and she would be well protected in the case of high winds.

On Friday, as scheduled, a taxi took us to Mount Pleasant

Airport, where we were due to fly on the military 'airbridge' service, bringing us directly to the UK. Pulling up at the terminal, the building was empty of passengers and the plane doors were already shut. At first we were confused and then upset to learn that the flight was leaving early. We pleaded unsuccessfully to be allowed to board. Instead, we were offered an apology by the officials, who had apparently tried to contact us to let us know that the plane would be taking off early due to the weather.

We returned to Stanley to try to book alternative flights in the knowledge that the one weekly scheduled flight was due to leave the next day. Fortunately we were in luck, managing to secure some seats. On Saturday 21st December, we finally took off from the Falklands, feeling a sense of relief that we were on our way in good time for Christmas. The plane made a stop in Rio Gallegos, southern Argentina, before continuing to Punta Arenas, southern Chile, and then onwards north to Santiago.

On landing that evening in the Chilean capital, I received a call that my father had passed away. It was naturally a blow to hear this news, but it had been anticipated. Brigitte and I said our cheerios to Ian, who continued on his way back home to the UK, while we took a night flight from Santiago to New York City to attend the funeral.

On the plane, I pondered over my father's love of the sea and how it had come about. In 1945, after the end of the Second World War, at the age of eighteen he went straight from Rugby School to join the Royal Navy. He was posted to the Mediterranean and served on various ships during his national service. He returned home in 1948 to begin his career and before too long he acquired a traditional yawl, named *Eala*, and my mother Louise became the main crew. Over the course of his life he would own eight boats, all sailing vessels, including *Cinderella II* on which he sailed around the world.

Although the year was drawing to a close on a sad note, I could hardly wait to be heading back south, ready for further exploration and to discover far-flung destinations in the Southern Ocean. In the back of my mind I knew how much I owed to my father, who had instilled in me his passion for the sea, and how lucky I was to have caught the sailing bug from him.

Chapter 3 – The Big South
Stanley, Falkland Islands to South Georgia, Antarctica and Ushuaia, Argentina

Cumberland East Bay, South Georgia

On Thursday 2nd January 2014, the day of my fifty-eighth birthday, I left home and later boarded a plane at Heathrow with my brother Lloyd. Our journey would take us via São Paulo to Santiago, where our family friend André Annicq would be joining us. Anne-Marie, André's wife, would meet up with us later in the month for the voyage to Antarctica. As a young boy growing up in Belgium, where my parents had moved to during the 1960s, I spent many happy times sailing in Breskens, a small Dutch village that lies on the south side of the River Scheldt opposite Flushing (Vlissingen), where our yacht *Cinderella* was moored. Our family's friendship with the Annicqs arose out of a shared passion for sailing.

In Santiago, we were also joined by Hamish Laird, who was to be our pilot and guide for the duration of the trip to South Georgia and the Antarctic Peninsula. We had been introduced to Hamish by Richard Haworth of High Latitudes, a company specialising in polar yachting. He ran a course for people who were contemplating sailing in Antarctica or the Arctic, which Brigitte and I attended over a winter weekend in Lymington, Hampshire. Hamish had a deep knowledge and experience of these parts, having spent more than two decades living and working on yachts in Antarctica, which would prove to be of inestimable value throughout our voyage. We soon discovered he was a very calm and erudite character.

On Saturday 4th January, Lloyd, André, Hamish and I boarded a plane from Santiago for the last leg to Port Stanley. The LAN Airlines flight took off on a bright summer's day, heading directly south over the Andes mountain range to the most southerly airport in mainland Latin America at Punta Arenas. After refuelling, the plane continued on its way to its final destination – Mount Pleasant Airfield on the Falkland Islands. Following a safe landing, we were met by Morgan before setting off by car on the one-hour drive to Port Stanley, East Falkland.

Because Stanley lacks facilities specifically designed for

visiting yachts, *Louise* was moored a brief walk out of the town, on the end of the large, rusty, steel FIPAS (Falkland Islands Port and Storage) floating dock. The plan for our journey into the 'Big South' was to divide the exploration into three parts. The first stage would involve a round trip from Port Stanley to go to the island of South Georgia and then back to the Falklands. After a break, this would be followed by crossing the Drake Passage to the Antarctic Peninsula, before returning to Ushuaia on Tierra del Fuego. Finally, during March we planned to navigate our way north through the Patagonian Channels in Chile to reach Puerto Montt from Puerto Williams, a short distance east of Ushuaia on the Beagle Channel.

Back on board *Louise*, the conversation turned very quickly to the subject of the weather in the Southern Ocean and the outlook for the coming days. Over New Year it had been very windy, and the locals had commented that summer had not yet arrived. Although it was pleasant on our return, a further strong blow was imminent, so we waited on standby in the Falklands for a better weather window. Sure enough, two days after our arrival in Port Stanley, a powerful gale blasted its way through, with the boat's anemometer recording a wind speed of 60 knots in harbour as the surface of the water turned white with spray.

We took full advantage of the free time available to visit the well-curated Historic Dockyard Museum in Stanley and had a conversation with Richard Cockwell OBE, a local resident who had experienced the 1982 Argentine invasion first hand. During those difficult days he was responsible for the local radio station. Along with his fellow islanders he remains patriotic, but at the same time feels a sense of disappointment regarding the incursion. Richard told us that before the war there had been growing ties with Argentina.

Sadly, the conflict put a stop to the chance of closer bonds emerging between the two peoples. Arguably this was a war that proper diplomacy could have helped to avoid.

With the strong weather system that had blown up from the Southern Ocean and crossed the Falklands now behind us, we were presented with a good window of opportunity to set off for South Georgia, 800 nautical miles to the east. Before us lay the open expanse of the Southern Ocean. On leaving Port Stanley on Tuesday 7th January, we sailed out into waters that are home to albatrosses and other seabirds which would become our companions during the passage ahead. A period of settled weather was predicted, and we had excellent downwind sailing conditions during the first two days at sea. A small front passed through on Thursday that would give us a north-easterly wind for a limited period, before the wind then backed to the west making the going easier.

After dinner on our third night at sea, we had the misfortune to suffer a little tear in our mainsail when we were shaking out a reef. Using all his skills, Morgan, assisted by André, set about sewing up the hole, making an excellent job of it despite the cold conditions out on deck.

Early on Friday, fog started to roll in, a sign that we were approaching the Antarctic Convergence where the water temperature drops to just over freezing. As soon as relatively warm air meets the cold sea, a dense fog results. Notwithstanding the low visibility, *Louise* continued on her way across an empty ocean. Unsurprisingly, we did not encounter any ships during this time. By late on the same day, while being accompanied by a pod of hourglass dolphins, we were approaching our destination under engine with the wind having died.

On Saturday 11th January the sun rose at 3 a.m., and although the fog hadn't yet cleared by breakfast, Bird Island

and the Willis Islands off South Georgia were visible on the radar screen about 20 nautical miles distant. Another sign that land was close by was the profusion of seals swimming around the boat. After the species was virtually driven to extinction by sealers in the nineteenth century, modern habitat management has helped to boost the seal population to the point of abundance. Now millions of fur seals live around South Georgia, breeding on land and fishing in the rich waters around the shoreline.

Our first sight of land was at lunchtime, when Hamish noticed the Fortuna Glacier emerge out of the gloom. There were another 30 nautical miles left to motor that afternoon, before we reached the old Grytviken Whaling Station and now the principal settlement on South Georgia. By teatime we were tied up on the Tijuca jetty, used by visitors, in front of the old Norwegian Whalers' Church. Our four-day passage from the Falklands had happily been a good ride. We were of course very excited to step onto the island that Captain James Cook and Ernest Shackleton had made famous.

Grytviken was one of half a dozen whaling stations that reached the height of their activity early in the twentieth century. Whaling had been an important industry, providing oil for lighting and lubrication, material for umbrellas and much more. The land-based whaling stations in South Georgia were mainly controlled by Norwegian companies. Whaling ships hunted their prey at sea before towing them to the station for the carcasses to be hauled ashore and processed. With the development of whaling factory ships in the early twentieth century, it was no longer necessary to bring whales ashore, so by the 1920s this innovation had sounded the death knell for South Georgia's industrial activity. Grytviken Whaling Station has been partially restored and now stands as a reminder of the island's past history.

During our stay, we met Professor Bjørn Basberg from Bergen University, an expert on the history of the whaling industry. The friendly professor is a trustee of the South Georgia Heritage Trust and has led industrial archaeology studies on the island's historic whaling stations. Arguably the highlight of our visit to Grytviken was paying homage to Ernest Shackleton, one of the world's greatest polar explorers, who died during his final Antarctic expedition in 1922. He is buried in the cemetery on a hill overlooking the small bay at Grytviken. The ashes of Frank Wild, Shackleton's trusted deputy, are interred next to his leader.

After spending two days in Grytviken, we moved on to Husvik Bay, the site of Stromness Whaling Station, where we set the anchor for a night. It was here, following the epic boat journey from Elephant Island to South Georgia in 1916, that Shackleton was able to inform the whalers of the plight of twenty-two other members of his Imperial Trans-Antarctic Expedition who were still stranded.

We also made a day excursion with *Louise* to Prion Island, where we went ashore to get a good look at the breeding colony of wandering albatrosses. These impressive birds hardly moved when approached, even at very close range, so we were able to observe them preening their feathers and building nests with their beaks. Aside from these highlights, we also went on some great walks on South Georgia, absorbing the majestic background of the huge mountain range which rises over 9,600 feet into the southern sky.

On our last day on South Georgia, we spoke briefly to Martin Collins, the island's Chief Executive Officer. There was also plenty of activity at the King Edward Point base, as the Royal Navy's ice patrol vessel, HMS *Protector*, was being loaded with postbags full of greetings cards before preparing to leave for Port Stanley.

Aside from postage stamps, the most important source of revenue of this far-flung British outpost is represented by fishing rights. The management of the surrounding waters has resulted in one of the Atlantic's most acclaimed sustainable fisheries. Among other species, the waters are home to the prized Patagonian toothfish, which is highly sought after in restaurants and appears on the menu as Chilean sea bass. Fishing rights are auctioned a month at a time, producing an income of a few million dollars each year, which helps to sustain the budget of one of the UK's last remaining dependencies.

A team of around thirty people staff the island during the summer, and their activities include managing a number of environmental programmes, such as the de-ratting of South Georgia and removing non-indigenous reindeer. We were delighted when the island's CEO sold us a leg of 'government stock' reindeer before we left, which we enjoyed for dinner on our last evening in Grytviken. While tasting our fine supper, snow was gently falling outside, covering *Louise*'s deck.

Following an early night, by 4.15 a.m. we were up again on the morning of Thursday 16th January, lifting the anchor to begin our return journey to Port Stanley. Motoring along the northern coast of South Georgia, all morning we hugged close to the shore. We passed near to Salisbury Plain, known for its substantial king penguin colony, the second largest on the island. When they are not fishing in the sea, the 250,000 or so penguins spend their time on the beach or find higher ground on the slopes behind. Unfortunately for us, it was not calm enough to go ashore, so we motored out into the South Atlantic.

As the island faded out of view, we were left with images ingrained in our memories of one of the world's most remote frontiers, where the power of nature is very much visible to the naked eye. South Georgia and the surrounding cold Antarctic waters are home to many seabirds and mammals that depend upon each other's existence to sustain life. This outcrop in the South Atlantic is certainly not an environment made for man. Captain Cook discovered the place in 1775, naming it after King George III. Observing the desolate land mass, he noted in his diary that 'the wild rocks raised their lofty summits till they were lost in the clouds, and the valleys lay covered with everlasting snow'.

A low-pressure system was close by, passing over around lunchtime when the barometer dropped to 971 millibars, which was the lowest we had recorded thus far. By the afternoon the barometer was rising, signalling that the weather system had moved to our east and we could expect a southerly wind quite soon. That evening we put three reefs in the mainsail and set the storm jib. Although it was rough during the night, with gusts of up to 40 knots, *Louise* sailed well despite the conditions. Our main concern had been keeping warm, because the boat's heater had stopped working overnight. In the cold South Atlantic, the sea temperature was approximately 2°C, so the cabin soon became very chilly. Luckily, Morgan was able to solve the problem and restored the on-board heating. After being on watch outside, when we came back down below we could once again dry off our hats and gloves inside the snug cabin.

Settling into the passage back to the Falklands, we witnessed a magnificent all-day-long spectacle of seabirds twirling through the air and skimming the waves. Wandering albatrosses, giant petrels, shags and many more entertained us while we each stood watch on deck. The wind slowly eased during the second day, and we were making good progress in the south-westerly. Then, just after midnight on Lloyd and

Morgan's watch, the autopilot ceased working. While Lloyd steered the boat, Morgan installed the replacement drive unit. Inspecting the broken autopilot, we discovered that the teeth on the drive cogs had worn through; unfortunately, this mechanical problem would become a recurring issue.

On the third day of the return leg we experienced lighter conditions, but there was still one weather hurdle to overcome, thanks to another South Atlantic low-pressure system tracking to the north-east of the Falklands. It became rough again during the night, as the wind backed towards the north-west and strengthened. Fortunately, we had managed to gain enough northing to allow us the possibility of reaching our destination without tacking. Sailors in these waters must be alert to the chance of strong headwinds coming back from South Georgia. Returning expeditions often have to bear the brunt of South Atlantic gales accompanied by big seas. Our luck was holding out.

That evening we were hailed on the radio by a nearby ship. The voice spoke with a Russian accent and asked us to keep clear of an oil exploration vessel that was in our path and which they were guarding. During the era of high oil prices, the Falklands were considered as a new frontier for this industry, attracting investment in exploration. In the light of the Russian's request, we took evasive action and steered north of the group of three ships. Later that night, another technical problem arose when our staysail unfurled without notice, making a loud flapping noise. On hearing the concerning sound, we all leapt out of our bunks to assist, but Lloyd and Morgan, who were on watch, were quick to get the situation under control.

At lunchtime on Monday 20th January, after four days at sea, we were safely back inside the shelter of Port Stanley. *Louise* had handled herself well, covering 1,700 nautical miles of sailing during our round trip to South Georgia, and we had been lucky to have encountered generally good weather conditions for the two passages.

On our return from South Georgia, we were able to moor *Louise* in the heart of town at the Falkland Islands Company jetty, a significant improvement on the rusty FIPAS floating dock where we had previously been tied up. A couple of other small boats were also moored there, which provided some company. Stepping off *Louise*, we were greeted by André's wife Anne-Marie, who had recently arrived from Belgium. She had booked a room in the Malvina House Hotel, where André joined her, and Lloyd and I also decided to stay there to get a peaceful night's rest. That evening we all celebrated our safe return to Stanley. We planned to pack in as much sightseeing and exploration as possible in the Falklands before setting off on the next stage of our journey. Morgan, Cheryl and Hamish had a long list of jobs to attend to in preparation for Antarctica, and consequently were happy to have the rest of us out of the way.

The following day, the first stop on our excursion was Port Louis on East Falkland. Visiting the island's original settlement brought to mind how desolate a place the first settlers would have found the Malouines. The Acadians had erected a few little buildings facing the sheltered creek where they moored their vessels. No sooner had the French occupied the islands in 1764 than Spain started to make noises that the 'Malvinas' were by rights within Madrid's colonial sphere of influence. After acquiring first-hand knowledge of the archipelago, France no longer saw the Malouines as of strategic importance and therefore didn't resist the Spaniards' claims. Louis-Antoine de Bougainville was despatched to Madrid to handle the negotiations. Top of the list of issues for Bougainville was recovering the investment that he and others had made in establishing the small outpost. Once an agreement had been reached with the Spaniards, the next step was to remove the settlers from the islands and hand the territory over to its new masters in 1766.

In 1767, Spain first took title to the islands and renamed the original French settlement Puerto Soledad. The Spaniards held onto the Malvinas for forty-four years, abandoning their garrison in East Falkland in 1811 and leaving the door open for Britain to eventually take over the territory in 1833. With the arrival of the new colonists, the main settlement was moved. Port Stanley was chosen for its natural harbour, which is protected from the prevailing westerlies. The official name of the islands also changed from the Malvinas to the Falklands. In French and Spanish, they are still called Îles Malouines and Islas Malvinas respectively.

On the day of our visit to Port Louis, we were greeted by jovial sheep-farm owners Mike and Melanie Gelding. Melanie, whom we discovered was originally from Fife, proudly showed us how they managed the triage of wool that was sheared from their 3,000-strong herd. The Falkland Islands economy is partially dependent on sheep farming. Sheep steadings are found on both of the main islands, West Falkland and East Falkland. The archipelago is divided by Falkland Sound, a navigable channel that runs south-west to north-east, separating both land masses. There are numerous other smaller islands dotted around the jagged coastline, especially off West Falkland.

On the morning of Wednesday 22nd January, we hopped on board an air taxi at Port Stanley Airport and took off west, bound for Port Howard on West Falkland. The pilot invited me to sit next to him and we chatted about the forecast. He pointed out how his map showed wind speeds at different altitudes and what conditions we could expect during the very short flight. Air taxis are the most common means of transport used to reach West Falkland and the outlying islands of the archipelago, and they operate in most weather conditions. On landing, we were met by Sue Lowe and Wayne Brewer, managers of the Port Howard Lodge where we would be staying overnight. As they drove us to their property, we learnt that their many local duties included driving cattle off the airfield and routinely flattening cowpats to ensure the grassy strip was safe for take-offs and landings! After dropping off our bags, we set off for an afternoon walk that took us past a little harbour opening out onto the sound. Port Howard is dominated by a massive farm that is home to about 40,000 sheep, who considerably outnumber the twenty-strong human population.

After breakfast the next day, we left the tranquil surroundings of Port Howard behind and reboarded the air taxi to fly to Carcass Island, off the north-west tip of West Falkland. Further west of Carcass Island are a series of treacherous rocks within the Jason Islands Archipelago that were well known as a death trap for passing ships. The Carcass Island airstrip is on a field that faces west towards to the ocean. Thanks to calm flying conditions we had a smooth landing. The island's owner, Rob McGill, was waiting in his four-wheel-drive vehicle to meet us off the plane. We drove across some fields and headed to the modest guest house where we would be spending a couple of nights. Our accommodation looked out onto a sheltered bay where a fishing boat lay at anchor. This vessel would be our transport the following day on our trip to West Point Island to visit its albatross colony. That evening we met some other tourists who were also staying in the guest house and who would be travelling to West Point Island too.

On Friday morning, we endured a bumpy crossing as the fishing boat rolled uncomfortably in the ocean swell. Our fellow passengers, who were probably less accustomed to being at sea, couldn't hold back their breakfast and were seasick. We felt sorry for them. Any inconvenience, however, was compensated for by the spectacle of young albatrosses at the bird colony, which were perched precariously on a cliff side facing the Atlantic. The juvenile birds had hatched a few months earlier and had the appearance of fluffy chickens. Not yet able to fly, they were still dependent on their parents for food. Looking at the birds I marvelled at the fact that scientists had worked out how a grown albatross was capable of flying 10,000 miles in a single journey, enabling it to circumnavigate the Southern Ocean.

After returning from our excursion, Anne-Marie, André, Lloyd and I enjoyed a pleasant walk to the beach on the eastern side of Carcass Island. The sea sparkled in the bright afternoon sun and we discovered a colony of gentoo penguins at the waterside. The penguins had chosen to live in an area with pure white sand running gently down into a shallow bay, which looked idyllic.

The next morning, after breakfast at the guest house, we noticed the cook was down at the waterside feeding seabirds straight out of his hand. He told us that he gave food to the same bird every day, which appeared as soon as he called its name.

Leaving behind Carcass and the outer islands of the Falklands, the air taxi took us back to Port Stanley. As we flew along the coastline on a beautiful day, the reflection of the sun sparkled on the sea below. On its way east, the plane passed over Port Louis just before descending into Port Stanley Airport, giving us an aerial view of the island's first settlement.

Before our departure from Stanley, we were witness to the aftermath of a minor drama. On the BBC news website, Lloyd had read a report about a car accident in the Falklands earlier that week involving two retired Argentinian footballers. Ossie Ardiles, of Tottenham Hotspur fame, had been injured during the incident and the article revealed that he had been admitted to the local hospital. While Lloyd and I were sitting in the lounge of the Malvina House Hotel, we overheard guests opposite us speaking in Spanish with unmistakable Argentinian accents. After introducing ourselves, we discovered we were in conversation with Ricky Villa, the other famous footballer. The two players were absent from the team sheet in 1982 when Spurs had reached the FA Cup Final and the Falklands War was in full swing. We had a chat with the friendly Argentinians whom we learnt had come to the islands to make a documentary film. Shortly after our encounter, the noise of a helicopter landing near to the hotel, which was close to the Port Stanley hospital, signalled that Ardiles was about to be airlifted to Mount Pleasant, where a private aircraft would fly him back home to Argentina. This incident was surely proof that, in spite of any political differences between our countries, our relationship at a human level was good.

By Saturday 25th January, we were ready to say farewell to Port Stanley to head back into the Southern Ocean and set sail for Antarctica. Before leaving, we received a gift of a leg of guanaco from our neighbour in the harbour. Christophe Auguin, winner of the 1996–97 Vendée Globe, a single-handed, non-stop, round-the-world yacht race, had shot the guanaco on Beaver Island while visiting a friend, Jérôme Poncet, who lives in the Falklands. Jérôme and his wife Sally are amongst the most prolific sailors in these waters, and are at the heart of a small community of adventurers who have a passion for high-latitude exploration. Between them, the couple have received multiple medals for supporting science and discovery in Antarctica. We reciprocated Christophe's generosity by giving him a bottle of Scotland's finest and wished him well for his upcoming trip to South Georgia.

At teatime we let go our mooring lines and waved goodbye to a group of onlookers. In the open water we were greeted by a light south-westerly breeze and the remnants of ocean swell from the same direction. By the middle of the night, the wind had veered north-west and we could turn off the engine. About 100 miles south of the Falklands we were due to cross over the Burdwood Bank, an extensive shallow area where the sea floor rises to approximately 600 feet, which can be treacherous during a gale. Fortunately, we were able to pass over the bank the next day, during quiet weather conditions under clear-blue skies. To our south-west and over the Scotia Sea ahead, however, a low-pressure system was coming our way. It would bring us the benefit of westerlies and, as forecast, the winds started to strengthen on the third day of the passage, building up to a full gale with some rough seas.

As we were reefing the mainsail, one of the sliders that attaches the sail to the mast broke. In place of the mainsail we hoisted our bright-orange-coloured storm trysail, which made *Louise* stand out against the rolling swell and occasional dark skies that accompanied the regular squalls. During the last part of the journey, the conditions calmed down and we motor-sailed dead south.

Just before sunrise, at 3.40 a.m. on Wednesday 29th January, we sighted the mountains of the South Shetland Islands, which lie north-west of the Antarctic Peninsula. To reach our first stop at Deception Island, we sailed through the English Strait, a narrow stretch of water between Robert Island and Greenwich Island. Passing our first icebergs, which each had a unique sculpted form, *Louise* seemed surrounded by living nature. Pods of humpback whales, chinstrap and gentoo penguins, seals and a solitary minke whale all came to greet us.

By the evening we had reached Neptune's Bellow, the narrow entrance to Port Foster at Deception Island, and motored into the flooded caldera that is invisible from the sea outside. We moored in a sheltered bay in the far corner of Port Foster.

The island is a living volcano that still simmers with activity and this was made very apparent to us when, on Thursday morning, we awoke to discover that *Louise* had been dusted by volcanic ash during the night. After sweeping all the ash away and having breakfast, we moved her over to the anchorage at Whalers Bay where, to our surprise, we found *Leava* at anchor, the French boat that we had met in Caleta Hornos, our last stop in Argentina.

We set off ashore to walk along the beach and climbed the small hill to Neptune's Window. From this viewpoint, looking out over the Bransfield Strait, we savoured our first sight of the Antarctic Peninsula rising on the horizon 60 miles east. Looking down from the cliff towards the beach, we could see steam rising along the water's edge, proof of the island's volcanic nature. We then walked through the ramshackle and rusty structures of the old whaling station, which was opened by a Norwegian company in 1912. The factory only operated for twenty years before pelagic whale fishing took over. Slightly further from the beach were the ruined buildings of the British Antarctic Survey station that had been damaged in 1969 by volcanic eruptions.

By mid-afternoon on Thursday 30th January, we were back on board *Louise* and lifting anchor to head further south. Before leaving Port Foster, we motored past *Leava* to say hello to the owners. Alain and Bernadette were preparing to go north by way of Tristan da Cunha, one of the most remote islands in the South Atlantic, on their way home to France. Next season they were hoping to sail to Scotland. There is no holding back some people's natural sense of exploration, not even those well over retirement age such as this intrepid couple.

Leaving the huge volcanic crater behind, we motored due south towards Trinity Island. Entering the Gerlache Strait that evening, we slowed *Louise* down. On a virtually flat, calm sea we drifted gently in a southerly direction, enjoying the silence under a clear night sky. For dinner we ate the guanaco that had been gifted to us in Stanley, which had been prepared as a lovely stew, accompanied by some red wine. Taking it in turns hourly, we each stood watch while appreciating the serenity of our surroundings.

The strait was named after the famous Belgian polar explorer Adrien de Gerlache. He obtained his first command in Antarctica when, at the age of thirty-one, he led the Belgian Antarctic Expedition of 1897–99, which was notable for being the first-ever expedition to winter in Antarctica. Twenty-five-year-old Roald Amundsen joined the multinational crew as first mate, and was able to acquire vital experience that would serve him well in the future, as arguably the world's most successful explorer and Norwegian national hero.

The following morning, on Friday 31st January, we started to explore the coast of the Antarctic Peninsula. This vast stretch of land, which protrudes into the Southern Ocean, is over 600 miles long. The peninsula separates the Bellingshausen Sea in the west from the Weddell Sea to the east. Our objective was to track the west coast of the peninsula as far south as the ice and time would reasonably allow. Hamish, our pilot, pointed out that flexibility was advisable to allow for possible changes in the weather conditions. But, so far, we felt spoilt as the sun had shone most days. Also, there was hardly a breath of wind, making it easier to explore close to the shoreline.

Passing Cierva Cove tucked under the black cliffs of Cape Sterneck, which the British refer to as Cape Herschel, we encountered pods of humpback and killer whales that seemed oblivious to the boat. Stopping for lunch, as we sat outside in the cockpit eating, *Louise* drifted while we absorbed the scenery to the fullest. Later that afternoon we reached Enterprise Island, a sheltered location chosen by whalers, who made the anchorage at the south side of the island at Foyn Harbour a major centre of summer industry from the First World War to 1930. A Norwegian whale ship called the *Gouvenoren* sank at her moorings in 1916, becoming a convenient jetty for yachts to tie alongside. The rusty shipwreck is the only mooring available on the Antarctic Peninsula and we had the fortune to experience a perfectly calm day for our visit. Lloyd took his camera and climbed up the mast on the bosun's chair to take in the view. *Louise* remained exceptionally still during our night tied up alongside the wreck.

On Saturday, after a short morning stroll over the snow-covered island, we motored gently through Wilhelmina Bay, encountering a pod of twenty or so humpback whales. As they circled on the surface it was clear that they were bubble-net feeding, a technique involving two whales diving together. When they start to surface, they swim in a circle emitting bubbles. This forms an underwater spout that encourages krill, their favoured food, to swim to the centre. The whales then filter the water as they come up, collecting krill in their baleens.

Following another lunch, sitting outdoors in the cockpit that was bathed sunlight, we passed two boats in quick succession. The first was a Russian exploration ship, *Akademik*

Sergey Vavilov, which looked very well maintained. In the latter stage of the Adventure, we would take the opportunity to go on board her sister ship, the *Akademik Ioffe*, in Cape Breton, Canada. A little while later, we passed *Kotik II*, a yacht owned by a couple who had been cruising in these waters for many years. Hamish spoke briefly with them and learnt about the ice conditions further south.

By the evening, Hamish had guided us to a sheltered spot at Cuverville Island where we could carefully moor *Louise*. Dropping the anchor from the bow, as normal, using the dinghy we pulled our floating mooring lines and tied them securely ashore. Hamish and Lloyd, who manned the dinghy, also had to push some large chunks of ice out of *Louise*'s way. By fixing the position of the boat, we would guard against changes in the wind or current that could expose her to the moving ice.

After breakfast on Sunday morning, we set off to climb to the top of the island. Although it was only 820 feet in altitude, when we made it to the summit we were sweating from the effort. In the afternoon we travelled further south, stopping for the night in the serene soundings of Paradise Bay. Tying *Louise* by the stern to the land once again, we made a shore visit onto the peninsula mainland for a special team photo on the continent of Antarctica, as all our other overnight moorings had been on islands off the peninsula. In the evening, we celebrated Hamish's fifty-second birthday with a freshly baked cake that Cheryl had made.

Another treat in Paradise Bay was courtesy of a National Geographic cruise ship, which was anchored close by but hidden just out of sight. One of their inflatable dinghies came by *Louise* and its crew offered us hot chocolate with alcoholic flavourings, which we gratefully accepted. Later, when we were back in the UK, we discovered that a picture of *Louise* moored in Enterprise Bay had been posted on Facebook. Unbeknownst to us, our friends Craig and Beth Armknecht from Atlanta, Georgia had been travelling on that particular cruise and taken a photo of our boat. None of us had been aware at the time that our paths had crossed so closely in Antarctica.

Lying in our bunks that night, we heard occasional cracking sounds as the huge glacier shifted and ice broke off into the water. The boat was gently rocked each time a wave was set off by the falling ice.

The following morning, on Monday 3rd February, we passed though the Lemaire Channel. Sheer mountains of dark, exposed granite, rising on both sides straight out of the sea, make this one of Antarctica's most striking stretches of water. We proceeded slowly with *Louise* through the strait that, in part, was clogged up with floating pieces of ice known as brash ice. Slowing down to snail pace at one juncture, we managed to find a path through. We passed the Dutch sailing vessel *Oosterschelde*, which we had been moored close to in Port Stanley before New Year. She is the only remaining Dutch three-masted topsail schooner and was on her way north. We were able to stop for a short while and speak over the water with the captain, wishing him and his crew a safe passage.

Later on, we sailed by a number of raft-like pieces of ice that crabeater seals had commandeered and were lying prostrate on, taking in the sun. Killer whales often take advantage of such scenes when they launch an attack by rocking the ice floes, which then causes the seals to take to the water where they become ready prey.

Further south, we arrived at our stopover on Pleneau Island, where we moored in a little inlet. Before dinner we made a dinghy excursion to a nearby gentoo penguin rookery. Our attention was grabbed when we noticed a leopard seal lying on a small ice floe and took some selfie pictures with the seal in the background. These creatures are dangerous predators, always on the lookout for their next meal.

Continuing south on Tuesday, we stopped to make a trip by dinghy into Circumcision Bay. In 1909, Jean-Baptiste Charcot's French expedition overwintered in this tiny bay on their ship *Pourquoi-Pas? IV*. Charcot's team rigged a chain across the entrance to the inlet to stop icebergs entering from the sea and potentially causing damage to their vessel. By the time that winter had fully set in, the crew could walk across the ice to the mainland opposite their winter hideaway.

We were now approaching our most southerly point at Vernadsky Station on Galindez Island. Originally established by the UK as the Faraday Station in 1947, the base was used for research before being handed over to Ukraine in 1966 and renamed Vernadsky. The UK Antarctic Heritage Trust maintains the station's original hut, which is located nearby on Winter Island and named after the Scottish geologist James Wordie, who was chief scientist and geologist on Shackleton's *Endurance* expedition of 1914–17. During our visit to the hut, we met a friendly British couple who had volunteered on behalf of the UK Antarctic Heritage Trust to do some restoration and repair work, and who gave us an informative tour of the tiny site.

When deciding where to moor the boat on Tuesday, we chose the sheltered anchorage of Stella Creek, a narrow, winding passage lying between Winter Island and Galindez Island, close to the old explorers' hut. Between 1935 and 1936, it had been used for overwintering by the *Penola*, a three-masted schooner that sailed in the British Graham Land Expedition of 1934–37.

Marking the occasion of reaching our furthest point south at 65 degrees latitude, we prepared a traditional Scottish

Burns Night dinner. With some foresight, while stocking up with provisions in the Falklands we had bought tins of Grants of Speyside haggis. It was just over a week since our country's evening of national celebration on 25th January, and I made the address to the haggis before we enjoyed a jolly dinner. After supper we had a brief walk ashore, where we marvelled at the mountains on the peninsula's mainland that stretched as far south as the eye could see, well beyond the Antarctic Circle at the latitude of 66.5 degrees south. In the fading light at the end of the day, while standing on the ice overlooking the anchorage where *Louise* floated almost motionless at her mooring, the view was simply beautiful.

We had been invited to visit the Vernadsky Station base later that evening, and made our way over there at 9 p.m. The officers welcomed us in and gave us a short tour of the premises before we all retired to the Faraday Bar, one of the world's most southerly drinking establishments. Customers are expected to bring their own bottle, so we chose to take some Reyka vodka from Iceland, which we thought our Ukrainian hosts would appreciate. Soon after the first toast, the hosts offered us another round. They produced a bottle of Grant's whisky and filled our glasses, which we raised again for another toast. I replied, thanking the Ukrainians and complementing them on their choice of brand, while also adding that the contents of the bottle did not taste like Grant's Scotch. Laughing, they revealed that what we had just drunk was their home brew, the original whisky having already been consumed.

We were then challenged to a snooker and darts tournament. Splitting into two teams, the men on *Louise* played really well and ended up winning the competition. Once the games were over, a magnificent evening was concluded and, after thanking our hosts, we retired to the boat.

After breakfast on Wednesday, we returned to the station to post some greetings cards to friends and family back home. We then prepared to leave to head north, accepting that this would be the most southerly point that we reached in Antarctica at 65°15'S, 64°16'W. The weather conditions were very smooth as we motored back towards the Lemaire Channel. Later in the morning a light breeze appeared, which provided us with our first chance to sail. We were keen to take some pictures of *Louise* under sail in Antarctica, so André volunteered as cameraman and Hamish drove the dinghy while the rest of us remained on board the boat. By the time the dinghy party had returned, they were frozen. But the filming was a success, capturing *Louise* as she sailed with penguins bobbing up and down in the water all around her.

In the afternoon, with the cloud cover becoming thicker, we continued north through a small channel that led towards Port Lockroy on Goudier Island. This base has become the most visited destination in Antarctica. A British research station from 1944 to 1962, it fell into disuse and eventually was taken over by the UK Antarctic Heritage Trust. The Trust developed the site into a first-class visitor centre, comprising a museum, souvenir shop and post office within Bransfield House. Its staff at the time of our arrival were all female, in stark contrast to Vernadsky where only men were employed at the station.

Another visitor that day, anchored close by *Louise*, was the Royal Navy ship HMS *Protector*. Following our first encounter with the vessel in South Georgia, and then again in Port Stanley, we were crossing paths with it for the third time. We talked to Commander Richard Bird, comparing our itineraries, and discovered that he and his crew were also heading to Chile.

That evening, to celebrate our last night in Antarctica,

we ate a delicious meal of Patagonian toothfish and talked about our extraordinary week exploring just a fraction of the frozen continent. Afterwards, Hamish, Lloyd, Morgan and I set our alarms for 4 a.m., for the purpose of an early-morning consultation on the weather. Although it was tempting to prolong our stay in Antarctica, a strong weather system was approaching from the west, which would provide us with a good opportunity to cross the iconic Drake Passage. Named after the sixteenth-century English privateer Sir Francis Drake, the stretch of water that lies between Cape Horn and the Antarctic Peninsula is 500 nautical miles wide and is also the boundary between the Atlantic and Pacific Oceans.

Remaining in Antarctica would likely result in us being stranded on the boat moored at anchor, waiting for the wind to subside. So, on Thursday 6th February, we took the decision to depart, and soon we were motoring out into the open sea. As we left, we were fortunate to see *Pelagic* at anchor. Captained originally by the sailing explorer Skip Novak, she was one of the first custom-built polar exploration yachts. Our pilot Hamish had skippered her for a number of years, before building his own boat with his wife. While sailing *Pelagic* he made countless voyages in the Big South.

Throughout our first day back at sea, we focused attentively on keeping an eye out for any icebergs as, at this time of the year, ice may be expected even in the warmer waters to the north. On our second day into the passage before lunch, at around 61 degrees south, a huge iceberg was sighted. The sea was settled initially, but as we progressed north the signs of the advancing low pressure became more apparent. A northerly wind gradually built up as we approached the depression. As planned, we had gained plenty of westing while motoring.

During the early hours on our second night at sea, the centre of the low-pressure system passed over and the wind strengthened, backing to the west. Over the next 400 miles to Cape Horn in southern Chile, we faced classic Southern Ocean running conditions, with strong winds accompanied by big waves, and *Louise* moved well through the water. The wind eventually strengthened to become a full gale with a large swell that the boat could nicely slide down. The conditions crossing the Drake Passage can often be rough and our experience of the 'Drake Shake' was true to form, but we were none the worse for it.

On Sunday 9th February, we all awoke in keen anticipation of the landfall that we were about to make. Out on deck we could see the iconic headland of Cape Horn to the north. It was a cloudy morning but visibility was good. At 7.40 a.m., the most southerly point of the Americas was abeam. Hamish was master of ceremonies for the traditional topping of the bottle of champagne, which he neatly severed with a confident swipe of the knife's blade. We all crowded into the cockpit to toast our safe passage, after which Cheryl prepared a full cooked breakfast. Late in the afternoon, we entered the Beagle Channel and anchored at Puerto Harberton on Tierra del Fuego in Argentina. Just after mooring that evening, André accidentally slipped in the cabin and cut his hand badly. Fortunately, the *Oosterschelde* had also just arrived from Antarctica and had a nurse on board who kindly provided some first aid.

The following morning, to stretch our legs we went ashore for a stroll, taking the opportunity to visit the grounds and outbuildings at Estancia Harberton. During the evening, in calm conditions, we motored the last few miles to Ushuaia where we tied up at the AFASyN yacht club pier. Already gathered there was an eclectic collection of yachts, and the pontoon was busy with their crews. We were introduced to Roxanna Diaz, the friendly Ocean Cruising Club port captain, and the next morning she accompanied us to the Naval Prefecture building in town to complete the paperwork for formal entry into Argentina, which went smoothly.

On Wednesday 12th February, it was time to take our leave and thank Morgan and Cheryl, who would remain on board *Louise* until my return in March. The Annicqs, who had been most friendly companions during our Big South adventure, flew north to a mountain resort near Bariloche to relax after their Antarctica experience. Lloyd and I were bound for Buenos Aires, from where we would catch a plane home to London. Taking off from Ushuaia over the Beagle Channel, from the plane window we had a clear view of the Chilean islands stretching out to the south, with Cape Horn in the distance.

Chapter 4 – Land of Fire
Ushuaia, Argentina to Puerto Montt, Chile

Caleta Beaulieu, Tierra del Fuego, Chile

By early March 2014, we were heading back to South America for the final stage of our travels in the Big South. Two of my oldest friends, Klaus Diederichs and Errikos Abravanel, had agreed to join Brigitte and me for our northwards passage through Chile's Patagonian channels. En route, we spent one night in Buenos Aires, where we enjoyed staying in the tiny Jardin Escondido Hotel. After the flight to Ushuaia, we met up with Morgan and Cheryl on the boat before dealing with the formalities involved in checking ourselves out of Argentina.

Back on board *Louise*, we were pleasantly surprised to find that, thanks to the generosity of the Annicqs, she had been restocked with some fantastic locally produced wines. Late afternoon on Monday 3rd March, we cast off from the AFASyN pier in Ushuaia and waved goodbye to the other crews on the dock. Just a few hours away, a short distance to the east, lay our first stop: Puerto Williams on Navarino Island in Chile, the most southerly settlement in the Americas.

That evening we rafted with other yachts alongside the *Micalvi*, a small ship which, now retired, doubles up as a mooring vessel and clubhouse. The *Micalvi* started life plying the River Rhine in Germany with modest cargoes and in 1928 she was bought by the Chilean Navy to transport arms to the country. Today she sits on the mud in a little creek in the town of Puerto Williams, where she acts as a floating yacht club. Meeting on the bridge of the *Micalvi*, we ordered a round of pisco sour cocktails, a favourite in Chile.

On Tuesday morning, we strolled along the waterfront and passed a well-painted building flying the Chilean flag. It turned out to be the coastguard office that we were seeking and here Morgan dealt with the necessary paperwork. Not long afterwards, we moved *Louise* alongside the town quay where a road tanker was waiting to supply us with fuel for the upcoming journey. There would be no possibility of taking on further diesel between here and Puerto Chacabuco, over 1,000 miles north, so we made sure that we had every drop of fuel possible. We had purchased a 400-litre-capacity orange-coloured diesel bladder that we also filled and put on the foredeck. This would prove invaluable during the weeks ahead, when we relied almost 100 per cent on the motor. While we were busy filling up the boat's tanks, the local naval commander came down to inspect what was going on and introduce himself. We had a brief conversation, during which he admired *Louise* and paid several compliments.

Fuelled up and formalities completed, we were ready to move on. Our next stop was at Caleta Ferrari, 45 miles west, a little beyond Ushuaia on the south side of Tierra del Fuego, just over the border in Chile. We motored up the Beagle Channel in flat, calm conditions and laid anchor in the early evening, opposite a small, brightly painted farm building. The anchorage was very well protected and the wind was light. Caleta Ferrari is located in the Estancia Yendegaia, one of the properties owned by Doug Tompkins, which would become a National Park after his death in 2015.

Tompkins, a successful American outdoor-clothing entrepreneur, was passionate about restoring these lands to their natural state and had acquired vast tracts of wilderness in Chilean Patagonia. He became the focus of criticism from people who were unhappy to see such a considerable amount of their country fall into foreign hands. After he died following a kayaking accident, lands were transferred into a public-private collaboration between the Government of Chile and the foundations established by Tompkins and his second wife, which helped to ensure that the unique environment of southern Patagonia was preserved and protected from unwanted development.

After taking the dinghy to go ashore on Wednesday morning, we had a walk. Knocking on the door of a low-lying building facing the beach, we were invited in by a European-sounding voice. As we stepped into the kitchen a man, who introduced himself as José, was butchering some cattle meat that he had just slaughtered. We also greeted his partner Anne-Mieke, a softly spoken lady from Antwerp. She had met José about ten years earlier, while visiting on a sailing expedition, and had decided to stay in Tierra del Fuego so they could live together. The couple, who resided on the Estancia, looked after it on behalf of the owners. They generously offered to take us on a horseback ride, which we had to turn down as we would be leaving the anchorage imminently and didn't have enough time. Looking at the freshly cut meat, we asked if we could buy some. They refused our request, instead insisting that we should just take a bit with us. Not wishing to be impolite, we fetched a bottle of whisky from the boat, which we offered them in return, thus concluding a friendly barter arrangement. Everyone was now happy and so we thanked José and Anne-Mieke before setting off back to *Louise*.

The Beagle Channel is divided into two main branches that run north and south of Gordon Island, and we planned to take the Brazo Norte. This branch has steep sides along its shoreline and many inlets set into Tierra del Fuego. When we cast our eyes to the north, looking up from sea level to the skyline, we could see Mount Darwin. Covered in snow, the mountain range rises to 8,200 feet and forms a majestic panoramic backdrop.

Our destination that afternoon was 50 nautical miles away. Seno Pia, a large fjord cut out of Tierra del Fuego, had been formed by the glaciers that flow down from the mountains. Entering the fjord under motor, we passed over a shallow sandbar, a natural feature created by the glacier's moraine. Inside the fjord, we were greeted by a pod of dolphins that escorted *Louise* towards the anchorage. High above was the vista of the Ventisquero Romanche flowing down into the water. We approached the face of the glacier very slowly and with great care, as we were surrounded in the water by little pieces of ice that had broken off it.

Tucked away on the eastern arm of the fjord, facing the glacier, lay Caleta Beaulieu where two other yachts were moored. We located some sturdy trees to tie our stern to and dropped the anchor from the bow in the shallow water to settle down for the night. From the boat we had an exceptional view of the glacier, while Mount Darwin loomed in the background.

Thursday's forecast was for strong westerlies, which would hamper our progress, so we decided not to move the boat while conditions were windy. This gave us the chance to explore ashore and take some exercise. So Errikos, Klaus, Morgan and I set off in our walking gear to climb the hill overlooking the anchorage. It was well worth the effort once we had reached a clearing up the slope. From our vantage point we had amazing views of the fjord, as well as the mountains covered with ice and snow as a backdrop. Later, we took the dinghy to travel deeper into the fjord. We discovered huge waterfalls and saw fallen trees that had presumably been knocked down by avalanches. Taking advantage of our icy location, we collected some pieces of ice from the water in readiness for our daily cocktails. Klaus's Germanic roots were having a strong influence, as the national tradition of enjoying a 'Festmacher' drink once the vessel is tied up at the end of the day had already been adopted on board *Louise*. As the other yachts in the anchorage had left in the afternoon, we were able to experience the peaceful surroundings all on our own.

At first light on the morning of Friday 7th March, we lifted anchor to make an early start. We had 100 miles to run to reach the western end of Tierra del Fuego at Brecknock Peninsula, and so we continued our journey along on the northern arm of the Beagle Channel, which resembles a labyrinth, with countless nooks and crannies leading off on both sides. Leaving the fjord, we accidentally collided with some chunks of ice, but on inspecting the bow we found no damage to the boat's aluminium hull.

The day was mostly overcast, with a few breaks in the clouds, and the wind was coming from the north-west, blowing off the land. In these conditions the sea was quite smooth, making progress good. We passed a few colourful fishing boats, as well as the rather ugly-looking Yaghan ferry. The ferry service provides the principal link between the Chilean mainland and Navarino Island, shuttling between Punta Arenas on the Magellan Strait and Puerto Williams.

As we travelled west, the mountain range on Tierra del Fuego gradually reduced in height, but the scenery was just as stark and desolate. We wound our way through channels that separate South America's largest island from the myriad smaller islands in the surrounding archipelago dotted here and there.

During the afternoon, I was on watch when a strong gust hit the boat. Klaus was at the helm and while we were furling in the working jib, the sail tore itself. The damage we sustained proved the old sailor's maxim: 'Flappy sails are not happy sails.' By early evening we had motored into Seno Ocasión, a little fjord at the western extremity of Tierra del Fuego. *Louise* was accompanied by seals frolicking around on the surface as if to entertain us.

Hidden away at the end of the fjord is a well-protected anchorage named Brecknock. It lies a stone's throw from the open sea in the South Pacific Ocean, and is an ideal spot to shelter when travelling around the west of Tierra del Fuego. Well known to yachtsmen, this bolt-hole is surrounded on three sides by sheer rock faces, creating a scene of great natural beauty. A strong gale was forecast, so we had to ensure we were safe from the elements. Williwaws, or katabatic winds, are powerful gusts that blow down the backs of mountains. Sailors are fearful of these phenomena, where wind bursts can reach over 100 miles per hour. With *Louise* anchored near the western side of the creek and her stern facing the shore, secured by three mooring lines, this gave us the shelter we needed.

Errikos, Klaus and I set off for a walk ashore, climbing up to a vantage point where we could see the boat moored below, while the view out to the west took in the tip of Tierra del Fuego. Almost overlooking the anchorage was a neatly formed lake with a waterfall. Back on *Louise* we stayed snug and entertained ourselves by watching films on the boat's television and playing board games, while outside the odd hail shower came and went. We spent two nights sheltered from the elements before the wind backed to the south-west, which meant we could safely proceed onwards to reach the Magellan Strait.

On Sunday 9th March, we left Brecknock before breakfast and motored out through a heavy shower of sleet. Rounding the westerly end of Tierra del Fuego, we emerged into a stretch of water named the 'Milky Way' by the Canada-born sailor and adventurer Joshua Slocum. During Slocum's solo circumnavigation (1895–98), while leaving the Magellan Strait he was blown south off course in a storm as soon as he sailed out into the South Pacific. In an attempt to survive, he chose to point his boat east, towards the treacherous weather shore, and tried to find a way back into the strait. As he neared land, he found himself surrounded by exposed or semi-submerged rocks with waves crashing all over them. Although it was night-time, he managed to survive the ordeal. He came up with the name 'Milky Way' because he thought the white water was like the starry belt in the sky that can be seen on a clear night.

On *Louise*, instead of heading out into the Pacific, which was now visible to our west, we changed course, turning into Canal Cockburn, the rocky stretch of water that separates the Brecknock Peninsula, the westernmost projection of Tierra del Fuego, from Clarence Island and Aracena Island to the north. Before long, we had reached one of the minor channels running north of Canal Cockburn and took a shortcut into the Magellan Strait. By Sunday lunchtime, the boat was going full steam north along the small Canal Acwalisnan, approaching the Paso O'Ryan narrows. The passage is about 100 yards wide at this point and shallow, so the falling ebb tide carried *Louise* through the strait at over 12 knots.

Soon we emerged from the narrow channel into the open expanse of the Magellan Strait. Cape Froward, which is the southernmost point on South America's mainland, was clearly perceptible to the east. The grey headland had a dusting of snow on the higher reaches and stood out prominently on the partially cloudy sky. We drank a toast to celebrate reaching the Magellan Strait, first navigated in 1520 by the Portuguese navigator Ferdinand Magellan, during his expedition's circumnavigation. Once in the strait, we motored west towards the Paso Inglés, crossing paths with a large cargo ship heading in the opposite direction. The strait is still a route for commercial traffic, albeit not so heavily used.

It was getting late in the afternoon and we had already travelled 100 miles, so we decided to stop for the night at Bahía Tilly, a convenient anchorage. We slept well there, unlike our hero Joshua Slocum, who had a few skirmishes with the Fuegian Indians, a nomadic people with canoes who lived on the water's edge. After once being attacked aboard his boat *Spray*, the next night he placed tin tacks on the deck to alert him to the presence of unwanted intruders. When one of them later stood on the tacks in bare feet, the man screamed and jumped overboard into the water, warning Slocum of the potential threat.

Anxious not to be held up by bad weather, we pushed on early the following day, motoring in calm waters. Gradually, the Magellan Strait widened again as we proceeded further west through Paso Largo, before reaching the Boca Occidental and the gateway to the Pacific at Cabo Pilar on Desolación Island. Beyond this point lies the whole of the Pacific, stretching out to the west.

For explorers like Magellan, making a clean getaway from the strait required considerable seamanship and also a generous dose of luck in getting the right weather. In a strong westerly gale, ships of old struggled to gain enough sea room to distance themselves sufficiently beyond the danger zone that is the rocky and jagged Chilean coastline. In 1578, Sir Frances Drake ran into such conditions after he had exited the Magellan Strait and, just like Slocum centuries later, he was forced to run south and face a momentous struggle against the storms. At this point, Drake deduced that Tierra del Fuego was an island and the sea to the south was an open stretch of water linking the Atlantic and Pacific.

We passed a yacht named *Firiel* making its way east and talked to the French couple on board, who revealed they were headed for Punta Arenas and the Atlantic. We continued our course towards the tip of Tamar Island, where Canal Smyth branches off to the north.

Shortly before we were about to change course north to leave the strait, we encountered another yacht. Seeing that it was a small boat, we slowed down to hail it. The yellow-hulled vessel was motoring slowly against a building sea. Flying a German flag, she was registered in Rostock, on Germany's northern coast. A young man wearing traditional yellow foul-weather gear stood on deck. After exchanging polite greetings, we continued on our way. We were anxious not to lose time as the wind was picking up from the west. A few minutes later, however, the VHF crackled with the voice of the German sailor. He came straight to the point: 'Would *Louise* be obliged to give *Phoebe* a tow?' Our natural instinct was to assist him, as he looked as though he would struggle to make it past the end of Tamar Island, which was not ideal when bad weather was forecast.

We turned *Louise* and prepared the towing line. *Louise* drew up close by *Phoebe* and the young sailor, who was standing on the bow to take our line, was completely soaked as the bow bobbed up and down in the chop. Fortunately, the tow went fine and by early evening we had reached Puerto Profundo at the entrance to Canal Smyth. We let go the tow line from our newfound buddy, whom we named 'Abschlepper' (from the German verb *abschleppen*, which means 'to tow'), and after parting company we slipped through a very tight entrance into the secluded anchorage of Caleta Teokita. The narrow cut led into a well-enclosed and pretty expanse of water. Both sides of the entrance were thick with dense vegetation. Reaching out, we could almost touch the tree branches as *Louise* motored slowly into the little bay.

Next morning, on Tuesday 11th March, we left our secluded hideaway to continue our journey via the channel that leads north. During the day we motored in windless but overcast conditions, passing *Phoebe* once again. The owner, whose name was Jan, called us by radio thanking us for the tow. We also passed another larger German yacht, *Nuno*, which we had seen a few months earlier in Argentina.

Moving only 40 miles further north, we moored *Louise* in Caleta Mallet. With more wind expected, we tied the boat's stern to the shore at three different points, making sure that she was secure for the night. The anchorage was on the western side of the Zach Peninsula, a long isthmus that borders Seno Unión channel on the east side, which leads to Puerto Natales, a gateway to one of Chile's most famous national parks, Torres del Paine. With more time on our hands, we would have made the detour through the windy channels to Puerto Natales, but there were still more than 600 nautical miles to cover before reaching Puerto Chacabuco, where we would be dropping off Errikos and Klaus.

Early on Wednesday morning, Errikos and I went ashore, and after a brief walk we reached a beach on the east side of the isthmus at Ensenada Oracion, looking onto the Seno Unión channel leading to Puerto Natales. Back on board *Louise*, we continued north, but the wind was on the nose and strengthening. Motoring along we enjoyed spectacular views of the Torres del Paine mountain range, but the going was getting harder, so we broke off the journey and moored up in Caleta Dixon. Because a wind of 50 knots was forecast for Thursday, we prepared to spend two nights sitting tight in this tiny creek at the southern end of Newton Island.

We decided to get some fresh air and exercise the next day, and climbed a nearby hill. The most difficult part of our hike was finding a path into the open ground above, which involved negotiating some dense mossy undergrowth that went all the way down to the sea. After some effort we managed to hack our way through. Reaching a vantage point well above the anchorage, we were rewarded with a fantastic view of the Collingwood Strait, as well as Seno Unión stretching out to the south-east with mountains all around.

Later, after returning to *Louise*, we made a dinghy excursion and discovered a small boat moored around the corner from us, off a little island. The brightly painted vessel was loaded high with a cargo of timber and the two sailors on board greeted us. The boat was on its way south and was also sheltering from the strong weather. Back in the bay where *Louise* was anchored, a pod of three Peale's dolphins quietly swam and played with the bow wave of the dinghy. We made a few circles of the bay, filming the mammals as they frolicked in the water. We also spotted the *Zandaam* cruise ship steaming along the channel, having previously seen this ship in Puerto Madryn. In the summer, she shuttles holidaymakers on cruises to and from the Chilean city of Valparaíso and Buenos Aires via the Magellan Strait.

Watching another movie together that evening, the time passed quickly and the following day we were once again heading northwards. Lifting the anchor on Friday morning, we dragged up a large clump of kelp with it. Seaweed is extremely prolific in these cold waters, but we soon got rid of the weed using our home-made kelp cutter, a tool like a garden hoe with a sharp, steel cutting edge.

Taking advantage of calmer conditions, we motored north on Canal Sarmiento and later passed a yacht named *Balbao*, owned by two French doctors to whom we spoke. We would meet them again in Puerto Eden where we learnt that their wives, who were also keen sailors, had decided to leave their husbands on their own to enjoy their Patagonian expedition. Our journey took us 60 miles further north to Puerto Bueno, which is sheltered on all sides and where we stopped for the night. We all went ashore and climbed up to a freshwater lake which offered an excellent panorama of the bay below, where *Louise* was swinging at anchor. Down at the shore we discovered a little rapids where a stream, flowing out of the lake, emptied into the sea.

Early on Saturday morning before full light, we left Puerto Bueno, passing a small cargo ship and a fishing boat that were both moored just outside our bay. Some smoke was rising from the latter and as we went by we could see that the fishermen had lit a fire to keep warm in the darkness. The smell of the burning wood was very pleasant.

As we exited Canal Sarmiento later that morning, we passed Peel Inlet, a place that was made famous by H. W. Tilman, the passionate mountain climber, sailor and author whose adventures have inspired many. In December 1955, Tilman sailed his 45-foot Bristol Channel pilot cutter *Mischief* into this fjord, having travelled all the way from England. He moored the yacht and left two of his crew on board before setting off to climb the Andes with the other crew members. In his absence, the boat-bound men were careless and allowed *Mischief* to run aground in a narrows. At the end of January 1956 (the month and year of my birth), on Tilman's return from a successful mountaineering expedition, the irate skipper discovered what had happened. Furthermore, he learnt that the hapless crew had been obliged to remove 3 tonnes of ballast from *Mischief* to refloat her and the cutter had also sustained a damaged propeller.

On the day that we passed through the inlet, chunks of floating ice that had broken away from glaciers in the fjord were drifting out into the main channel. We steered the boat around a few of these blocks to avoid any collisions. In the late afternoon, we stopped at Caleta Colibri, an anchorage that had been recommended to us during our Falklands stopover. After reaching the narrowest part of the cove, we managed to tie *Louise* to trees both fore and aft. Snug for the night, we relaxed and took in the calm surroundings.

On Sunday 16th March, we set off in the early hours in order to arrive at the Seno Eyre fjord during the afternoon. Motoring before the sun was up, the moon cast a beautiful beam of light over the sea. At the entrance to the fjord, we encountered a considerable amount of ice flowing out of Falcon Inlet. Our limited view prevented us from seeing the base of the glacier in the distance, but higher up there was a clear sight of a glacier flowing down from the mountain peaks far above to the east. The panoramic scene of the Andes range, visible from *Louise*, was majestic.

We had now branched north, later passing two other yachts, *Balboa* and *Finisterre*, who were both on their way to Puerto Eden, having already visited the glacier towards which we were headed: Ventisquero Pio XI, the largest glacier in South America. It was gleaming as we approached its face, which stretches almost 2 miles across at the head of the fjord. After launching the dinghy into the water, some of us set off to explore the glacier up close. We also drove *Louise* near to it, feeling the odd roll of the boat when pieces of ice dropped into the fjord and created a small wave. After enjoying a cockpit view of the glacier and surrounding scenery, we retreated to Elizabeth Bay close by, where we moored for the night in Caleta Sally in still conditions and had the bay entirely to ourselves. The sky was clear with the moon shining brightly that evening.

Next morning, we left our anchorage at dawn escorted by a pod of dolphins. The mist that hung over the hills to the west had not yet burnt off, so the atmospheric scene was further enhanced by a spectacular sunrise over the mountains to the east. Reaching the exit into the main channel, we discovered that the ice was thicker than when we had entered the fjord. Slowing down to find a way through the maze of ice, our passage was far from easy. Using the dinghy, we tried to shunt blocks out of the way to create a path for *Louise*, but with little success. Eventually, our patience was rewarded and we found a route through to reach flat water where, once again, there were dolphins seemingly everywhere. This offered a great photo opportunity from the dinghy and we motored around, filming the mammals while they swam at speed in front of us.

By late afternoon we had reached Puerto Edén, the only settlement along the Chilean channels with a population of around 200 people. The locals are mainly descendants of the Indian tribes that first inhabited this region. Sadly, the population of canoe people declined very sharply when the first colonisers arrived, largely due to the spread of disease. The village is made up of wooden houses built on stilts arranged in a semi-circle around the bay, facing the waterfront.

Entering the small anchorage, we found four other yachts already moored. We invited the other crews to join us on board for drinks before we all went ashore for dinner in the *hostería*. One of the yachts, *Esprit d'Équipe*, originally built for the Whitbread Round the World Race, had lost its mast near Cape Horn and the owner was heading north to find a convenient harbour where he could repair the rig. He had one other crew member, a friendly French lady who had joined him for the passage north. We had just reached the shore when we noticed a yellow hull approaching the anchorage, which we recognised as *Phoebe*. So, of course, we invited Jan to join us for dinner. Sitting down at a big table in the local guest house, thirteen of us ate a delicious meal of salmon and potatoes, with apples for dessert. Saying our farewells, we returned to our respective boats for a good night's rest.

Just north of Puerto Edén the channel narrows and winds itself snake-like over a short distance. On Tuesday, as we entered this stretch of water named Angostura Inglesa, we crossed paths with the Navimag ferry, which would be making a brief stop at Edén before journeying on south towards Puerto Natales. Passing *Louise* at full steam, the ferry sounded its horn to greet us.

Having cleared the narrows, where there was a current running against us, we emerged into Canal Messier, which was considerably wider. Lying grounded in the middle of the channel was a Greek ship, *Capitán Leonidas*, which had foundered on submerged rocks in 1963 while carrying a cargo of sugar from Brazil during a passage to Valparaíso. It was discovered that the captain had deliberately tried to sink the vessel to claim the insurance and he was eventually sent to prison. The water was completely calm around the wreck, so we stopped *Louise* and got in the dinghy to row over to the rusting ship, where we climbed on board and strolled around the sloping deck that was overgrown with grass. The wreck had rather an eerie feel, so we were glad to take leave of it and continue our journey.

On Tuesday night we laid anchor at Caleta Point Lay. Located in the lee of Isla Little Wellington, it was well sheltered from the elements. We tied up *Louise* in the usual way with two lines led from the stern and attached on the land. Klaus and I were in charge of using the dinghy to run the lines ashore to secure them on trees, and by this stage of the trip we had mastered this art. That evening the Dutch boat *Finisterre*, which we had seen previously, arrived and anchored beside us, also putting a line ashore for safety.

We were now just 50 miles from Caleta Ideal, our final stop before the Golfo de Penas. The next day's motoring was slower due to a northerly wind funnelling straight down Canal Messier. However, we managed to make progress under a dull and overcast sky. A lone fishing boat passed us, perhaps on its way back from the Pacific. When we stopped that evening, the anchor dragged at first, presumably because the sea bottom was muddy, but eventually it took hold. Our mooring in Caleta Ideal was on the western shore of Bahía Tarn in the lee of Isla Wager, named after a Royal Navy frigate wrecked off this coast in 1741. We settled down safely for the night in anticipation of sailing out the following day for the first time into the South Pacific.

Ahead lay the Golfo de Penas, a large horseshoe-shaped bay, which faces straight out onto the Pacific. It is the only stretch of the Patagonian coast where passing vessels must expose themselves to the open expanse of ocean with possible high winds and rough seas. A check of the weather report revealed a strong wind was forecast, but fortunately one that was blowing from the south-west. After lunch on Thursday 20th March, we donned our oilskins, readying ourselves to be out at sea, and lifted anchor. We hoisted our sails in the shelter of the island, putting three reefs into the main, and set a course northwards into the Pacific. Once we were in open water, we found the sea in a somewhat confused state, with waves criss-crossing each other.

After dinner I went to rest in my cabin, but I couldn't get to sleep due to the motion of the boat and felt uncharacteristically queasy. I got out of my bunk and went back into the cockpit to breathe in the fresh air. This was the only time during the entire *Louise* Adventure that I felt any seasickness. I sympathise with anyone who is chronically seasick, which often spoils the enjoyment of time spent on the waves.

During Klaus and Cheryl's watch during late evening, seawater filled the cockpit twice, with one wave coming over the bow and another wave later crashing over the stern. However, the wind was happily in our favour, with a brisk south-westerly around Force 7. *Louise* was still tossed around, but she made steady progress in the confused conditions. Though the ride wasn't very comfortable, we consoled ourselves with the fact that we were making good speed and we only had about 100 miles to run before reaching shelter.

At midnight we drew parallel with Cabo Raper, which

marks the most westerly tip of the Chilean mainland. Bearing away onto a more easterly course, the wind now came from astern and the rest of the night's sailing was much smoother. During my night watch with Errikos, we spotted a couple of ships pass by, both heading south. One of them was the *Zandaam*, with whom we had crossed paths on a number of occasions during *Louise*'s passage in the Big South. With a cloudless sky, we were treated to a magnificent display of the southern hemisphere's stars and planets.

Around Friday lunchtime, the air seemed to warm up as we sailed into the Darwin Channel, leaving the open sea behind us for the time being. We passed by group of minke whales who played around *Louise*. Still under sail, we began to penetrate the inland channels hidden away from the wrath of the Pacific. By dinner time we had reached the narrows at Isla Quemada, and found an anchorage for the night at Caleta Sucupira where we moored the boat to end our passage across the Golfo de Penas. It had been about thirty hours since we had left Isla Wager, and everyone was happy to put their head down for the night in calm waters. The following day, Saturday 22nd March, we motored the remaining miles left to run to reach Puerto Chacabuco, where we tied up that afternoon at the main jetty.

We had travelled over 1,000 miles since leaving Ushuaia, through arguably one of the most spectacular coastlines on our planet. Hemmed in by the jagged creeks of the Andean mountains on one side and the empty expanse of the South Pacific on the other, the narrow stretch of land that is Chilean Patagonia is virtually uninhabited. Its archipelago, stretching for mile after mile, endures a harsh climate, often buffeted by the howling westerlies hurtling in from the Southern Ocean. Trees and bushes bend over east-facing like hunchbacks. Constant rain and melting snow are soaked up by the vegetation, which can be as dense as tropical jungle. There are virtually no highways or roads, so accessing these parts is generally done by sea. The native population, such as the Fuegian Indians whom Slocum encountered, has reduced to a tiny handful of people, leaving a void that no one appears to want to fill. All this we had just left behind.

Puerto Chacabuco is a small port lying at the entrance to the Aysén River, and mainly serves the salmon farms that are numerous in southern Chile. On Saturday afternoon we visited the nearby town of Aysén. The main street was broad, rather like that of a frontier town, with shops selling every sort of commodity interspersed with bars. Like cowboys entering town after a long ride, Errikos, Klaus and I picked one of the saloons and ordered a round of beers. That evening we had booked a table at the modern-looking Chacabuco Hotel. There were very few other guests in the restaurant, but when we retreated to the bar, we found a few people having drinks. A live band was playing music and soon everyone was dancing. We toasted the end of our Patagonian cruise with Robbie Dhu twelve-year-old Scotch whisky, which is sadly no longer produced, and ended up finishing the bottle while we reminisced about the trip. The next day, we invited Mauricio Lagos and his wife, a couple whom we had met in the bar, on board *Louise* together with their friend and enjoyed more conversation. Coincidentally, they would be leaving for Santiago on the same flight as Errikos and Klaus later in the day.

Early in the afternoon, we set off to drive to Coyhaique, the capital city of the Aysén region, where Brigitte and I would be staying for the night in the friendly El Reloj Hotel. After being dropped off, we said goodbye to Errikos and Klaus who continued onwards to Balmaceda Airport, close to the border with Argentina, from where they were catching their flights home.

On Monday, under a very bright blue sky, Brigitte and I drove out of town in a rental car to explore the local area. Descending into a valley towards the east, we discovered the picturesque Lago Frío, where we stopped and had a walk through a field and down a gentle slope to the edge of the mountain lake. A light breeze was blowing, which made the water sparkle in the afternoon sun. We then had a leisurely drive back to our Coyhaique hotel by way of the narrow Rio Simpson valley.

Rejoining *Louise* back in Puerto Chacabuco, where Morgan had managed to refuel the boat, after lunch on Tuesday 25th March we cast off and motored all afternoon before finding an overnight anchorage at Caleta La Poza, north of Puerto Aguirre. The next day we continued our journey to Puyuhuapi, motoring up the fjord formed thousands of years ago during the Ice Age. At the head of the fjord we slowed down to cross the shallow sandbar at the Galvarino Narrows, created by the volcanic moraine. Ahead we could see a well-built summer house with a little pier, referred to as a 'marina' in our sailing guide. We moored *Louise* alongside the pontoon to which a rather neglected motorboat was also tied. Puyuhuapi township was originally founded by a group of German settlers in the nineteenth century. That evening we ate pizza in the Rossbach restaurant, which was the only establishment in the small community that we found open.

On Thursday morning, Brigitte, Cheryl, Morgan and I, together with a local guide, set out on a hike up one of the steep paths running off the side of the fjord. Our objective was to reach the viewing platform to observe the waterfall that runs off the Ventisquero Colgante, a hanging glacier located high above the Puyuhuapi fjord. After the trek, our guide took us back to her house where we ate sandwiches sitting on stools outside on the pavement.

By mid-afternoon, our old friends Andres and Marcela Kemeny had arrived. They had flown to Balmaceda Airport from Buenos Aires and then driven north to Puyuhuapi. Much of the road remains unsealed with a rough surface, so the going was slow at times. With our new guests settled on *Louise*, we pushed off to Caleta Dorita, 10 miles down the fjord, to be there in good time for dinner. On arrival, our anchor wouldn't hold, unfortunately, even after numerous attempts, because the seabed was soft and muddy. Another yacht was moored in the little bay nearby and its owners generously agreed to move it, which made it easier for us to anchor in shallower water. We got there in the end, but not before putting down two anchors to ensure we were safe for the night. We invited the owners of the other boat, Rick and Elaine from Seattle, on board for a drink to thank them.

After breakfast on Friday, we all went ashore to experience the thermal springs at the well-appointed Puyuhuapi Lodge. Two outdoor natural spring pools faced out onto the sea: one had a temperature of approximately 30°C and the second was considerably hotter at 40°C. We enjoyed sitting in both, interspersed by short dips in the sea, which was a much cooler 12°C.

Feeling relaxed after our morning hot spa, by lunchtime we were back on *Louise*. All afternoon we motored, before finding a small bay, Caleta Pozo de Oro, where we planned to stop for the night. Coming in through a narrow entrance to the bay, we passed a house with a well-maintained lawn running down to the waterfront. On the shore, a lady surrounded by a group of excited beagles that were jumping up and down gave us a friendly wave. As soon as we were anchored we went ashore, and the owners of the property, Benjamin and Jacqueline Saavedra, invited us inside their home.

Over the next hour or so we listened to their story.

After a coup d'état in 1973, which heralded the collapse of democracy in Chile, they decided to leave Santiago and relocate to Patagonia. In their thirties at the time, they left behind their home and careers to bring up their young family in this remote place. Now living alone in their waterfront house, they grow various fruit and vegetables together, while Benjamin maintains a stock of shellfish and Jacqueline is passionate about looking after their six beagles. The couple would not let us leave without giving us some salmon and vegetables. We reciprocated by offering them a bottle of whisky, at which point they insisted that we also should also take a bucket of clams. Benjamin proceeded outdoors to open the cage near to his jetty where he stored his clams, which turned out to be quite big. Ending our delightful conversation with the Saavedras, we bade them farewell and returned to *Louise*.

It was rather grey when we lifted anchor at breakfast time on Saturday 29th March, to leave the bay where the Saavedras lived and motor further north. That afternoon we reached the quaintly named Bahía Tictoc, where we tied the boat up in a quiet spot for the night. We made a dinghy excursion around some little islands nearby that were full of wildlife, including sea otters, Magellanic penguins, cormorants, kelp geese, caracara birds and a few playful Peale's dolphins. The plant life on the shoreline was also abundant and featured some bright-red flowering firebush. After absorbing so many different aspects of nature in this isolated spot, it was time for a quiet evening. Morgan had prepared a dish of spaghetti vongole using the Saavedras' clams. None of the ladies were keen on the shellfish, so the men were left to savour the delicious meal all for themselves.

The following day, we planned to reach the southern end of Chiloé Island. There was a light but contrary wind, so we motored all day. Crossing the Golfo de Corcovado, which is partially open to the Pacific, we had the fortune to sight a blue whale, which made a number of appearances not far from *Louise*. Its long back was clearly visible as well as its dorsal fin. The blue whale is the largest of all mammals and has a relatively small population, although in this area of the Chilean coast there are regular sightings recorded.

By the afternoon we had arrived at our anchorage in Puerto Queilén, and we soon went ashore to report our arrival to the coastguard. Perhaps because it was Sunday, the streets in the little seaside town were deserted. After dealing with the formalities, we found a little bar with an upstairs room and a sea view, where we each ordered a pisco sour. It took a while for the drinks to be served, but it was worth the wait as they tasted superb. Later, on leaving the bar, we looked across the anchorage and saw the yellow hull of *Phoebe*, lying at anchor, and remarked on how her young skipper Jan was making good progress.

On Monday morning, at a civilised hour, we moved off to continue north, following the eastern shore of Chiloé. The island relies heavily on farming, and from the sea we could see fields full of cattle and sheep grazing. Fishing is also an important activity, but sadly we found that many of the beaches were polluted, with white polystyrene strewn over the sand. The plastic material is used by fishermen to buoy their nets, but they don't appear to recycle the material once it is no longer fit for use.

Our next stop on the island of Mechuque was one of the highlights of the whole trip. Anchoring in a sheltered spot in Caleta Anihue, away from the strong current, we moored the boat then rode to the small village in the dinghy, passing under a bridge at the entry to the inlet. We found ourselves surrounded on both sides by traditional houses with wooden walls and tin roofs, many of which stood on stilts suspended over the water. In the middle of the inlet, black swans were quietly swimming around, adding to the beauty of the scene.

During a brief walk ashore, we almost got lost in the forest while exploring, before finishing our excursion with a stroll through the village. The summer was drawing to an end and the apple orchards were full of ripened fruit. As we walked past a house, a lady kindly offered us some freshly squeezed apple juice, which she poured into large soft-drinks bottles.

Heading back on the dinghy to *Louise*'s anchorage, as we came round the corner into the inlet where she was tied up, we were surprised to find *Phoebe* nearby. The German sailor's boat was moored within talking distance and we invited Jan over for tea and apple juice. The juice was simply delicious and we finished it in very short order. Meanwhile, we listened to the story of Jan's voyage, which included a fifty-day non-stop trip from the Canaries to Mar del Plata in Argentina. After regaling with us his fascinating tale, he took his leave and we wished him the best of luck. Later, we would learn that when *Phoebe* had departed to cross the South Pacific her engine had started to develop problems, and so sadly Jan had to make his way back to Chile.

For our last on-board dinner of the Big South cruise, that evening Cheryl had prepared some tasty Falklands lamb with all the trimmings. To accompany the meal, we enjoyed a couple of fine Argentinian wines, including an excellent bottle of the Bianchi Malbec Reserva that Andres had given us.

Waking up the next morning, on Tuesday 1st April, it was apparent that summer was drawing to an end. But it was a bright and sunny day with smooth conditions, during which we motored for 50 miles to reach our final stop in Puerto Montt. Clearly visible on the skyline to the east was the magnificent Calbuco Volcano, the top of which was covered in snow. The sheltered port of Puerto Montt was the first city of any real size that we had visited since leaving Buenos Aires four months earlier. Docking in the Oxxean Marina, we secured *Louise* and finally brought our adventure into the Big South to an end.

During our evening meal at a restaurant in the fish market, we noticed that the television show on the big screen had been interrupted by an announcement regarding a strong earthquake, measuring 8.2 on the Richter scale, in the north of Chile. Viewers were informed that a national tsunami alert had been declared. Finishing our dinner, we made our way back to *Louise* where the marina staff informed us that we should report to a nearby tsunami muster point. As there was no apparent danger that Puerto Montt would be affected, no one appeared to be taking the warning seriously, so we returned on board and had a perfectly safe night in the marina.

The following day, together with the Kemenys, we caught a taxi to the local airport to board our flight to Santiago and head home.

Chapter 5 – The Horse Latitudes
Puerto Montt, Chile to the Marquesas Islands, French Polynesia

Easter Island, South Pacific

Mankind's relationship with the sea has evolved over thousands of years. The South Pacific encompasses the world's largest expanse of ocean, and when combined with the North Pacific, the two oceans represent 44 per cent of the surface area on Earth covered by sea. Over centuries, people have overcome seemingly impossible barriers to create communities spanning the Pacific across thousands of miles. Sharing many ethnic and cultural ties, the inhabitants of the Pacific shores built craft that were capable of making long and often hazardous passages, then mastered the science of navigation to journey across great stretches of water to find landfall, when all they could see around them was the sea and the sky above. The commonwealth of Pacific nations is triangular-shaped, with Easter Island, New Zealand and Hawaii at each of the three corners and Polynesia at the centre. These seafaring peoples, driven by ambition and at times fighting for survival, developed strong bonds of community and blood supported by their maritime knowledge and bravery.

When Ferdinand Magellan, the first European to enter the South Pacific, contemplated his future voyage as he sailed west from the South American coast, he underestimated the massive area of water that had to be covered to reach his destination in the Spice Islands. He was unaware that what lay ahead was over twice the width of the Atlantic, the only ocean with which he was familiar. But with regard to its weather patterns, the Pacific had a lot in common with its smaller oceanic siblings. The Spaniards soon discovered that the easterly trade winds also blew in the Pacific.

A new path to access the riches of Asia, the Manila Galleon trade route linking Mexico to the Philippines, would emerge around 1565. Ships would set sail west from Acapulco to cross the Pacific, then return from Manila laden mainly with Chinese goods and other valuable commodities. But long before Europeans had risked crossing this vast stretch of water, it is speculated that little groups from South America had done likewise. The Kon-Tiki expedition, undertaken by Norwegian ethnologist and explorer Thor Heyerdahl, sought to prove that people had been able to reach Polynesia sailing from Peru on an open raft. In 1947, Heyerdahl's handmade balsawood raft carrying six men spent 101 days in Pacific waters before grounding on a reef in the Tuamotu Islands.

Setting out from Chile on Tuesday 13th May 2014, our aim was to trace the steps of the great European explorers, including Bougainville, and in doing so to learn about the peoples and places of some of the main islands of the South Pacific. *Louise* had been resting, moored in Puerto Montt, while Cheryl and Morgan took some well-deserved time off and went to the Galapagos Islands, a place that Brigitte and I would unfortunately not have the opportunity to see during this circumnavigation.

Accompanying us on the next stage of the trip was Jean-Louis Peyreyre, who had sailed with us at the very start of the Adventure between Jersey and Lanzarote. After flying out together from Paris via Santiago to join *Louise*, we took advantage of our short stay in Puerto Montt to go to the local fish market, where large and delicious fresh crabs were available in abundance.

In readiness for our crossing, we had lightened the boat by offloading some of the extra gear that we had needed in the Big South, such as mooring warps. The fuel tanks were fully replenished for the 5,000-mile journey ahead, as there would be no filling stations en route, and then we were ready to set sail. Motoring towards Chiloé Island, which we had visited on our way north back in late March, we headed for the Chacao Channel, a narrow passage between the mainland and Chiloé. The channel has a strong tidal flow caused by the Golfo de Ancud, an enclosed area of water to the east of Chiloé that empties and fills every twelve hours courtesy of the Earth's gravitational pull. Charging through the straits into the Pacific, we encountered some steep waves caused by overfalls on the sea bottom and *Louise* was carried along by the powerful tidal ebb.

Following our quick getaway from the mainland, we settled down and expected a good crossing north-west to the Juan Fernández Islands. A stable pressure system was kindly sitting to our west, off the Chilean coast, creating ideal weather conditions for our three-day course. At the beginning we motored, and during the first night, while the moon was out, it soon became cloudy. On Wednesday morning, we were able to turn off the motor and, with the wind filling in from the west, *Louise* began getting used to sailing in the Pacific.

By our second night at sea, we were into the high-pressure area and the wind slowly deserted us. But the next day, we picked up wind again, thanks to a deep low-pressure system that was quite far off in more southern latitudes, and could switch off the engine. With the new breeze, we were tight on the wind at first and as the front passed through it rained a little. However, by Thursday afternoon the weather had cleared up, treating us to a splendid blue sky, and we tacked as the wind backed to the west. We spotted a large school of whales spouting on the surface, though we were not close enough to identify the species. As evening approached the wind strengthened, then backed further to the south, creating magnificent downwind sailing conditions. The waves gradually grew in height, but the Blue Lady, as Cheryl and Morgan had affectionately begun to call *Louise*, easily took it all in her stride.

During the night we were running almost straight downwind, and in these conditions the boat rolled a fair bit, but in the morning we gybed, as the wind backed and settled down as a steady south-easterly. This made for an easy end to the first relatively short leg of the crossing, when Morgan sighted Robinson Crusoe Island about 30 nautical miles away on Friday 16th May. At teatime we came around the eastern tip of the island, at which point the wind died, being completely shadowed by the land. Soon we had dropped our sails and anchored *Louise* in Cumberland Bay.

I first heard about Alexander Selkirk and the tale of Robinson Crusoe when I was a boy, while playing on the beach in Lower Largo in Fife where my cousins had their holiday house. Selkirk was a sailor and buccaneer who was born in the very same seaside village on Scotland's east coast, which looked out onto the North Sea. It was during a voyage to the South Pacific in 1704, while his ship was stocking up on supplies and fresh water in the Juan Fernández Archipelago, that Selkirk refused to get back on board until repairs were made, as he was certain the vessel was unseaworthy. His captain duly left him behind on the shore and Selkirk found himself stranded there for almost four-and-a-half years. The Scotsman's fascinating story became the inspiration for Daniel Defoe's bestselling 1719 novel *Robinson Crusoe*.

On Saturday morning, which happened to be Brigitte's birthday, we set off to climb up to Selkirk's Lookout, at a height of almost 2,000 feet above sea level, which was on the ridge of island overlooking the water on both sides. After asking around ashore, we had managed to find Rosamaría Recabarren, a very friendly guide, who showed us the way while sharing her knowledge about the island and its history. Arriving at the lookout after the ascent, we gathered our breath and sat down to take in the incredible view that our eighteenth-century fellow sailor and compatriot would have experienced. Once the initial euphoria of escaping his ship had faded, for days on end Selkirk sat at this spot and prayed that a vessel would stop, allow him on board and enable him to continue his journey. To the west we could see Isla Santa Clara, also known as Île aux Chèvres, where goats were bred as a source of meat for starving sailors. Cows and horses now graze on the green pasture above the island's south coast. On our way back down we saw Selkirk's hut, overlooking the small village below, where he would have had plenty of time to reflect upon life and its meaning while regarding the view across the little bay.

Down in the village we visited the memorial close to the shore that commemorated the loss of life on the German light cruiser SMS *Dresden*. At the onset of the First World War, the Royal Navy knew that Germany had a powerful group of battleships stationed in the South Atlantic. In December 1914, a lighthouse-man on duty in Port Stanley spotted ships in the distance that were steaming past the Falklands. His intelligence was relayed to the Royal Navy, whose fleet at anchor in Stanley were immediately sent out to sea in pursuit of the German vessels. The lighthouse-man's information was so accurate that, within hours, shells fired from the Royal Navy ships had crippled most of the German convoy. Hundreds of German sailors died in a watery grave during the Battle of the Falkland Islands. But one ship, the *Dresden*, was able to slip away and evade the hunters, before rounding Cape Horn into the Pacific. Her escape would prove only temporary, however, as the *Dresden* became stranded when she ran out of coal and, after being tracked down and attacked by a British squadron, she was scuttled by her crew in Cumberland Bay on Robinson Crusoe Island in March 1915. The modest but well-preserved memorial is one further reminder of how the nations of Europe came close to total destruction during the twentieth century.

Our guide Rosamaría extended a kind invitation to join her and her family for dinner that evening. Naturally we accepted the offer, and at sunset we arrived at their house overlooking the bay. *Louise* lay in view at anchor facing the beach. We were introduced to Rosamaría's partner Leopoldo, or 'Polo', Charpentier, of third-generation French descent, whose very own Parisian ancestor had been shipwrecked on the island. Polo had been mayor of the Juan Fernández Islands and had only recently retired after twenty years' public service. For dinner we were treated to some salted goat cooked in an open fire pit above the beach. The goat had been hunted by their nephew on Isla Alejandro Selkirk, about 100 miles to the west. After having a delicious meal while sitting around the glowing fire in front of the sea, we thanked our hosts for their hospitality and returned to *Louise*.

Back on board, Cheryl produced a lovely cake for Brigitte and we opened a bottle of champagne to toast her birthday. Following our eventful day on Robinson Crusoe Island, we settled down for a much-needed rest. The boat rolled gently for much of the night, but we woke up refreshed in the morning. Although the conditions were quite settled, an Italian yacht moored nearby had not fared so well, dragging its anchor in the dark.

After breakfast on Sunday, we collected Polo and Rosamaría and brought them aboard for morning coffee. As a souvenir they gave us a small map of the island, which we gladly accepted. We later dropped them back ashore with the dinghy and then started to prepare *Louise* for the next leg of our passage. Once the checkout formalities had been taken care of with the authorities, we were ready to continue our journey westwards.

Weighing anchor to leave Robinson Crusoe Island after lunch on Sunday 18th May, we hoisted the sails to head north-west initially, to sail a little closer to the equator. Our destination, Easter Island, only lay 5 degrees latitude further north than the Juan Fernández Islands, so the course we set would more or less be pointing west over the coming days. Happily, our departure coincided with settled conditions.

The Chilean high-pressure weather system was lying to

our south and gave us some excellent sailing on port tack for the first two days at sea, though the wind strength was up and down at times. These conditions are typical of the subtropical areas in both north and southern hemispheres that are known colloquially as the 'horse latitudes'. The term is thought to originate from olden times when sailors, who would often spend their money in the first few days of a voyage, would subsequently incur debt from advances paid to them by the ship's paymaster, known as 'dead horse' time. A month or two later, they would usually have managed to pay off their 'dead horse' debts, and to celebrate they would parade a straw-stuffed effigy of a horse around the deck before throwing it overboard. Sailors gave this unusual name to the zone of high pressure lying between the easterly trade winds in the tropics and the westerly winds experienced in higher latitudes.

In the subtropical high, there is generally little rain and cloud formation, and variable winds mixed with periods of calm. We were kept on our toes dealing with the changing pattern of winds, and the times we spent on watch were busier than normal. Reefs had to be taken in and out of the main, requiring at least three hands on deck. Headsail changes were frequent too, although both the larger yankee and smaller working jib can be furled and unfurled from the cockpit, making the job fairly simple. Between the sail changes, sheets still had to be trimmed to keep the boat moving.

By this point in the Adventure, the watch rota system was well established. The three men on board, Jean-Louis, Morgan and I, each kept watch three hours in the day and two-and-a-half hours at night, while Brigitte and Cheryl covered slightly shorter periods of time.

We were making good progress across the vast emptiness of the Pacific towards our destination further west, but on Tuesday 20th May, the third day at sea, just before lunchtime our autopilot motor gave up the ghost for the second time. Morgan set about removing the broken unit, while Jean-Louis and I alternated at the helm, manually steering *Louise* until the new motor had been fitted. It was during such moments that we realised how much we took the autopilot for granted. Before the invention of automatic steering systems, a ship's helm had to be constantly manned. For the long-distance sailor, this mechanical aid makes sailing so much easier because the helm can be left unattended while the crew, as they keep watch, can also go about doing other things. We added the autopilot steering to the list of problems that we would try to resolve when we reached Auckland.

We were also less than happy with our fishing performance, despite having our lures out for most of the day. We attributed our poor success to the depth of the ocean where we were sailing, which was thousands of feet deep, as well as the lack of available nutrition for the fish that live near the surface. Fortunately, our fridge was very well stocked with fresh food and vegetables, and there was little chance of any one of us going hungry.

With the temperature on board gradually starting to rise, we no longer needed duvets on our bunks, and during the daytime we could now wear just T-shirts and shorts. Sailing had become easier too, with a long spell of easterly winds, so *Louise* ran nicely with the wind in our back. On some days we were able to use our big reaching sail, or Code 0, which flies from the bowsprit like the spinnaker. When the wind changes and the sail can no longer be carried, it is simply furled in. If the sea state and weather are good, the sail can be left aloft, allowing it to be easily redeployed.

After a week of consistently good conditions, the weather threatened to take a turn for the worse with the approach of a front. We were becalmed during the night of Saturday 24th

May and had to put the engine on to motor, but then after sunrise on Monday, the wind picked up with some force from the south-west. We shortened sail, putting two reefs in the main, and with the smaller storm jib unfurled in place of the working jib, we made decent progress in the building sea. Far away to the south the powerful low, which we were on the edge of, was making its way eastwards across the Southern Ocean. We were only feeling a mere fraction of this depression's huge strength.

At breakfast time we caught our first fish in the Pacific, which we hoped was a good omen; it also indicated that we were in warmer subtropical waters. Hauling in the line, we found we had hooked a mahi-mahi or common dolphinfish, easily recognised by its bright colours. A tasty lunch was prepared by Cheryl and included our first-ever tropical ceviche.

The wind continued to shift on Monday, and around teatime a big group of dolphins passed by *Louise*, entertaining everyone on deck. In the evening the front passed over, heralded by squalls and rain, after which the wind backed to the south-east. Having run with the wind behind us that night, the following day we closed in fast on our next destination.

On Tuesday 27th May at 9 a.m., we sighted Easter Island. Rapa Nui, as it is known locally, was translated by a French ethnologist in the nineteenth century to mean the 'Navel of the World'. The island takes its modern name from the Dutch explorer Jacob Roggeveen, who discovered it during an expedition sponsored by the Dutch West India Company and landed there on Easter Sunday in 1722. This marked *Louise*'s arrival at Polynesia's most easterly island.

Rapa Nui was originally populated by people who, thanks to an exceptional ability in building seaworthy craft, had crossed the vast Southern Ocean from islands further west, such as Pitcairn, Mangareva and the Society Islands. The migrating seafarers brought with them not only plants and animals, but also their Polynesian culture and skills including stone-carving. Between the tenth and sixteenth centuries, the Rapa Nui people built over 900 stone monuments to honour their ancestors and leaders in the shape of head-and-torso figures known as *moai*. Each clan erected platforms, upon which they raised the magnificent statues that stand with their back to the sea. Watching over their people, the *moai* were believed to guard against hunger and misfortune. Passing under sail along the northern side of the island, we had our first glimpse of the incredible structures that are the hallmark of Easter Island.

By Tuesday lunchtime we had dropped anchor at Hanga Roa, the main town on the western end of the island. After maintaining an average of just over 200 nautical miles per day, we were very pleased to have completed our passage across this empty expanse of the South Pacific. Before we could disembark, we had to wait on board for the local authorities to come over and give us clearance to land. Until then, we spent time preparing the dinghy in readiness for going ashore to explore one of the world's most isolated islands. Our first thought was to seek out the comfort of a bar to share a celebratory toast to our arrival in Polynesia and then find a good tour guide to show us the main highlights of this UNESCO World Heritage Site.

Two other yachts lay at anchor in the otherwise deserted bay, including *Dana Felicia*, a 60-foot Danish sloop that had left Puerto Montt ahead of us. This sturdy yacht is owned by Sven Aaen, who has criss-crossed the Pacific a number of times. The other boat, *Karma Waters*, was a smaller 40-foot cruising boat owned by solo-sailor Ray Reinaud, who was on his way to Patagonia. On our second evening at anchor, we invited our neighbours aboard for a drink.

Ray, a laid-back Western Australian, had landed on Rapa Nui after travelling from Mexico about one week previously. We learnt that before our arrival the wind had been westerly and Ray had had to confine himself to his boat for a full week at anchor on the eastern side of the island, waiting for the wind to shift so he could move to Hanga Roa on the west, where the little harbour makes landing easier. When we met him, he was busy preparing for his voyage to Valdivia in Chile, bringing fresh water and provisions on board. Once in Chile, his plan was to visit the Patagonian Channels together with his wife. Some weeks later, he emailed us to report that his journey to Chile had been fraught: when he had hit the Roaring Forties, problems emerged with his rigging, but it was too late to turn back as he was already too far east to sail close-hauled back to Easter Island.

Early on Wednesday, Cheryl and Morgan went to watch the sun rise above the mysterious *moai* statues at Tongariki, at the eastern end of the island. While they waited, sitting in the dark, it was rather cold, but their patience was eventually well rewarded when the sun appeared over the horizon.

Later in the morning, Jean-Louis, Brigitte and I met with José, our guide for the day. A former soldier in the French Foreign Legion, he was originally from Portugal and had married a local Rapa Nui resident. We managed to explore the principal sites of interest including Rano Raraku, a volcanic crater where the stone for the statues was mainly quarried. It was here, towards the east of the island, that the iconic *moai* were carved, each representing a living person who had been revered in society. One of the unresolved mysteries regarding Easter Island is how the statues were transported from the place where they were crafted to the many locations where they stand.

When Captain James Cook landed in 1774, four years

after a Spanish expedition had taken possession of the island, his estimate of there being 600 or 700 inhabitants suggested that something had happened to trigger a collapse in the population, for at the peak of the Rapa Nui civilisation there were believed to have been about 10,000 islanders. Historians point to the exhaustion of resources; in the space of a few centuries the environment had gone from being heavily wooded with a sizeable bird population to a state of denudation, and therefore unable to sustain so many lives on such a small area of land. This impoverishment in resources seemingly led to clan warfare and human slaughter. Some see a parallel with today's planet, where nature is at risk and being steadily thrown off balance due to global warming and other threats to the environment.

Another sign of tensions within the old Rapa Nui society was apparent in the toppling of many of the statues after 1770, with clan members damaging the *moai* of opposing tribal groups. The symbols of the old civilisation were gradually destroyed, after which a new pagan birdman culture was introduced.

Jean-Louis and I were keen to go diving in such a remote island location, and so we made arrangements with the local scuba club. Heading to the site on Thursday morning, we jumped off the little dive boat into the sea to find plenty of life underwater, including a large turtle, stonefish and moray eels. Most notable was the exceptionally clear visibility, as the waters around Easter Island are clean and there are no rivers flowing into the sea from the land.

Our visit to Rapa Nui coincided with a weekend of local sporting activities, including a football tournament. Before the kick-off, Polynesian dancers dressed in traditional costume entertained the crowd of onlookers. Dressed in a brightly coloured warrior-style cloak, the island's mayor also made a brief speech. Once the game had got under way, we retired to a local restaurant where Jean-Louis treated us to an enjoyable dinner. Although it felt like we were no longer in Latin America, this was our final opportunity to experience Chilean hospitality.

On the morning of Friday 30th May, we set off on the next leg of the passage, which would take us further north-west and closer to the tropics at Pitcairn Island. *Dana Felicia* had left the day before, headed for the same destination. On our first night back at sea we were accompanied by a starry sky. We sat in the cockpit, marvelling at the constellations and the stars sparkling high above the South Pacific.

On Saturday, we passed through a weak weather front that produced a headwind for a short while. After the front had left us, the wind backed to the south-east, bringing some useful easterly winds that held up for the following 1,200 nautical miles until we had reached Pitcairn. The conditions made the voyage easy-going and relaxing for all on board. We could concentrate on our favourite pastimes, including fishing, reading and backgammon, as well as enjoying good conversation.

Apart from the times when we had been at anchor, we had not seen any other boats since leaving the coast of South America, which allowed us to savour the vastness of the ocean completely by ourselves. The presence of seabirds was also noticeably less frequent in these waters, although we had visitations from the odd sooty tern and one giant petrel.

In warmer seas, fish are easier to come by for the pleasure cruiser and so it didn't take us long to land a pair of wahoo and a skipjack tuna. Our lucky streak continued with the catch of a 45-pound white marlin. When the latter was gutted on deck, we found that its recent diet had included squid, baby bonito and a thin eel-like deepwater fish.

Passing above a number of seamounts, where the bottom rises from around 3 miles to over 3,000 feet, we expected to find fish in greater numbers. On one occasion, we heard the ratcheting sound of lines running out and rushed to grab the rods at the stern, only to discover that whatever had been on the end of them had escaped. When we brought in the lines for inspection, both of the lures had gone, so maybe this was a case of the fish just being too heavy. With fish in abundance, our meals had turned into culinary feasts and the catch was prepared in a variety of ways, including ceviche, sashimi and pan-seared. On our new diet we were truly spoilt, especially one evening when Morgan and Cheryl regaled us with a sushi dinner that undoubtedly rivalled the best that Tokyo could offer.

As we progressed further west the trade winds strengthened, but the wind was still in our back and so we were pushed nicely on our way. Five days after leaving Easter Island, we were drawing close to Pitcairn. We reduced sail for the night to slow down, in order to make landfall in daylight when the shoreline would be more visible. In the early hours, approaching dawn, we were able to pick out the silhouette of the tiny outcrop in the South Pacific.

Pitcairn Island was rendered famous by Fletcher Christian and his band of mutineers on HMS *Bounty*. They had landed there on 15th January 1790, several months after Christian had declared a mutiny on 28th April 1789, forcing the *Bounty*'s captain, William Bligh, off the ship along with a number of loyal crew members and setting them adrift in a small launch. Before the mutiny, the *Bounty* had just begun its return voyage from Polynesia after spending five months in Tahiti, carrying breadfruit plants destined for the Caribbean. In September 1789, the mutineers made a return visit to Tahiti, where they picked up several Tahitian men and women before taking to the sea again and eventually ending up on Pitcairn. Afraid of being tracked down by the Royal Navy, Christian decided to burn the ship eight days after making landfall, in the place now known as Bounty Bay. Within a decade almost all the crew had died. Only John Adams would be found alive when, in February 1808, a ship from Boston, Massachusetts landed on the island. Pitcairn's capital, Adamstown, is named after him.

On the morning of Thursday 5th June, *Louise* sailed past Bounty Bay and drew into the shelter of Pitcairn Island at Tedside where we anchored. Two other boats were already moored there, including *Dana Felicia*, who had arrived the day before, making the journey in good time. The island's supply vessel, *Claymore II*, was also riding at anchor, rolling gently in the swell. She had come from the Gambier Islands after picking up passengers bound for Pitcairn. Visitors to the island are taken to and from the shore courtesy of a little, aluminium, open-craft longboat, which passed by *Louise* carrying people from *Claymore II*. We waved at them enviously. With the brisk easterly trade winds, it wasn't going to be easy to get on and off *Louise*, and the longboat service didn't want to come alongside our hull for fear of causing any damage. Using our dinghy wasn't permitted either, as Pitcairn doesn't have a suitable jetty for landing and yachtsmen are only allowed to come ashore using the longboat service.

Over the radio we spoke to Brenda Christian, who was friendly but uncompromising, advising us that it would not be possible to be ferried ashore for a few days. Brenda has been a long-standing member of the Island Council which, led by its mayor, governs the lives of the fifty inhabitants in this the world's smallest democracy. Reluctantly, therefore, we took the decision to leave for the Gambiers that evening, but before heading off we spent the rest of the day relaxing at anchor, savouring the view of Pitcairn. Of course, without stepping ashore it was hard to get a real sense of the island's atmosphere, though we were struck by its tiny size at only 2 miles long.

Although Britain held considerable sway in this part of the South Pacific centuries ago, nowadays this is no longer the case. Today the Pitcairn Islands, which are a group of four volcanic islands – Pitcairn, Henderson, Ducie and Oeno – form the sole British Overseas Territory in the Pacific Ocean. Perhaps our nation's best legacy was the creation of the Pitcairn Islands Marine Reserve in 2015, when the British Government established a marine-protected site covering the waters surrounding the Pitcairn Islands. At more than twice the land area of the British Isles, it's the world's largest marine reserve and extends over 324,000 square miles (834,000 square kilometres). All commercial activities, such as fishing, oil and gas exploration and mineral mining, are prohibited, making this one of the first regions in the Pacific where the pristine waters and coral reefs are managed and protected in this wholly sustainable way.

Sitting at anchor off Pitcairn, we were just 300 nautical miles to the east of the Gambier Archipelago. The Gambiers are the most easterly of the islands that are part of the huge area of French Polynesia, which stretches over 1,000 miles from east to west in the middle of the South Pacific. As well as the Gambiers, French Polynesia is made up of four other island groups: the Tuamotus form a massive band of low-lying atolls running from the Gambiers all the way west to Rangiroa; to the north lie the high-peaked Marquesas Islands covered with lush tropical vegetation; to the west is Tahiti and the rest of the Society Islands, including Bora Bora; and most isolated of all are the remote Austral Islands, which lie further south.

Following a short and smooth 300-mile passage from Pitcairn, we dropped anchor mid-afternoon on Saturday 7th June at Rikitea on Mangareva, the principal settlement in the Gambier Islands, just to the north of the tropic of Capricorn. We were pleased to be back in the tropics six months after leaving Brazil. It felt as if we had already crossed a substantial part of the Pacific Ocean, but in fact we had only reached the midpoint.

During the Cold War, the Gambiers served as a staging post for French nuclear testing activity in Mururoa, approximately 250 miles away, which brought French Polynesia under the international spotlight for negative reasons. There is only a trickle of tourism, which means that new arrivals to these shores are guaranteed an exceptional welcome, with local residents offering handshakes in the streets. Today, the small population of just over a thousand people makes their living primarily from pearl farms, which we were looking forward to discovering.

For the first time since leaving the shores of Chile, we found ourselves in the company of a number of other boats. We recognised *Moksha*, a Shipman 72 that we had first admired back in the UK when she had been moored on the south coast of England, and there were other yachts flying Canadian, Dutch and French ensigns. But when we went to look for our French courtesy flag, a burgee that is flown by a visiting ship in foreign waters as a token of respect towards the host country, we discovered that we didn't have one on board. On Sunday, we met a Dutch couple cruising on a beautiful 55-foot boat that they had built themselves. Joining us for drinks that evening, they had noted the absence of a courtesy flag raised on *Louise* and surprised us with a gift of a French burgee. Trees, a most friendly lady, had made the flag with her sewing machine that afternoon. We hoisted the burgee below the port mast spreader, thanking our new friends.

The next few days were spent relaxing and experiencing our first taste of French Polynesia. Our stay in Rikitea coincided with Whit Sunday, which was a day of great celebration at St Michael's Cathedral, the largest church in the South Pacific. While attending Mass in the packed cathedral, and listening to the melodious singing of the worshippers, we couldn't help but notice the beautiful altar that was decorated with mother-of-pearl shells.

After the service we went to a village fete, where we indulged ourselves eating churros. Our other activities included a tour of one of the main pearl farms hosted by the owner, Dominique Devaux, who explained how he had grown the business from scratch.

Commerce has barely changed over the last 300 years since the first Europeans arrived in these waters. When commenting on Polynesia, Bougainville recorded in his diary: 'I only know one object of rich commerce; and that is the very beautiful pearls.' Centuries later, the cultivation of black pearls is still the mainstay of economic activity in the Gambier and Tuamotu Archipelagos. The pearls grow in the *Pinctada margaritifera* (black-lip pearl) oyster and come in different shades and colours, but are generally dark and iridescent.

During an afternoon stroll one day, we met a local resident who stopped to speak to us while passing by in his pick-up truck. Introducing himself as Yves, he offered to take us on a tour of the area, which we were more than happy to do. Brigitte sat up front next to the driver, while Jean-Louis and I clambered onto the back of the pick-up and we set off around the island. Along the way we made several stops, and guided by Yves, whom we learnt was a former French Foreign Legionnaire and rather handy with a machete, we harvested some produce, picking limes, grapefruit, bananas, chillies and various spices. We also collected breadfruit, which is another staple of the islanders' diet, and found pits where the locals used to bury this fruit to preserve it.

Another amenable citizen with whom we made friends was Nico, a local Mr Fixit, who provided visiting boats with foodstuffs such as vegetables. He also had a ready supply of cheap pearls, mainly seconds, so we bartered a bottle of whisky and fish from the freezer for some pearls. Unfortunately, our freezer had broken down, which meant we had to offload much of the fish that we had caught.

Before leaving Rikitea we walked up Mount Duff, which overlooks the town's picturesque anchorage. Having enjoyed many of the activities on Mangareva and profited from perfect weather conditions, on Wednesday 11th June we moved to moor within the eastern side of the outer reef that surrounds the Gambier Atoll. The next morning, Jean-Louis, Morgan and I were able to go on a dive outside the reef. The rest of the day was peaceful and we passed the time exploring a few small uninhabited islands and beachcombing, finding hermit crabs concealed within bright-red shells.

We spent our last night in the Gambiers anchored at Anganui Bay on Taravai Island. After sundown we were treated to a full moon that rose over the island, bathing the boat and surrounding water in beautiful light.

On Friday morning, before our departure we did some more beachcombing and discovered a family of pigs living under the palm trees on the beach. Ever-athletic, Morgan climbed one of the trees, shaking it in the hope of causing some fresh coconuts to drop off, which they did. Slicing open the ripe fruit, we refreshed ourselves with the milk and threw the husks to the pigs, who seemed to appreciate this morning feast.

After our six-day sojourn in this beautiful archipelago it was time to move on. We lifted anchor after lunch, and motored out through a cut in the reef on our way to the Marquesas, 800 miles north-west of our current location, and heading ever closer to the equator. On leaving the atoll, with the wind still blowing nicely from the south-east, we experienced some smooth sailing during our first night back at sea. On watch before midnight the moon shone brightly, illuminating *Louise* as she glided along through the water. The following morning we encountered a few rain showers, which are common when sailing in the tropics. The conditions remained ideal, with the wind on our beam pressing well on the sails.

That afternoon we noticed a little sail on the horizon, travelling in the same direction as we were. On catching up with the sailing boat, which was going quite slowly, we discovered it was *Noroue*, whom we had last seen in Rikitea. In fact, we had spoken to Karmin Poirier, the owner's daughter, on the quayside before our departure. She was from British Columbia in Canada, and together with her father, Jim, was heading all the way to Hawaii, from where they planned to continue their passage to their home port of Ladner, BC. We passed their boat to leeward, exchanging a few words before waving farewell. This encounter was the only time we saw another vessel at sea during the entire leg from South America to French Polynesia.

Thanks to the strong easterly trade winds, we were making excellent progress. Around the halfway point to the Marquesas there were showery spells to deal with, but they quickly blew through. At night, these squalls kept the person on watch on their toes, changing course, trimming the sails and so on. But getting soaked while working out in the cockpit wasn't too taxing in the warm tropical weather. *Louise* was thriving in these sailing conditions and although we had a reef in the main, we were achieving a good speed.

On the third day at sea, at dinner time we encountered a dwarf minke whale, a most inquisitive species. Our visitor was about 20 feet long and swam in our wake, easily keeping up with the boat. We watched with fascination as the grey-brown shadow of the adult whale was discernible just below the surface, surfing down our stern wave.

That evening the wind picked up strength, but *Louise* took it in her stride. By this stage, we were settled into our watch routines and had become creatures of habit. On the last morning at sea, I handed over to Brigitte at six o'clock, retreating to my bunk to get some rest ahead of our arrival in the Marquesas. While Brigitte was enjoying the company of a large school of dolphins that was swimming alongside the boat, without any warning the autopilot gave up the ghost once again. It was clear that some changes were required to make our steering system more reliable. But happily, the weather that accompanied our voyage across the South Pacific had been everything that we could have hoped for, as following winds and blue skies had been our companions for the most part.

The first view of one of the Marquesas Islands was of Tahuata off to the east, which was sighted on my early watch after dawn on Tuesday 17th June. The Marquesas stand out sharply from the surrounding Pacific Ocean, with peaks rising up to almost 4,000 feet. We were initially struck by the presence of some very rich vegetation, though in the lee of the islands the ground can be dry. Due to limited rainfall, drought often affects the archipelago. With the nearest continental landmass being Mexico, located around 3,000 miles over the horizon, we were surprised to learn that at the height of the Marquesas' civilisation, approximately 100,000 people lived on the islands. Sadly, the arrival of European explorers nearly resulted in the loss of the entire population, with only 20,000 recorded inhabitants by the mid-nineteenth century and an all-time low of just over 2,000 by the mid-1920s. Most deaths had been caused by the influx of infectious diseases, including smallpox and measles. Today, the small local population of just over 9,000 people makes a modest living primarily from tourism and fishing.

As we approached Nuku Hiva, the largest of the Marquesas, we were particularly excited about the prospect of learning about Herman Melville's visit in 1842, when he jumped ship as a young man and spent around a month there as a castaway. The events that followed would inspire the future author of *Moby-Dick* to write his first book, *Typee*, which became a bestselling novel and launched his literary career.

During our last morning at sea on the passage from the Gambiers, we passed a string of islands within the archipelago as we headed north-west to Nuku Hiva. At 4.30 p.m. on Tuesday 17th June, we finally dropped anchor in Taiohae Bay. Taiohae is the main settlement on the island, as well as the administrative capital of the Marquesas. To our surprise, there were a number of other yachts moored in the shelter of the bay.

We were really happy to have reached these islands, after successfully sailing 5,000 miles during the last five weeks, and felt enriched by the opportunity of exploring such an isolated and watery part of our world. As we stepped ashore in the early evening, apart from yacht crews sat at the dockside cafe chatting to each other and checking their emails, the town seemed quiet. These islands are off the beaten track and attract very few tourists, which maybe explains how the Marquesas have retained an exotic image.

And so, it was sadly time to say farewell to *Louise* and leave her for five weeks in the care of Cheryl and Morgan, who would be staying on board to keep her safe, carry out maintenance and prepare her for the next leg. After waving goodbye to the crew, who had dropped us on the dock, Brigitte and I set off on the long journey home together with Jean-Louis, who had been our trusted friend and companion on this memorable trip.

For the 12-mile journey to the airport, we picked up a rental car and drove along narrow roads through the steep mountain range that fell away deep into the valleys below, giving a feeling of vertigo as soon as you looked over the edge. At the airport we did some souvenir shopping and Jean-Louis acquired a carved wooden model of a traditional outrigger boat. The shopkeeper introduced herself as a princess and we had no reason to doubt her. With smiles all round, we bid the lady with royal blood farewell and boarded the plane for our three-hour flight to Pape'ete on Tahiti, from where we changed aircraft and flew to Paris.

* * * * *

Back home we caught up with family and friends, and I managed to compete with my Dragon in the Edinburgh Cup, the UK's national championship for the class. The previous year I had decided to restart competitive racing in this classic keelboat, which was originally designed in 1929. On the international circuit, fleets of around forty or fifty boats are not uncommon, coming from every corner of Europe as well as further afield, including Hong Kong and Australia. My goal was to get a foot on the bottom rung of the ladder and begin absorbing the intricacies of racing an old-fashioned keelboat. My good friend Klaus Diederichs had won the Dragon World

Championship in 2013 at Weymouth, so I hoped to be able to learn from his experience.

Klaus and I had previously co-owned and jointly campaigned two racing boats over a twenty-year period. We formed a true sailing partnership when working together on our team's performance and had huge fun competing on the circuit. Our coach Jim Saltonstall MBE, author of *Race Training*, ensured his philosophy on sailing – that it is the most challenging sport in the world and requires commitment and discipline to achieve your ultimate aim – was deeply ingrained in our minds. Finishing the Dragon Edinburgh Cup at Lymington a long way behind the leaders, therefore, was a sign that I had a lot to learn if I was to reach a top ranking in the Dragon fleet.

Chapter 6 – Islands of Paradise
The Marquesas Islands to the Society Islands, French Polynesia and Auckland, New Zealand

Bay of Virgins, Fatu Hiva, Marquesas

On Sunday 20th July 2014, following the long journey over from Europe, Brigitte and I touched down in Tahiti together with Brigitte's sister Isabelle. That day our eldest daughter Juliette also arrived, combining her sailing holiday with a stopover in Tokyo during a brief visit to Japan. Then in the evening we were joined by our friends Cherry Chau and Philippe René-Bazin, who had come from Hong Kong. All six of us flew from Pape'ete to Nuku Hiva on Monday morning, a three-hour journey overflying the Tuamotus before reaching the Marquesas.

After landing at the tiny airport, we picked up two cars in order to reach the other side of the island. Leaving the airport on the unpopulated north side of Nuku Hiva, the land was brown and arid. Along the way, we kept catching glimpses of the ocean that sparkled in the sunlight. We stopped for lunch and enjoyed a meal in a community cafe where the only other patrons were a group of ladies playing a leisurely game of bingo.

Eventually, we were back in Taiohae Bay where we rejoined *Louise*, who was lying at anchor almost in the same spot where we had left her five weeks earlier. The crew had been working hard in our absence and all the repairs had been carried out, including the fixing of the freezer.

On Tuesday morning, we checked out with the authorities and motored a short way west to Daniel's Bay. Once ashore, we set off on foot to see the settlement, where the gardens of the houses running up the luscious Hakaui Valley were abundant with fruit trees. An enthusiastic villager, sporting a traditional warrior-style face tattoo, gave us lessons in opening coconut shells. Traditionally, copra was the main commodity sustaining the local economy, and the following day we would observe locals drying the coconut shells on the surface of the road. Tropical fruits are another source of income for the islanders.

On Wednesday we had our first sail, covering the 30-mile trip to Ua Pou, a smaller island that lay south of Nuku Hiva. After an early start, we hadn't gone too far before we caught a 30-pound mahi-mahi, which Juliette held high for a photo once it was safely on deck. In the gentle trade winds we made light of the distance and by breakfast time had reached our destination. From our anchorage in Hakahetau Bay, the view of the mountains was impressive.

It was a busy day for Ua Poa as the supply vessel MV *Aranui* had arrived, together with its modest contingency of passengers who were cruising around the area, visiting the populated islands one after another. Ashore we could hear the sound of drums; a group of musicians and young Haka dancers were practising for the finale to the July Marquesas Festival. In spite of the crowds we managed to secure the services of a guide named Jerome. A retired French marine with the build of a fitness fanatic, he was talkative and keen to share his knowledge of the islands. Driving along the twisting and narrow roads, we were surrounded by dense vegetation. We stopped at the ruins of an historical village named Te Lipona that had been well restored.

Having spent much of the day ashore, we retreated to the boat where we ate an early supper. After doing the dishes and storing everything away, we prepared for a brief overnight sail to Hiva Oa. Good fortune had it that the winds were not very strong for the journey. Although we sailed close-hauled, we made good progress all night long. At dawn on Thursday, it was wonderful to behold daybreak against the backdrop of the islands. We found that we were following the *Aranui*, which prevented us from getting inside the little harbour at Atuona when we arrived. Luckily, the supply ship didn't stay long and we were able to anchor closer to the shore, next to the other visiting yachts.

In modern times, Hiva Oa's history has been marked by two prominent figures of francophone culture: Paul Gauguin (1848–1903) and Jacques Brel (1929–78). Both had chosen to spend their final years in the Marquesas, living in Hiva Oa. They are buried close to one another in the small Calvary Cemetery and their gravestones overlook the bay at Atuona.

We took a walk through the cemetery after looking around each of the cultural centres that celebrate the men's lives. In the Brel exhibition was a picture of the yacht *Askoy II*, which the Belgian singer sailed from Northern Europe to the Pacific. As a boy I have memories of seeing this ketch-rigged yacht on the North Sea coast of Belgium. At that time my family and I lived in the 'capital' of Europe and were members of the Brussels Royal Yacht Club. The former British Prime Minister and then member of the European Commission, Edward Heath, was a fellow club member and an accomplished yachtsman, winning competitions such as the Sydney Hobart Yacht Race. During my teenage years, boats were a passionate topic of discussion in the family and with friends. Living among a mixture of nationalities, we hung out together growing up as Europeans and sharing common values.

We dedicated the whole of Friday to visiting the island and viewing some of Hiva Oa's historic ruins, a reminder of the former glory of the Marquesas before the arrival of any Europeans. To access some parts of the island and climb the steep roads requires the use of a four-wheel-drive pick-up, so we hired one for that purpose. Reaching the northern edge of Hiva Oa, the views were spectacular. The island has an abundance of statues known as *tikis*, especially concentrated near the village of Puama'u on the north-eastern coast. We marvelled at the majesty of the carved statues and neatly ordered plinths, imagining crowds congregating in these places centuries ago.

On our way back to Atuona, we collected grapefruit and starfruit to add to our stock of fresh tropical produce. The locals gladly gave us permission to help ourselves to the yield of the well-laden trees. At the end of the day, the owner of the car rental company enquired if we needed more fruit, and the following morning he delivered two huge sacks bulging with avocados and papayas. With these wholesome stores safely stowed, we were ready to leave Hiva Oa.

Fatu Hiva was our final destination in the Marquesas and after breakfast on Saturday morning, we set off to sail 40 miles further south. This breathtaking island has a very steep coast and the main village of Omoa is only accessible by foot from the other settlement at Hanavave due to the mountainous terrain. We anchored *Louise* at the famous Baie des Vierges (Bay of Virgins) in Hanavave, which is the northernmost landing place on the island and one of the most picturesque sites in the South Pacific. We set two anchors, as the water was deep and we didn't want to risk the possibility of the boat accidentally drifting while we were ashore. Joining us on board for drinks were a Dutch couple, who had sailed their boat from Holland via the North-West Passage in Alaska and down the west coast of North America before crossing to the Marquesas.

The following morning, we left *Louise* to visit Hanavave, and on discovering that the local church was filling up for Sunday service, we went inside and listened to the congregation singing in harmony with great conviction. Afterwards we did a little shopping in one of the nearby houses, where we bought some wood carvings from a resident artisan. On our way back to the waterside, we joined some locals at the cafe next to the football pitch, where half a dozen goats were tethered and grazing on the lush grass.

Our stopover in Fatu Hiva brought to an end our trip to the Marquesas, which had been notable for their mountainous beauty. Across the four islands that we had spent time on, we had found their citizens to be so friendly. It is hard to believe that only a few thousand visitors come to this archipelago each year. How lucky we were to be among the privileged few to have first-hand experience of places that most people can only read about in the novels of Herman Melville or Robert Louis Stevenson, or see in pictures.

In the late afternoon on Sunday 27th July, we lifted the anchor and slipped out across the calm water towards to the ocean, beginning our passage south-west to the Tuamotus. Before dusk we passed Point Teae, the southern tip of Fatu Hiva, leaving the Marquesas astern as we savoured a beautiful sunset.

The trade winds were blowing in from their regular easterly quadrant and were strong enough to give us a good start to the 550 nautical miles that lay ahead. The two-and-a-half days in open sea passed by quickly and we settled into a gentle rhythm that allowed everyone to read or just catch up on sleep. Cherry, Isabelle and Juliette were on their first long passage on a sailboat, and each took everything in their stride. We were able to do some fishing and caught a tuna every day. In terms of sailing, the journey was quite straightforward, occasionally switching headsails from the small working jib to the larger yankee when the wind dropped or vice versa when it strengthened.

By the third morning at sea, the eastern end of the low-lying Fakarava Atoll had drawn into sight. The wind had dropped during the last night of the passage, so we motored for the final stretch. On our approach to the narrow entrance through the reef into the atoll, known as the 'cut', a heavy shower reduced visibility, but once the rain had cleared we spotted the cut and proceeded to motor through.

The Tuamotus are a chain of atolls in French Polynesia that cover an area about the size of Western Europe. Early explorers such as Bougainville feared these low-lying islands with their coral reefs, and generally avoided attempting to navigate their vessels into the lagoons. Perhaps the best-known landing was that of Thor Heyerdahl who, together with five companions, sailed a raft across the Pacific Ocean before grounding on a reef at Raroia in the Tuamotus in August 1947. Heyerdahl's Kon-Tiki expedition helped to demonstrate the hypothesis that people from South America could have settled Polynesia in earlier times.

Our point of arrival was at Fakarava, the second largest of the archipelago's atolls in the west of the Tuamotus. We had opted to pass through the southern cut which is well known for the presence of sharks, as hundreds of mainly reef sharks enjoy the feeding ground there. The cut forms a route for water to flow in and out with the rise and fall of the tide, and so around the entrance the water is usually rich in nutrients and small fish, which attracts bigger fish from the deep and encourages sharks to come hunting.

It was breakfast time on Wednesday 30th July when we lowered our anchor in the shallow waters, and were soon surrounded by reef sharks that had come to inspect the boat. A few other yachts were moored in the turquoise lagoon, sheltered by little islands with swaying palm trees. The divers among us, which was everyone except Brigitte and Isabelle, were keen to start exploring underwater, so we all kitted up to view the southern cut. Once we had prepared our gear and lowered it into the dinghy, we set off to the cut where we went on our first dive in the Tuamotus. Underwater we discovered lots of marine life, including sharks and rays, schools of pelagic fish and colourful reef dwellers.

Later on, we spotted a few people kitesurfing on a sandy spit not far from where we were anchored. In the afternoon we all got into the dinghy and headed over towards the shore, and as we neared the beach we were approached by a young kitesurfer who landed directly on the back of our dinghy. The Frenchman, whose name was Adrien, offered to give us lessons, which Cherry and I accepted and arranged to do the following day.

On Thursday morning, Cherry and I set off as novices to our kitesurfing class with Adrien and although we both eventually managed to get up onto the board, by the end of the lesson we had still not fully mastered the technique. After a fun few hours, during which we strayed quite a distance from the beach, we were towed back to the island. Nursing a few scrapes from encounters with the coral, we thanked our enthusiastic teacher for his expert guidance.

On Friday 1st August, which was Swiss National Day, Brigitte and her sister Isabelle, who are both Swiss, hoisted their national flag after breakfast to mark the special occasion. In the morning we motored inside the Fakarava Atoll, stopping for lunch at a sheltered anchorage where we swam in the warm waters. In the afternoon we continued towards the northern entrance to the atoll, anchoring at the main village of Rotoava near to a larger elegant-looking yacht named *Nefale*. Saturday was spent ashore, exploring, and we also decided to rent bikes for some easy-going cycling, as there are no hills or slopes in such low-lying areas.

On Sunday morning, we left Fakarava at first light for our next stop further west, at the slightly smaller and less populated Apataki Atoll. Entering the island's southern cut by the little settlement of Niutahi, towards the end of the ebbing tide there was a current of 3 knots against us. Inside the lagoon we found much of the water surface was covered with buoys that marked the pearl oyster beds.

We took the dinghy to a pearl farm that stood on stilts above the water, where we were warmly welcomed by the staff and given a guided tour. Twenty or so people were busy with various tasks involved with harvesting pearls. We learnt that after the pearl fishers have brought in the nets containing all the oysters, the shells are then removed for opening and careful inspection. The task of inspecting is a skilled job, requiring a long apprenticeship. Most of the workers carrying out this job were Chinese and not local Polynesians. As in the Gambiers, black pearl cultivation is an important activity in the Tuamotus, although overproduction has weighed on the fortunes of the industry.

The following afternoon, we experienced one of our best dives outside of the lagoon and encountered an adult bottlenose dolphin who started to play with us. He splashed his tail while circling around near enough to touch him. His skin was quite scarred, which suggested that he had suffered his fair share of battles. The friendly mammal swam really close by and we were able to film his movements and the sounds he made, which seemed as though he was talking to us.

On Tuesday 5th August we motored further west to Rangiroa, the largest atoll in the Tuamotus and one of the biggest in the world. On our way we were fortunate to catch two fish – a mahi-mahi and a wahoo – so our freezer was exceptionally well stocked.

The passes at lagoon entrances, particularly the main ones where large volumes of water flow in and out, can be challenging to negotiate. When we arrived at the Tiputa Pass at Rangiroa on Tuesday afternoon, the tide was ebbing with the current running out into the sea at about 5 knots. We had to motor full speed ahead in order to get *Louise* inside the lagoon. The strong current created breaking waves in the cut that we were careful to avoid. Meanwhile, a pod of dolphins was jumping through the waves, providing a very entertaining spectacle. Once we had navigated the pass safely and were inside the huge atoll, the waters were smooth and calm. We anchored *Louise* at Avatoru, close by the lagoon entrance, and the shallow waters inside stretched away from the narrow strip of land for miles towards the horizon. For the next three days this place would be our home.

The following morning, we joined a local dive-shop group for an expedition outside the reef. Along with a few other divers, we explored the coral reefs close to the entrance of the lagoon that were teeming with fish. Back ashore we discovered a little restaurant for lunch where we ordered mahi-mahi. The simple meal was excellent and we enjoyed listening to the tales of the owner, Michel, who used to serve in the French Army. Now collecting a monthly pension, he was apparently living a happy retired life in Polynesia, while his wife ran a small mobile ice-cream parlour.

A visit to Rangiroa would not be complete without seeing the Blue Lagoon. We set off with *Louise* on Thursday morning, motoring across the atoll towards the western side where the lagoon lies inside the main reef. Once we were anchored, all of us boarded the dinghy to get to the Blue Lagoon, whose vibrant colour contrasted against the white sandy bottom. Its depth is mostly only waist-height and a maximum of no more than 15 feet. During our excursion we swam in the warmth of the shallow waters. On our way back, we passed a family of fishermen who were gutting some of their fresh catch. They managed to entice Morgan to taste the head of a raw fish, though the rest of us declined. Noticing that a basket was floating in the water nearby, we asked one of the fishermen, named Zoro, what was inside. He promptly pulled out a good-looking lobster. After giving it a quick inspection, we decided to buy one lobster for each of us.

Back on board *Louise* the wind had got up a little and, although we were inside the lagoon, waves were forming and the boat was beginning to ride up and down on anchor. We decided that we would sleep better if we backtracked to Avatoru in the north-western part of the island, where we had been moored before. It was getting dark, so we had to carefully follow the route taken on our journey to the Blue

Lagoon to ensure we avoided any coral heads. By dinner time, we were safely moored in a calm spot and able to savour a tasty meal of freshly cooked lobster, boiled in the pan, which was accompanied by some delicious Chilean Sauvignon Blanc.

Waking up on the morning of Friday 8th August, our last day in the Tuamotus, we prepared for a final dive outside the cut. We spent almost an hour in the water and saw some interesting sights, including a well-disguised stonefish. Returning to the boat, we stowed away our dive gear and got ourselves ready for the passage to Tahiti over a distance of about 200 miles. We motored until the mid-afternoon, passing outside the reef close to the Blue Lagoon. At that point we were able to hoist the sails to do some gentle sailing. Just before 6 p.m., as we drew away from Rangiroa, the sun was setting beautifully in the west.

Passing the Makatea Atoll, we set a course south in the direction of the Society Islands. The first recorded European to reach the tropical island of Tahiti was the English naval commander Samuel Wallis on HMS *Dolphin* in June 1767, days after discovering the Tuamotus. In quick succession, less than a year later our hero Bougainville had also arrived in Tahiti, and then in 1769, during his first visit to the Pacific, Captain James Cook made landfall and bestowed the name of 'Society Islands' on the archipelago. Cook had previously been given some useful information about the islands by Wallis. But it was not until the nineteenth century that Tahiti became a French colony, when Admiral Abel Aubert Dupetit Thouars established a French protectorate over both Tahiti and the Marquesas Islands.

On Saturday afternoon, we moored *Louise* at Taina Marina in Pape'ete on Tahiti. Attaching our stern lines, this was the first time that *Louise* had been tied up at a marina in over 6,000 miles, since our departure from mainland Chile. It felt rather like getting back to civilisation as we know it, even if we had landed on a smallish island in the middle of the South Pacific, very far away from any mainland. That evening, Cherry and Philippe treated us to a celebratory dinner ashore, which we all enjoyed.

With a day to spare before we flew back to the UK, on Sunday 10th August we hired a car and set off on an exploratory island tour. Making our way to the easterly end of Tahiti, we came across a little crowd that had gathered to watch a round of the World Surfing Championships that were about to take place. While there, we took a picture of the reigning world surfing champion, Gabriel Medina, who kindly posed for our camera together with two of his fans. After a light meal, we retraced our steps back to Pape'ete, stopping at the Harrison Smith Botanical Garden, next to the Paul Gauguin Museum that was closed.

We had packed in a considerable amount of activities during our 1,000-mile cruise through the Marquesas Islands and the western part of the Tuamotus. Filled with so many new memories, we were happy to start our homeward journey, taking with us images of a tropical island paradise. After twelve months and 20,000 nautical miles, *Louise* had finally reached the destination that European explorers had prized – the heart of French Polynesia.

At this halfway point mid-Pacific, now was a good time to draw breath and leave Cheryl and Morgan to have a well-deserved break. With the boat tied up in the marina and services available locally, it was also an ideal place to prepare the boat for the second part of the South Pacific cruise. Meanwhile, the rest of us could return to our daily routines and lives back home, and make the most of the end of the northern hemisphere summer.

* * * * *

Just as autumn was about to show its face in Europe, we were all set to continue our travels and journey back to the South Pacific. This stage would see the completion of our Pacific crossing and was due to end in New Zealand, but first we wanted to explore a bit more of the Society Islands. For this part of the trip, Brigitte and I were joined by our youngest daughter Claire and her best friend Natasha Dyer. We were also reunited with my friend Klaus Diederichs, who was returning to the Adventure for a second time, but on this occasion he was accompanied by his charming wife Alice.

The six of us flew out together from London on Saturday 20th September 2014 and were glad to reach Tahiti late that evening, after twenty-four hours of flying via Los Angeles. The first thing we did the next morning was to go to the market in Pape'ete. Local Tahitians get up early on Sundays to buy fish and other fresh produce; the brightly coloured market is full of stallholders neatly displaying their goods and happy to give you a taste. We took the opportunity to sample some freshly squeezed cane juice that was offered to us by a Chinese vendor. He also made his own rum and invited us to try it, but it was still breakfast time and a little early to drink alcohol.

Later in the day we did some more sightseeing, accompanied by a local guide named Diana, which included a visit to Point Venus, a peninsula on Tahiti's north coast that owes its name to Captain Cook. During his first circumnavigation, it was at this location in 1769 that Cook and his crew set up equipment for the official observation of the transit of Venus in early June. In the afternoon, we went for our first dip in the water, and swam close to the reef where locals were making the most of the last of the daylight aboard their boats.

On Monday we set off to the neighbouring island of Moorea, which is very laid-back and a more interesting place than Tahiti. During the brief sail over, we were entertained by some passing whales. These mammals are a common sight in the Society Islands, which is a breeding ground for the species and where young whales can spend time close to their mothers learning to swim and being prepared for a life of travel.

We anchored in the beautiful location of Cook's Bay, where we found ourselves in the company of a few other boats. Named after the famous British navigator, Cook's Bay is a deep inlet carved into the mountainous landscape that dominates Moorea. One of the nearby vessels was a motorised catamaran belonging to the solo Swiss sailor Laurent Bourgnon, who in June 2015 would sadly lose his life in a diving accident in the Tuamotus.

We also met an old friend of Cheryl and Morgan, a Canadian-born artist called Douglas Hazelton, who had been sailing around the world in a converted Danish small-cargo vessel named *Sindbad*. Visiting his boat, which doubles up as a floating art studio, we found Doug to be witty and most likeable. He shared the latest artworks that he had produced, all of which were made using metal and inspired by the sea. His works captured the movement of fish, often depicted in shoals. In the evening, Doug joined us for dinner aboard *Louise* as we lay for our second night at anchor in Cook's Bay, one of the explorer's favourite spots in the entire Pacific.

The other highlight of our Moorea stopover was swimming with the manta rays that played inside the reef near our second anchorage at Opunohu Bay. We all stood in the shallow waters while the rays swam around, often touching us.

Leaving at dawn on Thursday 25th September, our next stop in the Society Islands was Huahine, a quiet island where we made an excursion ashore by road and went to Maeva, a little historic village with a good heritage centre. During the afternoon, while being ferried on a motor boat across the lagoon to visit the local pearl farm, a couple of whales made an appearance. We were able to get close to the mother and her young offspring, who would soon be heading back out to sea and eventually starting the long journey to their feeding grounds in Antarctica.

During our stay on Huahine, we also made our first dive of the trip with Claire and Natasha, who really enjoyed the experience of diving in calm waters away from any tidal currents. After the dive, Claire, who had been struggling to decompress underwater, began to develop a minor ear infection and had to stay out of the water for a few days.

That evening we made a rum cocktail with the sugar cane juice and lime that we had bought from the Chinese stallholder in the market at Pape'ete, and named our newly created cocktail recipe Sugar Daddy. Afterwards we had dinner ashore in the Huahine Yacht Club, a fashionable restaurant and bar. It was a really fun night and by the end of the meal, with the holiday spirit well and truly unleashed, we were all dancing.

Heading further west on Saturday, we stopped at the lovely island of Taha'a. It shares the same outer reef as its larger neighbour Raiatea, which would be the final stop on our visit to French Polynesia. On arrival, we discovered that the Shipman 72 *Moksha* was anchored inside the reef.

Much of our time on Taha'a was spent in the waters surrounding the reef, swimming and snorkelling. While moored on the west of the island, we witnessed magnificent views of Bora Bora on the horizon at sunset. We had also discovered that the best restaurant on Taha'a was reputed to be Chez Louise, so of course we had to book a table. The 'surprise' menu on offer that day consisted of local seafood and fish, including lobster, crab and tuna, which was served in bamboo dishes with rice as an accompaniment. The meal was delicious and the friendly owner Louise also entertained us with some of her life stories.

Most of Sunday's activities involved snorkelling on the coral reefs, sunbathing and generally relaxing on board *Louise*. Then on Monday we were met by Aro, a local guide, who took us on a fascinating tour of Taha'a, which included going to Joe Dassin Beach, a well-known spot on the south-west of the island, and a trip to a vanilla orchid farm, as these islands are renowned for their production of vanilla pods.

For the near-final leg of our cruise in the Society Islands, an element of competition was introduced after Morgan and Cheryl, who were friends with *Moksha*'s skipper and crew, discovered that the Shipman 72 would be travelling in the same direction as *Louise* when we left Taha'a. So, for a bit of fun, it was agreed that we would race one another the 30 or so miles to Bora Bora. Before leaving the island, Claire presented Brigitte and me with a simple black-and-white illustration of Taha'a that she had drawn herself and which we have kept as a lasting memory of our visit.

After breakfast on Tuesday 30th September, both boats lifted anchor and we motored outside the reef, hoisting our sails ready for our private race to Bora Bora. The easterly trade winds were obliging, so all the sailing was downwind, but tactics would certainly be involved as both yachts needed to gybe at some point. Displaying excellent teamwork on board *Louise*, we set our red-and-white spinnaker and got off to a great start. However, our luck soon began to run out when we sailed under a cloud and found ourselves wallowing with almost no wind. *Moksha* was taking a more direct course, but we were not going to give up, so we gybed and found wind once again, and started to win back some of the lost distance.

By the time that both yachts were abreast off the reef at Bora Bora, it was still anybody's race. Approaching the cut where boats can pass through the reef and on into the lagoon, *Louise* finally took the lead to win.

The charm of Bora Bora lies in its amazing topography, with a central island that rises quite steeply, surrounded by the azure-blue waters of the lagoon. The spectacular scenery certainly matches people's perception of a tropical island paradise. The romantic appeal of this faraway South Pacific island draws honeymooners and couples from all over the world. As long as the sun shines no one should be disappointed in such a place, whether staying on a boat or in a resort.

We went to the main town of Vaitape, but most of our time was spent exploring anchorages where we swam and enjoyed the serene waters of the lagoon. Moored close by at Vaitape was a 100-foot Oyster yacht named *Sarafin*. We spoke to the owner, Will Vickers, who was from Sydney, and learnt that he was keen to look at *Louise*, so we invited him on board. A highlight that evening was dinner in the fun setting of the Bora Bora Yacht Club, where we toasted *Louise* on completing the first 20,000 miles of the Adventure.

Our last anchorage on Bora Bora was in a shallower part of the lagoon on the north side of the atoll at Motu Tafari. Entering it required us to pass over a shallow ledge on the reef with a depth of only 9 feet. Once inside we discovered some of the clearest waters that we had ever seen, which made for great swimming. Klaus, Claire and Natasha each climbed the mast in turn to get a bird's-eye view of Bora Bora. That evening, Klaus and Alice treated us all to a meal in the Four Seasons resort where they would be staying for a few days on a belated honeymoon after their wedding in June.

Early the next day, on Friday 3rd October, we bid farewell

to Bora Bora, the Pearl of the Pacific, and started to make our way back towards Raiatea, the final stop on our Society Islands cruise. With an easterly trade wind blowing 20 knots, the short passage took five hours, sailing all the way on the wind. Claire was a little sick during the crossing, but was happy once we had reached our destination by mid-afternoon. Our last night on board with the girls was spent quietly at anchor. On Saturday morning, Claire and Natasha packed their bags and we went ashore for lunch together. Later on, we dropped the girls at the airport, saying cheerio and leaving them to catch their flight to Tahiti and begin the journey beyond.

Brigitte and I then checked in at the Raiatea Lodge, where we had decided to stay for the weekend. The staff were really friendly and the surroundings were extremely pleasant. I managed to do some paddle-boarding in the lagoon and we also made the most of the hotel pool. The following evening, we were joined by Luigi Rosselli, an old friend from our student days in Lausanne. We had also shared experiences in Australia, when we moved there in November 1980 to start new jobs. Luigi, a highly acclaimed architect, subsequently decided to settle down and to make a living in Australia.

On Monday morning, we checked out and set off to explore the ancient historical sites of the old capital of Polynesia. At the height of the Polynesian civilisation, which began to develop after these islands were populated from approximately 1000 AD onwards, Raiatea became the hub from which activity resonated to the three corners of the Pacific. The Society Islands were at the centre of a triangle that stretched to New Zealand in the south-west, Easter Island to the south-east and Hawaii to the north. Taputupuatea, a cultural landscape and seascape comprising a number of sacred ceremonial and social spaces, is the most impressive of all the sites and was the epicentre of political, ceremonial and religious activities during ancient times. Filled up with a dose of history, and having contemplated the skills and knowledge of this old civilisation, we returned to *Louise*, who had been moved from her anchorage to be docked in town.

Klaus and Alice had flown back from Bora Bora after a wonderful holiday, and while he would be joining me for the onward passage to New Zealand aboard *Louise*, Alice had stayed at the airport to meet up with Brigitte. The ladies then boarded the same flight together to start their journey back home.

A cruise ship had berthed at Raiatea earlier in the day and the small town had been quite busy with visitors. That evening there was lots of noise coming from the vessel's aft deck, with a party seemingly getting underway as it cast off its moorings. The Society Islands have long been regarded as a special place where sailors could unwind and regain their health after long, hard days at sea, and they seem to offer a similarly restorative quality in modern times. We had certainly managed to relax and unwind during our short cruise around them, but the seasons would soon be changing and it was time to leave behind the tropics for now.

On the morning of our departure, on Tuesday 7th October, *Louise* motored out of the reef in calm conditions with Klaus, Luigi, Morgan, Cheryl and me on board. We passed the Miri-Miri cut just before midday, leaving behind the Society Islands and French Polynesia. We had spent four months in these waters, visiting fourteen different islands and learning about the diversity of the archipelagos that occupy this vast expanse of the South Pacific. While we hadn't been able to go to the remote and sparsely populated Austral Islands, which lie further south, we had touched on parts of the Tuamotus, Marquesas and the Society Islands, with each having their own special charm.

Leaving astern the centre of Polynesia, we set course for New Zealand, approximately 2,200 nautical miles south-westwards, from where settlers had crossed the waters in an earlier age, finding landfall and spreading the Polynesian culture. It was a hot afternoon, but our fishing got off to a good start when we landed a large mahi-mahi.

During our first night, while still motoring on a flat, calm sea, after midnight we were lucky enough to experience a total eclipse, when the moon was completely hidden from the sun. Going from full moon to total darkness, we watched as the Earth gradually shadowed the moon. We all sat on deck observing the sky above in awe, thinking how tiny we were on Earth in comparison to the enormous size of the universe. In the early hours, we passed another yacht that was sailing slowly in the same direction as *Louise*.

The first 200 miles were spent motoring until we picked up an easterly wind on the second day of the passage, which allowed us to begin sailing. A shift in the wind to the south heralded more steady trade winds, which we were fortunate to hold onto during the next few days. On our second day at sea, we passed the island of Atiu in the southern Cook Islands. Just north of here, on 11th April 1789, Captain William Bligh discovered the beautiful Aitutaki Atoll. Over a fortnight later, mutiny broke out on board HMS *Bounty* in Tonga on the ship's homeward journey. Cast out into the *Bounty*'s longboat alongside eighteen loyal crew members, Bligh and his men sailed for 3,500 nautical miles until arriving in Timor on 14th June 1789, an achievement hailed as an extraordinary feat of navigation.

By the third night at sea we were abreast of Raratonga, the largest and most populous island in the Cook Islands Archipelago, which we passed close by with the light of the main town Avarau plainly visible. Those on watch were surprised to find that their mobile phones were working and Klaus managed to speak to Alice, who picked up his call while sitting in a hairdresser's chair near her home.

The excellent sailing conditions continued and we hoisted the spinnaker, allowing us to make good progress during the day. We took turns at driving and Morgan managed the best top speed at 14.4 knots. Spirits were high, with the on-board entertainment including backgammon in the afternoon, which was hotly contested. The daily tournament would start as soon as self-appointed barista Luigi had served each of us with a post-lunch espresso.

The wind then shifted to the north, giving us a good wind angle to reach the following day and helping us to make further progress along the rhumb line straight to Auckland. Gradually, the wind veered back to the west, dying, so we dropped the sails and motored. Morgan kept a watchful eye on the weather, checking for low-pressure systems. The daily forecast revealed a deepening front ahead, albeit far to the south, so we decided to take evasive action by gybing onto starboard tack to move west. Happily, the weather remained good and we were still able to make headway almost directly towards our destination on New Zealand's North Island.

We crossed the tropic of Capricorn at longitude 165 degrees west during the evening of Saturday 11th October, which we had last passed four months ago, just before making landfall in French Polynesia. After a large rain squall, the wind backed to the west, steadily dropping. Due to the absence of enough wind, the next two days were mainly spent under engine.

On Monday 13th October, the sixth day of the passage, we reached the halfway point of our journey to Auckland, and a following wind picked up once again. Back under full sail, we charged on further west. As a sign that we had left the tropics, we sighted our first albatross. The majestic bird glided effortlessly in the light wind, while later in the day a giant petrel also made an appearance. That evening we crossed the International Date Line, and Morgan presented Klaus and Luigi with signed certificates. This meant that we had skipped 14th October, losing a day.

During the night, misfortune struck and we were woken from our sleep by Morgan, who announced that the yankee foresail halyard, the rope which keeps the sail hoisted, had broken and the sail had dropped into the water. We all rushed on deck and after thirty minutes or so, had wrestled the sail back on board and were able to get going again. After dawn the wind strengthened to over 30 knots and we reefed the main for the first time on the passage. Making the best of the strong wind, we were clocking up the miles under beautiful sailing conditions. Kelp also started to appear in little bunches in the water, indicating that land must lie somewhere not too far over the horizon.

On Thursday the wind moderated and the boat was fairly stable, allowing Morgan to climb to the top of the mast and recover the end of the broken halyard, which he pulled down to deck level. This meant we could re-hoist the yankee, which we unfurled later on.

A day later, on Friday 17th October, the wind had died, so we motored on over a calm sea. Just as our fishing line caught a small tuna late in the afternoon, a pod of whales emerged, blowing in a spectacle all around the boat. One of them disappeared under *Louise* and we saw the mammal's shadow in the water at our stern. We struggled to identify the exact species, but narrowed it down to either sei or Bryde's, both of which are rorquals, the largest group of baleen whales.

That evening, Klaus noted in the log, '*Louise* halfway around the world crossing the 180th meridian at 20.50', to record our passage from the western into the eastern hemisphere. Opening a whisky bottle, we shared a toast to celebrate this significant milestone in the Adventure. At midnight, a cargo ship overtook us and, on checking our chart plotter, the AIS signal showed that it was heading to Auckland, reassuring us that we were on the right track.

During the last full day at sea, we discovered that a gecko had stowed away on board, but sadly, in anticipation of the strict rules in New Zealand regarding animals, our little passenger had to be ejected overboard. In the evening, we were entertained by a big group of dolphins, a sign that we were getting close to coastal waters. During my watch at 11 p.m., I spotted the loom of the light beaming from the lighthouse on Cuvier Island, close to the entrance of the famous Hauraki Gulf. At 3 a.m., with Klaus and Morgan on deck together, we cleared Channel Island and altered course for the final run to our destination. The weather had taken a turn for the worse, with rain falling during the night, but we had just managed to scrape into New Zealand ahead of a depression, which thankfully saved us slogging to windward.

At 9 a.m., we tied up alongside the Auckland customs dock, celebrating our arrival on Sunday 19th October. This marked the end of our trans-Pacific crossing and the first half of the *Louise* Adventure. Our journey from French Polynesia had taken just ten days and twenty-two hours. Luigi had come closest to estimating the correct overall duration of the passage and so had won the competition that we had set, whereas the rest of us had been too pessimistic in our calculations. Klaus, who had been filming highlights of the trip, asked Luigi on camera to comment on his experiences of standing watch during both dawn and dusk. Answering philosophically, Luigi said that his role was to 'make sure that the sun came up in the morning and went down at night'.

After docking in Auckland, it was time to say farewell to Luigi, who had been a fantastic companion and crew member, as he had to get back to Sydney and his busy practice.

Klaus and I also flew to Sydney, where we made a brief stopover on our way back to the UK and met up with old friends Fiona and Jost Stollmann. The Stollmanns had emigrated to Australia, after making their own round-the-world voyage with their family on their Tripp-designed boat *Alithia*. Eventually, it was time to leave the southern hemisphere behind and board a plane bound for London.

* * * * *

A few days after my return home, Brigitte and I became grandparents for the first time. Our grandson Ivo Gakic was born to our second daughter Valerie and her husband Luka on 27th October 2014. The months that followed marked the happy beginning of our new role in life. The addition to the family also provided a good excuse for an interlude to the Adventure, allowing time to draw breath and enjoy being grandparents. My mind was never far from sailing, however, and the plan for the winter was to prepare *Louise* to compete in the Sydney Hobart Yacht Race.

Chapter 7 – The Race
Sydney to Hobart, Australia

Tasman Island, Australia

Every Boxing Day, one of the biggest events in the Australian sporting calendar occurs when a fleet of yachts sets off from Sydney Harbour to race to Hobart, Tasmania. We decided that we would take up the challenge and put *Louise* through her paces over the 600-mile passage across the Bass Strait to Tasmania. Much preparatory work would be required, including finding a crew, getting the boat primed for racing and doing the mandatory training in readiness for the start on Friday 26th December 2014 at 1 p.m.

Morgan and Cheryl worked hard in Auckland throughout November, and on Tuesday 2nd December they left New Zealand with *Louise*, accompanied by Morgan's brother Jonathan, also a very accomplished sailor, and another crew member named Stephen O'Shannessy, to cross the Tasman Sea to Sydney, where they arrived safely after a six-day passage.

After flying out to Sydney from various parts of the world, the rest of the race crew assembled for training during the weekend before Christmas. In our normal cruising mode we only ever sailed short-handed on *Louise*, so it felt odd to be back on the boat surrounded by thirteen other people, including my youngest brother Lloyd. Our training took place in light winds and included an overnight sail outside the Sydney Heads – a series of headlands at the entrance to the harbour – before we slipped back into Port Jackson Bay at first light. Surrounded by the city of Sydney, which was still asleep, the harbour was calm and there were no other boats on the move.

Taking a day of rest, I caught up with friends in Pittwater, north of Sydney, where I raced in the evening with John Bacon, Commodore of the Royal Prince Alfred Yacht Club. After the twilight race, John invited me to enjoy some great Aussie hospitality at the vast clubhouse, which was full of members attending their pre-Christmas party.

On Christmas Day, Lloyd and I walked on the beaches in the eastern suburbs, soaking up the festive atmosphere. Other sailing friends who helped to make up the team included Mike Greville, a former Royal Ocean Racing Club Commodore; Conor Roche, whom I had raced with on *Fever*, the Swan 45 that I co-owned with Klaus; and David Tydeman, whom I had met years ago when he established the Melges 24 racing circuit. Completing the crew of fourteen were eight more sailors: two from New Zealand – tactician Dan Slater and navigator Ed Smyth – and from Australia we were fortunate to have main trim and crew boss Simon Reffold, who was ably supported by Murray Gordon, Tommy Spithill, Tobias Wehr-Candler, Max Vos and Rob Human.

On a warm and sunny Sydney morning, we checked out of our hotel in Double Bay on Boxing Day and made our way to the Cruising Yacht Club of Australia in nearby Rushcutters Bay. Most of the race fleet was moored here and, as we approached, a sea of bright flags flying in the boats' rigging came into view. The atmosphere on the dock was buzzing, with crews keen to get to the start and out of the harbour to race south.

The customary pre-race briefing was packed and we listened attentively to the weather forecast, which sounded good, except for the fact that the wind was expected to drop during the first night. The fleet faced the prospect of being becalmed off the New South Wales coast while waiting for a new wind from the west. However, what startled *Louise*'s crew was when our boat's name was announced and we were warned that we had not passed the mandatory radio test, without which we couldn't join the race. Our Single Side Band (SSB) radio had been hired from one of the Clipper Challenge boats, and Morgan had installed it temporarily in the aft lazarette. SSB radios are part of the obligatory safety equipment carried on yachts competing in this race. Despite our efforts, we had not yet managed to complete the SSB radio check because one of the ground transmitters had been hit by lightning. We rushed back to the boat, hurriedly leaving the marina to get out into the middle of Sydney Harbour from where we could transmit. We could hear the voice of the radio handler who acknowledged our call, confirming that our SSB transmitter was working, at which point our sense of panic dissipated.

With an hour or so to go to the race start, we motored slowly around the harbour as the rest of the fleet began to assemble. In a state of full readiness for the race, *Louise*'s interior was almost unrecognisable and now resembled a sports team's locker room, as all the furniture had been removed and stored in a shipping container, the walls were covered in plastic board and an array of life jackets and oilskins were neatly numbered and hanging on a temporary clothes line in the saloon.

Following a final briefing in the cockpit, we hoisted sails ready to get underway. In the minutes leading up to the starter's gun at 1 p.m., we executed a near-perfect approach, and a few seconds after the starting signal, we crossed the southern end of the line just inside the 'pin' or marker buoy. In the Sydney Hobart Race, all the competitors begin racing at the same time, with smaller boats passing two separate lines further back inside the harbour. We were in the front row, together with the biggest competitors in the fleet, but one by one these sleek-looking racing boats began to pull ahead of us. The largest yachts, which are around 100 feet long, are naturally the favourites to be the first to reach Hobart and cross the finish line.

As we sailed out of Sydney Harbour between the Sydney Heads, spectator vessels were motoring close to our path, throwing up their wake, while helicopters buzzed noisily above. Hauling close to the wind after passing the turning mark buoy beyond the Heads, we pulled in the sails to travel south. *Louise* heeled to port and water was coming over the bulwark, flooding the deck as she was pressed onto her side by the building southerly wind.

Later in the afternoon, a sail change to the smaller working jib was required. Unfortunately, during the switch-over we tore the leech of our brand-new genoa sail and had to furl it in. The sail was out of use until we could take it down and stitch up the tear. We were fortunate that a forecasted calm period arrived as predicted during the night and we could take advantage of the wind dropping entirely to make the necessary repairs in the morning.

By dawn the next day, we had managed to sail in close to the New South Wales coast, while we waited for the new wind to fill in. We made our entry into Bass Strait near to Green Cape, the south-east tip of Australia. Fortunately, the wind gradually started to build from the north, allowing us to escape the conditions that had slowed down the entire fleet. The race was back on.

With the sea state remaining calm, the watches slept well during their rest breaks. Our rota system consisted of two hours on watch, followed by two hours on standby and then two hours of sleep. By daybreak on Sunday 28th December, the wind had freshened and we sailed nicely across the Bass Strait towards Tasmania. The wind picked up to around 20 knots and *Louise* made great progress, running downwind under bright blue skies. Both the drivers who were steering the boat and the trimmers who were constantly keeping the sails filled worked hard to ensure that *Louise* maintained speed. Ed, our talented navigator, was monitoring the weather feeds and the positions of our competitors to plot our strategy. During the afternoon, Conor, David, Mike and my brother Lloyd each had a spell on the helm, all doing a good job. Crossing the Bass Strait, we prepared for another night at sea and positioned ourselves for the final run into the lighthouse at the south-east corner of Tasman Island. This is the southerly turning point for the race, where competitors bear west to start their final approach to Hobart.

In the closing stages of the competition, we had a taste of why this event can be so challenging. A frontal weather system was approaching Tasmania from the Australian Bight, bringing ahead of it strong northerly winds. Running with the growing breeze, Dan and Ed decided that we could gain on the fleet by heading out to the east, staying away from lighter winds in the lee of the Tasmanian coast. This gave us a faster angle to sail on our approach to Tasman Island and moved us up nearly ten places in the overall rankings.

We found the stronger breeze in the early hours and discussed a change to the smaller spinnaker. When *Louise* hit a top speed of 23 knots while surfing on a wave with Dan at the helm, it began to feel as if the boat had too much sail area hoisted and was overpowered. While setting the smaller spinnaker chute, we had the misfortune to rip the sail. After switching to our reaching sail, we could see Tasman Island emerging from the morning glare, a foreboding sight with the sun shining onto the vertical cliffs. We changed headsail again and rounded up into a reach to cross Storm Bay. Disaster nearly struck when we heard a loud bang as one of the turning blocks, through which the sheet connecting the jib to the cockpit winch passes, ripped out of the deck. If anyone had been close to that side of the boat at the moment the block severed from the deck, a serious injury could have been sustained.

Finally swinging around north into the Derwent River, we made our approach to the finish line under bright blue skies. With all the crew hiked out on the windward rail, *Louise* crossed the line at 11.20 a.m. on Monday 29th December, completing the race in two days and twenty-two hours. As we entered the marina, the crowd of spectators burst into applause as *Louise*'s name was announced on the loud speakers and the team was welcomed to Hobart.

Participating in the race revealed that, as a yacht, *Louise* was very much capable of being taken offshore and put through her paces. The boat responded magnificently to the range of conditions, acquitting herself well and producing a great performance. Together with all the members of the team, we celebrated that afternoon and well into the evening.

Tragically, we would later discover that while we were toasting our success, a light aircraft carrying a race photographer who had earlier taken pictures of *Louise* crashed into Storm Bay at 6 p.m. Both the photographer Timothy Jones and his young pilot Sam Langford lost their lives.

Most of the crew left Hobart on Tuesday 30th December, heading home in time for New Year. I travelled to Melbourne to see my old Harvard friend Stewart Baron and his family, spending Hogmanay with them before catching a flight home on Thursday 1st January 2015.

Morgan and Cheryl were joined in Hobart by Morgan's brother Jonathan, their sister Sarah and Jonathan's girlfriend Maeva, to help sail *Louise* back to New Zealand. Unfortunately, they endured a tough passage while encountering some rough weather. Richard Dobbs' Swan 68 *Titania of Cowes*, which had also competed in the Sydney Hobart Yacht Race, followed a similar track to *Louise* on the return crossing to New Zealand, sighting each other on one occasion. On Tuesday 13th January, *Louise* safely completed the 1,500-nautical-mile sail across the Tasman Sea, arriving back in Auckland ready to resume her normal life of cruising. The next chapter in the Adventure would get under way at Easter, after an interval of approximately three months, when we planned to sail north for a return visit to the tropics.

Chapter 8 – The South Pacific
Auckland, New Zealand to Fiji and Cairns, Australia

Hitch-hiker, Coral Sea

At the beginning of 2015 we took a break from sailing, but our thoughts were never far away from what lay ahead in the *Louise* Adventure, fulfilling plans to discover more islands in the South Pacific before travelling towards South East Asia. During the three-month interlude, Brigitte and I flew to New Zealand to spend some time visiting the boat in Auckland. We also didn't want to miss the opportunity of seeing the country's South Island, which Captain Cook first set foot on during his first voyage in 1769. It would have been extraordinary to sail *Louise* in the fjords and follow in Cook's footsteps, but we didn't manage to do it on this occasion because she was back in the boatyard in Auckland, being prepared for the long journey home. Instead we hired a car to journey by road. During our trip we went to a variety of places, including Queenstown, Milford Sound and the Otago Peninsula at Dunedin, each of which was beautiful in its own way.

Back in Auckland at the end of March 2015, before the Easter weekend, we prepared to set sail for the tropics once again. Joining Brigitte and me for a third time on the boat was our good friend Ian Reid. One of the benefits of being in New Zealand was that we could stock up on some of the nation's extraordinary wines. An old business acquaintance of mine, Brian Cleal, who before retiring had worked in the drinks industry, helped us to source a wonderful selection of bottles. The evening before our planned departure, we caught up with him over a drink on board *Louise*.

Casting off early on Tuesday 31st March 2015, we sailed out into the harbour on a fine late summer's day with the city of Auckland looking beautiful in the morning light. Unfortunately, we discovered a technical glitch with the newly reinstalled forestay, so decided to return to the marina to have it looked at. We were fortunate to get underway again by lunchtime, and after covering approximately 90 nautical miles, we were still in good time when we reached Urquhart Bay in the lee of Whangarei Heads, where we moored for the night.

All was quiet as we lay at anchor on still waters, until one of the bilge pump alarms sounded, shattering the peace. On checking the stern compartment, we observed a tiny trickle of water entering the boat at the rudder posts. Although this didn't threaten our security, it was nevertheless a significant inconvenience. We came to the conclusion that when *Louise* was taken out of the water and the bottom was given a rigorous pressure-cleaning, a bit of dirt must have been pushed into the rudder seals, which then affected their ability to prevent seawater from seeping inside the hull. It made sense to fix the problem in Auckland, where all the necessary services would be available. To do the job, *Louise* would need to be lifted from the water in order to remove the rudders and replace the seals, all of which would take a few days.

Alongside every setback there is often a silver lining. The Easter weekend was approaching, and the country would soon shut down for business until after the holiday period. Now was our chance to go to the Bay of Islands, an outstanding cruising destination and a site of great natural beauty, before sailing *Louise* back to Auckland. Changing our plans, we decided to relax and enjoy some sightseeing in the town of Russell and go walking on a few of the nearby islands including Motuarohia, also known as Roberton Island.

Leaving Whangarei on Wednesday morning, we motored past Cape Brett where there is a spectacular hole in a rock off the point at Piercy Island. We dropped anchor at Roberton Island, where Captain Cook became the first European to visit the area in 1769 and used the place as his base from which to explore the archipelago of over 150 small islands. In our anchorage a couple of French boats were moored, including a large vessel named *G Force* – formerly *Gitana 13*, a 100-foot-long maxi-catamaran which broke numerous long-distance speed records in 2008, including the North Pacific Crossing from San Francisco to Yokohama and the old Tea Route from Hong Kong to London.

Venturing ashore, we said hello to a *G Force* crew member named Elena Aloisio who, two years later, would join *Louise* as crew together with her partner Richard Boutet, *G Force*'s then skipper. Also moored up was a smaller yacht called *Caval'où*, which was owned by a French couple named Pascal and Valerie Bussereau. Pascal had designed and built her himself, and for the last five years she had been their floating home in which they had cruised Patagonia and much of the South Pacific.

From our sheltered anchorage, we decided to take advantage of the calm conditions and make use of our new inflatable paddle-boards. While relaxing on *Louise*, we recorded a short video of Ian paddling near the boat and losing his balance before falling in the water. Never missing an opportunity to humour others with his antics, Ian shared the video with his family accompanied by Easter greetings.

Keeping true to the tradition of eating fish at Easter, Ian and Morgan set off later with the boat's dinghy to do some fishing nearby and came back with a sizeable haul of snapper ready to be cooked for dinner.

Ashore in Russell, the original capital of New Zealand, we visited a modest but well-proportioned house where a French Catholic mission had been established in the mid-1800s and a bible-printing factory was set up to help spread the Christian gospel. We also managed to find our way to the Omata Estate boutique winery, which had wonderful views over the bay between Russell and Waitangi opposite. Our detour to the Bay of Islands proved to be a relaxing and pleasant experience.

To ensure we would be back in Auckland by the end of the Easter break, on Saturday 4th April we began to head south early in the morning, stopping along the way on Great Barrier Island. Even though autumn was just around the corner, the day was still warm for the time of the year. Barrier Island lies north of the Coromandel Peninsula, helping to shelter the waters of the Hauraki Gulf and Auckland from the Pacific Ocean. The overnight anchorage where we stayed at Karaka Bay in Port Fitzroy was very peaceful. Off to bed early following our long journey that day, we resurfaced from our cabins around 1 a.m. to witness a total eclipse of the moon. There was not a single cloud in the night sky, which made the spectacle of the moon disappearing briefly into complete darkness a wonder to view.

After a lie-in on Easter Sunday, we lifted our anchor to motor a little way further south, passing through some narrow and picturesque channels, before anchoring again in Whangaparapara Harbour. From here we hiked over to the other side of the island, finding a plunge pool where we enjoyed a bathe in a hot spring. Being a land with plentiful volcanic activity, such thermal water sources are one of the great natural pleasures afforded in New Zealand, especially on the North Island.

Our last stop before our return to Auckland was in Man O' War Bay, on the eastern side of Waiheke Island, where we arrived early on Sunday evening. Lots of yachts were already anchored, many of which were rafted up alongside each other, but we managed to find a spot for *Louise*. People were taking advantage of the fine weather and celebrating the end of the long Easter weekend, which coincides with the beginning of autumn in the southern hemisphere, so quite a few floating parties were held that night.

The next morning, on Easter Monday, Brigitte, Ian and I left Cheryl and Morgan to organise *Louise*'s new rudder seals, and took a taxi through some beautiful vineyards over to the Waiheke Ferry Terminal where we boarded for a short ride over to downtown Auckland. Back on the North Island, we rented a car to make a side trip for a few days to explore further inland and around Taupo. During the tour, we experienced an exhilarating high-speed river-raft excursion at Huka Falls on the beautiful Waikato River. A trip to the nature reserve at Orakei Korako, with geysers, hot springs, mud pools and silica terraces, was another amazing attraction. Walking among the geysers, you could really appreciate the extent of the seismic activity that occurs within New Zealand.

When we rejoined *Louise* at the marina in Auckland on Wednesday, we found the boat fitted with a brand-new set of rudder seals and all ready to go. Because we had lost one week of our allotted time for this leg of the Adventure, we sadly had to take the decision to miss out on visiting Tonga.

On Thursday 9th April, a friendly lady from the immigration department came aboard and stamped our passports, after which we were ready to cast off from Auckland Harbour for the third and final time. Docking out at 10 a.m., we motored close by downtown Auckland, which lies south of the harbour, soon turning north towards the Hauraki Gulf. We kept our fingers crossed that this departure from the iconic City of Sails would go without any hitches.

With not enough wind to fill our sails, we had to rely on the engine until we passed Little Barrier Island late in the afternoon, where we came upon slightly more breeze and were able to motor-sail during the first night back at sea. At sunset we had our last view of New Zealand's North Island, which had been *Louise*'s base for almost five months. We left behind good memories of the time spent in the Land of the Long White Cloud, this magnificent island at the other side of the planet to our home.

During the first few days of our passage north from New Zealand, good conditions enabled us to make excellent progress towards the tropics. This next leg was the beginning of the long trip home, and we weren't sure of the exact route that we would follow nor how long it would take to complete our round-the-world Adventure. There was still so much of the South Pacific to visit, but over the coming months we chose to focus our cruising plans on Fiji, Vanuatu and New Caledonia. In the long term, we had decided that beyond South East Asia, which lay on our path westwards to the Indian Ocean, we would aim for Cape Town before turning north to head across the South Atlantic and re-cross the equator on our home-bound course.

As we set out, low pressure was established to our west in the Tasman Sea, bringing a steady north-westerly wind, which held for the first three days out of Auckland. With the wind angle ahead of the beam and the boat tracking north, *Louise* was constantly heeled over to starboard. But she moved nicely through the waves, making good speed in the breeze, and we were happy to have notched up over 600 nautical miles by lunchtime on Sunday 12th April. However, the wind began to drop and veered around onto our nose, so eventually we switched back to motor-sailing. Meanwhile, the weather chart was showing a tropical storm building over New Caledonia, which we started to keep an eye on as it was expected to make its way towards our current position.

Forewarned of the pending change in the weather, we maintained our speed to avoid the strong winds and seas that the tropical storm, now named 'Solo', would bring in its wake. With no sign as yet of the new wind, we continued to relax on board, playing games and fishing. A further boost to morale was that the temperature was gradually getting warmer as we moved closer to the tropics.

By mid-afternoon on Sunday we had our first catch of fish, courtesy of a fine mahi-mahi that Ian had hauled in. Overhead we noticed lots of seabirds circling around, which was a harbinger that prey was near the surface. Sure enough, a school of tuna became clearly visible and a few hundred feet to windward they began to thrash around, making a big commotion. One energetic fish leapt right out of the water. We spun *Louise* around in haste, casting a lure from one of the rods, and motored towards the shoal. One of the tuna immediately took our bait. Knowing that this species doesn't give up easily, we stopped the boat to stay as close as possible to our quarry. After tussling with his catch for about twenty minutes, Morgan eventually hauled it in close to *Louise*'s stern. Seconds before, Cheryl landed the gaff in the side of the poor creature. As it circled underneath *Louise*, we prayed that the line would not snap on one of the boat's rudders. Working together as a team, we finally managed to hoist the fish on board. The adult yellowfin had lost her struggle, tiring at the finish. Ian's suggestion that we should have New Zealand lamb for dinner was quickly forgotten as we contemplated our catch lying on the aft deck.

No sooner had we landed the weighty fish, which we estimated to be about 90 pounds, than work began in earnest to fillet it. The poop soon resembled a fishmonger's on a busy day. Morgan completed the task with great skill and panache, passing the neatly cut pieces to me, who was assigned the role of drying the fresh meat ready to be bagged for the freezer. Brigitte then carried the precious cargo down to the galley to hand over to Cheryl, who sealed the individual bags using our vacuum packer, which we had acquired without knowing just how useful it would become. Then Ian noted details of the contents, quantity and the catch date on each packet. Once the fish was frozen, its flavour would be captured for the delectation of future diners.

Dusk had fallen by the time the freezer had been loaded up. It was back to the business of sailing and reaching our destination of Fiji 400 nautical miles further north. Under storm jib and two reefs, *Louise* ploughed ahead on a close-hauled course, leaving 'Tropical Depression Solo' in her wake. During the night the wind gradually backed to the south, improving the boat's motion and on-board comfort.

The next morning, we passed close by the Minerva Reefs, reputed to be one of the finest diving locations in this area of the South Pacific, but sadly we didn't have the time to stop there and explore. In the evening, we crossed the tropic of Capricorn and could feel the temperature was improving.

Six days after leaving Auckland, during my dawn watch on Wednesday 15th April, we sighted the archipelago of Fiji, a country formed of more than 300 islands, two-thirds of which are uninhabited. For the rest of the day we motored, as the wind was too light for sailing, and by evening we were approaching our destination: Savusavu, a town on the south coast of Vanua Levu, Fiji's second main island. Swathes of lush forest cover the mountainous terrain of Vanua Levu and much of the rest of it is cultivated with sugar cane and copra. We dropped anchor off Savusavu just after midnight, finishing the 1,300-mile passage that had gone well overall and without major incident.

Early on Thursday, a group of at least half a dozen local officials arrived alongside *Louise* and asked to come on board. Welcoming us to the country the administrators, who all seemed to work in pairs, filled out reams of paperwork. Admiring *Louise* they were also keen, after seeking our permission, to take photos of her.

Once the mandatory admin had been completed, we headed ashore. The little town has a few hotels, one of which is owned by the Cousteau family. We tried to book a meal in the restaurant of the latter, but were rebuffed by the staff who didn't seem interested in the prospect of our custom. Our efforts to rent a car were more successful, however, and we set off by road to visit the island's main town, Labasa, located on the north-east side of Vanua Levu. While there, we walked through the main market at the end of the town, which was full of stalls selling spices, fish, poultry, goats and other local products. By the roadside we also passed various vendors who were selling fresh oranges.

We had arranged a rendezvous on the small island resort of Laucala with our friends Marcus and Caroline Blackmore from Sydney. To get there, we set off from Savusavu on Friday and sailed east between Vanua Levu and the island of Taveuni, stopping for the night at anchor adjacent to the Somosomo Strait on the 180th meridian. The waters there are best known for their high-quality dive sites, but we didn't have time to do any underwater exploration on this occasion.

The following morning, we motored further on towards our final stop at Laucala. After arriving late in the afternoon, we laid anchor for the night, but the resort staff asked us to move *Louise* away from the main beach and re-anchor out of sight of the island's guests. Of course, we did as requested and made ourselves comfortable for the evening ahead.

The next day, Sunday 19th April, was the date of Marcus's surprise 70th birthday party. Caroline had not told her husband that his friends would be coming, nor that we were bringing *Louise*. So when he saw the boat that morning, he was rather taken aback. As part of his celebrations Marcus joined us on board and we set off on a quick sail. We anchored at the nearby island of Tovuka, where we swam and had lunch aboard *Louise*. Marcus had just commissioned a Southern Wind 82 yacht to be built in Cape Town and so was glad to have the opportunity to see *Louise* and ask lots of questions about her design features.

In the evening, we were invited to join Marcus's party for a traditional Fijian celebration dinner, which included the ritual of the kava drinking ceremony, accompanied by music and dancing, and a sumptuous meal enjoyed with Marcus's closest friends. We were glad to see Terry Wetton, who had helped to manage our preparations and crew for the Sydney Hobart Yacht Race at the end of 2014.

After an amazing evening of fun, we retired for a brief rest on board *Louise* before an early-morning start to fly to Nadi, on Fiji's main island of Viti Levu, and catch our flight to London via Hong Kong. During our earlier visit to Labasa, we had managed to buy a compact cooler box, which we used to pack chunks of tuna meat in between several frozen bottles of water for safe transportation on the journey home. Dawn had still not risen when Brigitte, Ian and I arrived at the little airstrip, but despite the hour the resort manager, who was a friendly Scotsman, had arranged for the same group of musicians who had entertained us the previous night to play some more traditional Fijian songs before we boarded the plane.

Safely back in the UK, at short notice Brigitte and I organised a small dinner party in our flat, serving the big tuna steaks caught in the South Pacific to our guests. Our appetite was truly whetted and we looked forward to an imminent return to these friendly islands.

* * * * *

On Saturday 20th June 2015, Brigitte and I began travelling back to Fiji. This time, we took off from Heathrow accompanied by our daughter Valerie, son-in-law Luka and grandson Ivo. We were heading to the island of Taveuni, on the north-eastern side of the country, where we landed the following afternoon, on midsummer's day. *Louise* was anchored at the northern tip of Taveuni, near the little village of Matei, and we were delighted to be reunited with her. During our nine-week break from sailing, Morgan and Cheryl had made a leisurely round trip on *Louise* to the main island of Viti Levu, returning to Taveuni via Savusavu. There was a sense of excitement to be embarking on a family cruise with Ivo, who was only eight months old and had just begun to master the art of crawling.

Once we had recovered from our long journey, on Monday morning Valerie, Luka and Ivo set off to explore the island and saw the sign in Tavuki that marks 180 degrees longitude where the meridian passes through Taveuni. In the afternoon, we moved *Louise* to an anchorage slightly further east. Around teatime we saw a group of schoolchildren travelling home on a dinghy. They waved at us, noticing that there was a baby on the boat, and we invited them on board to talk while they admired Ivo. The youngsters seemed very happy and after a brief chat they were soon on their way back to their families.

Departing at first light on Tuesday, we travelled south-east to Vanua Balavu in the Lau island group, a remote part of the Fijian Archipelago with an extensive reef system. On arrival at any inhabited island, it is customary for visitors to request permission to come ashore from the local leader before one starts to explore. After the short passage, we moored *Louise* in front of the village of Daliconi in a beautiful bay that faced west and offered great views at sunset. Before setting foot on Vanua Balavu, we dressed ourselves in traditional 'pareos' – skirts worn by men and women in the South Pacific – some of which we had bought in Polynesia. On reaching the shore, we then had to ask around to find the village leader who would take us to the chief's house. Once there, we were invited to sit cross-legged on the floor for the Fijian 'sevusevu' welcoming ceremony, at which a gift is presented to the chief. The standard offering is kava, a dried root that is ground into a powder and mixed with liquid to create a mildly intoxicating drink. Cheryl had bought some in a local market before leaving for the cruise, so we were well prepared and ready to give the kava to the chief when required.

It was a busy time of the year, and three other yachts were anchored with *Louise* in the bay, whose crews also joined us for the ceremony. This was our first encounter with boats participating in the World ARC Rally, which had just arrived in Fiji on a fifteen-month circumnavigation, following the classic trade winds route.

After taking a walk around Daliconi, we settled in for a quiet night in the bay, then on Wednesday morning we moved the boat to the Bay of Islands, a secluded anchorage surrounded by magnificent rock formations. We were not alone, however, as the boats we had met the previous day had also sailed down that way. That evening we were invited for drinks on *Pacifica*, a catamaran owned by Janet from Australia. It was her seventieth birthday, and to celebrate she had asked the other crews of the yachts moored nearby on board. Yachties, many of whom are complete strangers, are usually at their friendliest at such impromptu parties and this occasion was no exception.

The next morning, we went on a dinghy ride to explore the bay, which was maze-like with small, rocky outcrops rising out of the water. When we looked more closely, we saw lots of bats suspended from trees overhanging the water. Wishing to see more of Vanua Balavu, before lunch we moved *Louise* to Soso Bay where we laid anchor completely alone. The water was flat calm and ideal for paddle-boarding, which Brigitte tried for the first time. Ivo was also able to experience a dip in the sea, which he enjoyed.

On Friday we took a walk ashore, climbing up through a forest to find a lookout over a cliff with a magnificent view across the Bay of Islands. On our way back we passed an enormous lemon orchard, with tall palm trees offering shade to the low-growing citrus bushes. In the bay itself there was a lone building with a jetty, flagpole and the sign REIYS, which stands for 'Royal Exploring Isles Yacht Squadron'. A man whom we spoke to on the jetty said that the owner of the property, whose identity would remain a mystery, was away on the main island. We spent a quiet evening in this secluded bay, located in a sparsely inhabited corner of Fiji on the far side of the Earth.

Over dinner, we debated the plan for the rest of the holiday. One idea was to sail south of the main island, Viti Levu, and visit Kadavu, a smaller island renowned for its wildlife and turtles. It was tempting to take this route, which was likely to offer excellent sailing conditions but would require travelling over a longer distance. In the end, our preferred option was to navigate our way through Bligh Water, the channel named after the famous English naval captain that separates Fiji's largest islands, Viti Levu and Vanua Levu, as this would mean spending less time at sea.

After breakfast on Saturday 27th June, we left the anchorage and set sail for the Yasawa group of islands, pointing the boat west towards Viti Levu and Bligh Water on the island's north shore. Our goal was to reach Yasawa Island on the western side of the archipelago by the following morning. We sailed all day downwind in the south-easterly trade winds and experienced a very smooth ride. By the evening we had changed course, gybing off Ovalau Island to head north-west towards Bligh Water. The channel is littered with coral reefs, so we had to be vigilant and maintain a good watch, while accurate navigation in the dark was also essential.

Our night watches passed by quickly, as *Louise* kept up good speed sailing downwind in the trades which reached 30 knots in the gusts. Ivo woke up during my watch in the early hours, but after I gave him his bottle of milk, he was soon back asleep. He appeared to be the happiest person at sea.

On Sunday morning, at breakfast time, we anchored safely opposite Nabukeru Village on Yasawa Island. The wind was gusty and the boat swung quite strongly on her anchor from one side to another. We had covered a little more than 200 nautical miles, sailing from the eastern side of the Fijian Archipelago to the most westerly islands in twenty-four hours. These western islands, or Yasawa Group, are distinctive for being more arid and therefore much less green. Once again, we readied ourselves for the customary presentation to the island chief at the local village. After the ceremony, which was quite informal, we were approached by a young man offering us crabs for sale. We paid no notice at first, but he insisted that we went with him to take a look at his catch. He lifted a cloth covering a bucket to reveal some mud crabs and we knew we couldn't pass up the chance to buy them. Our evening meal turned out to be simply delicious.

The following morning, during another onshore visit, we encountered local women from the island who had neatly laid out on the ground a selection of their handmade wares. Naturally, we bought a few trinkets from the smiling ladies. Afterwards, we snorkelled through a series of underwater caves. Luka and Valerie both enjoyed this excursion, taking pictures above and below water of the caves that were illuminated by shafts of light shining through a small opening to the sky above.

At midday, we moved a short way south to Nanuya Lailai Island, best known for *The Blue Lagoon*, where the water scenes in the classic 1980 film starring Brooke Shields were shot. Ivo went for his first proper swim on the island's beach. We just relaxed there, making the most of the calm and attractive surroundings. By chance we discovered *Moksha*, the Shipman 72 yacht that we had come across the year before in French Polynesia, anchored close by and so we invited her crew on board for drinks. The owners, whom we still hadn't met, were at home in Australia.

The next stop on Tuesday was Naviti Island, where we found another secluded anchorage and, after having some fun and games on the beach, we settled in for the night. Luka and I went ashore for a drink in the bar of the resort, where we met a friendly Australian couple who shared their travel stories, including the time when the gentleman got lost in Chile's Torres del Paine National Park and couldn't find the way back to his hotel.

After getting up early on Wednesday 1st July, we journeyed a little further south, hoping for the opportunity to swim with manta rays at Nanuya Balavu Island. Unfortunately, we were out of luck, but the local dive shop and two friendly, youthful diving instructors made up for this by taking Valerie and me for a great dive in Fiji's crystal-clear waters.

Moving off again that afternoon, we continued sailing south near to the chain of islands that form the southern part of the Yasawa Group. Along the way we encountered groups of fish thrashing around on the surface in a feeding frenzy. We tried and failed to catch some of them, by towing our lines as we passed through the shoals. Not having any success with fishing, we gave up and decided that, given the calm seas, we would attempt to take pictures of their vast numbers. Luka, Morgan and I jumped into the water from the dinghy and began swimming through the mass of fish. Small parr fish swam together in what looked like a cloud, while the bigger specimens chased around like mad, trying to snare the little ones. The spectacle reminded me of some underwater scenes in David Attenborough's first *Blue Planet* series.

That night we stopped at a rather uncomfortable anchorage, where *Louise* rolled like a pendulum from one side to another. Fortunately, we still managed to sleep well before sailing the next day to Musket Cove in the Mamanuca Islands. This destination is the most popular anchorage for visiting yachts in Fiji. Our arrival coincided with the farewell party for the World ARC Rally, some of whose participants we had seen earlier in Vanua Balavu. The yacht club was closed that evening as it was hosting the ARC event and, although tempted, we decided not to gatecrash it. Instead we found a restaurant where we ate an early dinner and Ivo tucked into a generous plate of scrambled eggs on toast.

On Friday 3rd July we motored to Denarau, a nearby resort with a marina on the western coast of Viti Levu. In the afternoon there was time for Ivo to take a dip in the resort's pool, where he played happily. On the last evening of our family cruise, we toasted the successful end of the trip, during which we had travelled 400 nautical miles while visiting ten beautiful islands. Sailing with our grandson on board had been a fantastic experience, especially for Brigitte and me, making these two weeks particularly memorable. We were awake fresh and early the following morning, ready to drop Luka, Valerie and Ivo at Nadi Airport to start their long trip home. It seemed very quiet aboard *Louise* when we returned.

Taking a short break from sailing, later on Saturday morning Brigitte and I set off to explore the north of Viti Levu by road. Our north-easterly drive took us past field after field of cane sugar, which had grown to full height and was beginning to be harvested. In colonial times, Fiji's economy was established on the cultivation and export of sugar cane. To man the plantations, British landowners established an indentured labour force brought by sea from India, most of whom would never return to their motherland. About 40 per cent of the modern Fijian population originated from the subcontinent. The country's ethnic division has led to political tensions in the past, but with a population of just under 900,000 people, Fiji now seems to be a peaceful nation.

On our drive we passed signs for the Fiji Water factory. This brand, which styles itself as 'Earth's Finest Water', has acquired a sizeable following among consumers, especially in the USA. Our attention was also caught by posters displaying options for a proposed new national flag to give Fijians their own distinctive identity. To date, the planned changed still hasn't happened, which shows how hard it is for nations to strike out on their own and discard the baggage of their colonial history. Close to our destination we drove past Ellington Wharf, and could see the remnants of the colonial-era pier that was used for importing labour and exporting sugar.

Late on Saturday we reached Wananavu Beach Resort at Rakiraki, facing Bligh Water. The small seaside location had a dive school where I signed on for a Sunday-morning scuba expedition. Heading out into Bligh Channel to the dive sites, I discovered some of the finest underwater coral and sea life that I had ever seen, and experienced some of the best diving in the Pacific. I also found out that my dive buddy, Chris Landry from Milwaukee, Wisconsin, was a most gifted underwater photographer as well as being great company. That evening we had a drink in the bar with Chris and relaxed in the calm setting of the resort.

Back in Denarau on Monday afternoon, we found that Cheryl and Morgan had stocked up the boat with fresh food in advance of our departure to Vanuatu. We didn't expect to be able to buy many comestibles before reaching French Caledonia, the place we were going after Vanuatu, which we aimed to reach in about a fortnight. With final preparations made on Tuesday 7th July, we motored to Vuda Marina on

Viti Levu to deal with the formalities involved in checking out of Fiji. The harbour was attractive, but very tight to enter and manoeuvre around with *Louise*. The local officials didn't seem too interested in dealing with clients, and kept us and other yacht crews waiting patiently, but eventually we received clearance to move on.

That afternoon we began our passage west, leaving behind a beautiful nation of islands. We had enjoyed our Fijian experience, finding the people friendly, the waters crystal clear and excellent opportunities for water sports, such as sailing and diving. Perhaps Fiji is a 'tropical paradise', if indeed there are places that can claim this accolade. We would miss hearing the greeting of 'bula vinaka', the Fijian expression commonly used when meeting people.

Motoring out of the reef at Wilkes Passage, we passed a few yachts moored at anchor in the clear water by the cut. Surf enthusiasts were taking advantage of the sunny afternoon and the well-formed waves thrown up by the ocean swell hitting the reef. The wind was unseasonably light, but before sunset the breeze filled in and we gratefully hoisted our sails. Light winds accompanied *Louise* for the next twenty-four hours until we encountered a minor weather front, which we got through before midnight on our second day at sea. The front was heralded by a torrential downpour of rain, which was followed by a huge shift in the wind direction. Turning 180 degrees without warning, it caused the boat to tack itself and immediately afterwards we were hit by a strong gust of wind. All this happened while it was pitch-black out on deck. Those off watch, who were resting in their cabins, suddenly had to move from one side of their bunk to the other. However, the silver lining was that the trade winds had returned and the boat set off like an express train straight for Aneityum, the most southerly island in Vanuatu.

The rest of the night was still bumpy, which made it a little harder to sleep, but that's one of the small prices that sailors have to pay during overnight passages. Indeed, such is the lot of the long-distance seafarer who logs mile after mile crossing open waters. While on watch, when you are not steering, trimming sheets or cooking, you can maybe snatch a moment to read, listen to music, fish or just contemplate the universe while being soothed by the waves. Far-from-land time is a luxury that is often in good supply for mariners who spend a while at sea.

Vanuatu is one of the least developed countries in the South Pacific and stretches over approximately 800 nautical miles from north to south, comprising around eighty-three islands. We had decided to focus on the most southerly islands in the chain, the area worst impacted by Tropical Cyclone Pam, which had struck with dreadful force just four months earlier. First stop for *Louise* in Vanuatu, on Thursday 9th July, was the anchorage at Aneghowhat Bay on the southern side of Aneityum Island. The bay is protected to the south by Mystery Island, whose unusual name came about following a visit made by Queen Elizabeth II in 1974. When reviewing pictures of the place, the Queen wasn't able to identify the location, so the photographer decided to call it Mystery Island.

Our hero Bougainville also passed through the archipelago in 1768, proving that the large island of Espiritu Santo wasn't the 'Terra Australis' that Portuguese explorer Fernandes de Queirós, who 'discovered' the islands in 1606, had thought. Captain Cook also came to these shores during his second Pacific voyage in 1774 and named them the 'New Hebrides'.

The first locals whom we met were more reserved than the Fijians, but no less welcoming. Apart from Bislama, the native language of Vanuatu, most people speak some English and

French, making communication relatively easy. For many years the country was a Franco-British condominium, making it a rare overseas collaboration between the UK and France. Once ashore, we were introduced to Wheena, a former teacher who was also a tour guide and musician. During a walk around the village of Aneghowhat, she explained how the lives of the locals were changing with the advent of visiting cruise ships, which helped them to earn a living but also put pressure on the natural environment and the traditional way of life.

After two nights in Aneityum, we departed on Saturday 11th July from the lovely anchorage under sail, setting a northerly course to Tanna, the next island up in the long chain. Arriving after 50 miles of good reaching, which lasted from breakfast through to lunch, we moored with a few other yachts in Resolution Bay, named after Captain Cook's ship. Congregating ashore in the afternoon, together with the other yachties we set off to climb the island's volcano, Mount Yasur.

Travelling in a four-wheel-drive vehicle, it took us an hour to reach the foot of the volcano. Most of the trails were very poor and we had yet to see a single road. Shattered tree trunks that had fallen during the tropical cyclone were strewn everywhere. But thankfully they had been cleared from the tracks, courtesy of the rapid intervention of the French military who had been sent over from New Caledonia after the cyclone had hit. Some members of the Ocean Cruising Club (OCC) who had sailed up from New Zealand also provided some much-needed assistance, albeit on a limited scale. Reaching the volcano just before sunset, we climbed up to the rim. Staring down into the crater, we watched it constantly erupting in small bursts accompanied by a boom, while molten lava lit up the sky.

Departing from Tanna on Sunday morning, we had an excellent sail to Dillon's Bay on the sparsely populated island of Erromango. Two other yachts followed our path, including Graham and Avril Johnson on board *Dream Away*, who are fellow OCC members and regular contributors to *Flying Fish*, the club magazine. A most friendly couple, they left the UK in 2002 and have been on the move on *Dream Away* ever since, including overwintering once in Ushuaia.

After dropping our anchor, we were greeted by one of the locals, David, the owner of an informal 'yacht club' whom every visiting sailor normally ends up meeting. He had rowed over to *Louise* in a dugout and extended an invitation for us to come to the island the next day. On Monday morning, we were welcomed ashore by Jacob, the village chief. We learnt that the village had fortunately managed to survive the cyclone without suffering casualties. Apart from ongoing repairs to damaged buildings, the main issue was the lack of root crops and fruit, as torrential rains and violent gusts of wind had destroyed a full year's supply of many essential foodstuffs. Although the villagers had already replanted their 'gardens', it was going to take at least another six months for the full variety of traditional crops to become plentiful once again. In the afternoon, David escorted us to Suvu beach, a short dinghy ride away, which was the burial site of his ancestors. Sitting in quiet contemplation in front of the skulls and bones, our thoughts were transported back to an era, not long past, where it was customary for locals to leave the bodies of their dead in caves.

That evening, along with the Johnsons, we had dinner at David's home where his family had prepared a wonderful spread. We sampled a great variety of delicious local foods including laplap, the national dish of Vanuatu, made from breadfruit, bananas and taro. David also played the guitar and, together with his wife and grandchildren, he sang some traditional songs for us. At the end of the meal we naturally offered some money as payment. Our donation was gladly accepted to help to fund the costs of finishing work on their home, which we discovered was affectionately known as Wowo Yacht Club.

On Tuesday 14th July we arrived in Port Vila, the capital of Vanuatu on the island of Efate, where we docked adjacent to the World ARC Rally fleet of yachts that were each neatly tied up next to one other with their sterns facing the quay. After mooring alongside the quay in the same way, we spoke to a number of the crews who comprised many nationalities. They were making final preparations to leave for Mackay in Queensland, Australia. From there the rally would continue into the Indian Ocean, heading almost directly to the Cape of Good Hope to enter the Atlantic and proceed towards the Caribbean. Our plan was to follow a similar route, except we aimed to cross the Indian Ocean close to the equator.

We also went to the national museum where we witnessed a demonstration of sand art, which forms part of the local culture, with the museum curator drawing a beautiful pattern in sand. The museum displayed Captain Cook's chart from when he surveyed the area in 1774. The document showed how his ship zigzagged up and down as he explored the archipelago from one end to the other. Another aspect of Vanuatu that the museum reminded visitors of was the role that the country played during the Second World War, providing a base camp for the Allied forces who were fighting to regain territory from the Japanese. Armed forces from Japan had pushed south of the equator to islands such as Guadalcanal in the Solomon Islands, which are north-west of Vanuatu.

With a bit of time on our hands we decided to continue heading north and were able to go to two more islands. Our first stop was at Nguna, where a local guide showed us around and talked about how his views regarding religion influenced his life and how small faith groups still have influence. We passed a lady who was preparing the family's evening meal, with food wrapped in coconut leaves ready to be put into a fire pit in the ground to cook. At our last stop, Epi, we hired a driver to take us on an island tour in a pick-up truck, in order to see some of the interior. We took the opportunity to visit a cocoa plantation that a young farmer had husbanded and was becoming successful. Women tended the cocoa plants, which the farmer said was good for productivity, as he had observed that local men were not so committed to working as hard.

During our stay in Port Vila, we had bought some locally made chocolate which tasted first class, but sadly we ate it all too quickly. Indeed, one of the on-board treats during the passages was savouring a piece of chocolate after dinner. It was a special time of the day when we sat chatting in the cockpit, often under the stars if the sky was clear. Having enjoyed our chocolate moment, those who were not on watch usually retreated to their cabins to get some rest, while the watch continued to keep an eye on the boat, monitoring wind changes and looking out for any obstacles that might need to be avoided.

As we picked up anchor before departing from Epi, a small taxi motorboat passed *Louise* and the passengers grinned with big smiles, waving at us, so we naturally waved back. On leaving Vanuatu on Sunday 19th July after our ten-day stay, we felt uplifted by the courage and character of the people we had met. Considering that Vanuatu was perhaps the least developed country that we had visited, its citizens seemed to be happy. Looking over our shoulders, the silhouettes of both Ambrym Island, with its volcanic peak, and Malekula Island to the north were magnificent in the morning light.

Now on our way to the Loyalty Islands, which are part

of the French territory of New Caledonia, our course was almost dead south. We were en route towards what remains one of the largest French outposts in the Pacific. During the journey of approximately 260 nautical miles, we encountered stiff south-easterly trades, which ensured a fast passage that lasted a little over a day. As we left Vanuatu, the weather had started to worsen and by evening the sky was overcast. But of course it was midwinter in the southern hemisphere, and in these subtropical latitudes the weather can be changeable.

During the night, the mainsail reefing line snapped, so we took in the third reef prior to repairing the broken line. At first light, sitting at the end of the boom and dangling his feet over the sea while the boat pounded into the waves, Morgan fixed the broken strop. Once the problem was sorted, more sail area could be raised by shaking out the third reef in the mainsail and we continued to make excellent progress.

Just after 1 p.m. on Monday afternoon, Cheryl sighted the low-lying island of Ouvéa. Our approach took us through the 'Passe du Taureau', entering into the northern side of the lagoon where a gap in the reef provided safe access. Once inside the reef, the sea became very smooth and we managed to sail across the flat water at a good speed. By teatime, we had anchored at Fayaoue off the long beach on the eastern side of the Ouvéa lagoon, which we discovered was vast and up to 25 nautical miles wide in places.

We had been expecting to rendezvous in the Loyalty Islands with our friends Sherry and William Spurgin, for their first cruise on board *Louise*, but after turning on my phone I read the unfortunate news that they would be delayed. However, we were still hopeful that they would be able to join us.

On arrival, there was the usual official business to deal with ashore, landing as we had in a French overseas territory which required clearing customs and immigration. Officially, boats are only permitted to enter and leave New Caledonia through its capital, Nouméa, located on the main island of Grande Terre. If we could get our papers to our agent on Grande Terre, she had offered to submit them to the authorities on our behalf and request the various clearances. The problem was how to get the documents there. As we hung around the little airport, it was clear that most people knew each other and could, we hoped, be trusted. Before long, we found a passenger who was happy to help us out and we entrusted the lady with an envelope. Later that evening, it was a relief to receive a message from our agent confirming that she had collected our passports safely from the passenger in Nouméa.

The following morning, Josué, a friendly taxi driver whom we had met the night before, picked us up at the beach and took us on a full tour of the island. We started with the copra factory, which relied on the sale of soap when it wasn't generating electricity. Copra is the dried coconut flesh from which oil is extracted, and historically has been an important cash crop for Pacific islanders. Its oil can be used as a source of power generation, alleviating the need to import other fuels to produce electricity.

After a snack lunch in a beachside cafe, we saw Ouvéa's impressive limestone cliffs that were showing signs of being eroded by the sea. We also stopped on a bridge to see turtles swimming in the fast-moving current. Before ending our tour, Josué insisted that we came to his house to meet his family. Around their small homestead they reared a variety of animals, including cows, goats, chickens and pigs, as well as growing a few crops. He proudly showed us the hut where the family all slept under a roof covered in coconut-leaf matting. Hanging on a wall in his barn was a flag representing the freedom movement of the indigenous Kanak people, but Josué didn't want to talk with us about politics.

The destination for the next stage of our journey was Lifou, located south-east of Ouvéa and also part of the Loyalty Islands. Moving our anchorage the night before near to Mouli Island at the southern cut, we left at first light on Wednesday 22nd July. With a robust south-easterly trade wind blowing, it was going to take almost ten hours to reach Lifou, even though it was only 45 nautical miles away. During the day we tacked eight times, the most we had ever done over such a short period. But we made good progress and by early afternoon we had reached the lee of the island at Santal Bay.

As we entered the bay we spotted a humpback whale, which was in its winter breeding ground. We went on to find a suitable spot to anchor at Drueulu, where later that afternoon we picked up the Spurgins who had just arrived from London. Before flying to Lifou, they had landed in Nouméa, where they liaised with the agent who had organised for our passports to be stamped by the authorities. That evening, when our friends settled down to their first night on board, I was most relieved and grateful when they handed over an envelope containing all our precious documents.

On Thursday we set off to explore and swim in the underground caves at Luengoni, which featured impressive underwater stalagmites. We were accompanied by our friendly guide Louise, who crawled down into the caves to show us the way.

In the afternoon, we drove to the north of Lifou where we met another charming lady named Janine Bole. Together with her husband, she owned a botanic garden and she shared with us some fascinating facts about the tropical flowers and plants that grew there. Most notable was the vanilla plant, an orchid that is the mother of the vanilla pod, one of the main cash crops on Lifou. We learnt how local customs and life on the island had profoundly changed in the nineteenth century with the arrival of Scottish Presbyterian missionaries.

The following day, William, Morgan and I set off in a rib with the local diving school to explore the reef on the northwest of the island. The two dives went well but didn't reveal anything of particular interest. In the evening, to celebrate our short visit to the Loyalty Islands we went to a restaurant in the north of Lifou called Fenepaza, where we savoured a delicious meal of local leaf salad and grilled lobster.

Next stop on the Adventure was Grande Terre, New Caledonia's principal island, located about 100 nautical miles to the south of the Loyalty Islands, and a UNESCO World Heritage Site that is surrounded by the world's longest continuous island barrier reef. With the trade winds still well established, the brief crossing promised to be fast, but a little bumpy.

Making an early start on Saturday 25th July, we raised the anchor at 5 a.m. and motored around the western side of Lifou. We hugged the shore as close as possible to keep in sheltered water, before setting our sails after breakfast and heading south. Before too long we had caught a mahi-mahi, which William landed safely onto the boat. Sherry and Brigitte sat out on deck for most of the day, enjoying the sunshine and fresh air, while *Louise* made good progress. We found ourselves all alone at sea with not a single other boat in sight. Late in the afternoon, we sailed through a gap in the New Caledonia reef to enter the lagoon and then anchored at Port-Boisé, tucked in at the south-easterly point of Grande Terre Island.

On Sunday morning, we awoke to flat, calm conditions, with the weather set to stay that way for a few days. We motored further east towards the Isle of Pines, so named by Captain Cook after the tall and slim native pine trees that he saw as he sailed past in 1774. New Caledonia was originally established as a French penal colony in the mid-nineteenth century, and the Isle of Pines Penitentiary was built to accommodate the inmates who had been transported from France to the far side of the world. Life for the long-suffering prisoners was tough and tropical diseases took their toll. On our way there, a pair of adult humpbacks swam close by the boat, our visit coinciding with the whales' winter mating season in these subtropical waters.

Kuto Bay on the Isle of Pines offered one of the finest anchorages in the area, as well as providing good shelter. We settled down there for three days to allow us time to explore the island. Other boats were also moored there and we managed to chat with some of the crews, including Eric and Dee Govan on *Sirena of Oare*, an English couple and OCC members who had been cruising the Pacific for a few years.

During our stay, we discovered the natural pool at Oro Bay with its clear, turquoise water. After seeing one of the island's prettiest sights, we walked along the bed of an old river that was now above sea level, which was covered in soft, white sand and lined with tall pines on each side. Later on, William, Brigitte and I set off to climb to the top of the Isle of Pines' highest hill. Brigitte accompanied us to the halfway point, leaving William and me to scramble up the last bit to the top where we experienced a beautiful 360-degree panoramic view of the island's shoreline and the sea beyond.

On another occasion, which I unfortunately missed, William went for an early-morning swim near the boat and spotted a dugong, more commonly called a 'sea cow', a shy marine mammal that was feeding off the grass at the bottom of the shallow bay.

The final stage of the New Caledonia trip would take us to the territory's capital, Nouméa. After three nights anchored at

Kuto Bay, on Wednesday 29th July we moved on and headed in a north-westerly direction, bound for Prony Bay at the southern tip of New Caledonia, where we were due to pick up Morgan's parents. We stopped overnight in the bay and at breakfast time the next morning, Morgan's brother Jonathan dropped off Roger and Jacqueline Morice at the small quay near our mooring, and we welcomed them on board. Our visitors had kindly brought some fresh croissants, which we savoured with our morning coffee. Roger was retired and living on his boat in Nouméa, and his wife Jacqueline, who had moved back to France, had come to pay him a visit.

Getting underway, we had a pleasant sail to Nouméa which lasted the whole morning. By early Thursday afternoon, we were tied up in the Port Du Sud Marina in time for a late on-board lunch. Jonathan, who had driven to Nouméa from Prony Bay, joined us together with their family friend Hugues, a local doctor and keen sailor. After lunch, while the Morice family continued with their reunion, Brigitte and I set off in a hire car with Sherry and William to explore the interior of New Caledonia.

Chloé, our friendly port agent who was originally from Espiritu Santo in Vanuatu, had recommended an itinerary for our two-day excursion and made a couple of hotel reservations along the route. Our first overnight stop was inland, close to the Parc des Grandes Fougères, where we took a walk after breakfast on Friday. Reaching a high point, we were rewarded with panoramic views of the island's interior, which revealed that much of the surrounding landscape was covered in thick vegetation. We had lunch in a little restaurant where we were served venison stew, a popular local dish that was really tasty. Deer were introduced to the island by colonial settlers, whose ancestors are known as the Caldoche. We passed through Borail, an area where many French prisoners had been given land at the end of their detention. However, the land in question had been seized from the indigenous Kanak population, so not surprisingly these measures resulted in tensions between the two groups.

By the evening, we were back on the shore and spent our final night in a modern resort near central New Caledonia on its southern coastline. On Saturday, William and I made an excursion around the lagoon on a glass-bottomed boat. Our guide explained the ecosystem of the reef that stretches over 900 miles around the whole of the island. We lazed by the pool for the rest of the morning, before saying cheerio to Sherry and William after lunch. The Spurgins' holiday was sadly drawing to a close and they would be starting their journey home, which included a stopover in Sydney, that evening.

Brigitte and I drove our rental car back to Nouméa, where later in the afternoon we visited the Jean-Marie Tjibaou Cultural Centre, built in honour of the assassinated leader of the Kanak independence movement. Designed by Renzo Piano, it opened in 1998, nine years after Tjibaou's murder. The centre was proposed by the then French President François Mitterand as a symbol of reconciliation with the Kanak people to celebrate their culture and traditions. The building, a modern architectural masterpiece, echoes the Kanak Grand Hut design, as well as the native pine trees of New Caledonia.

On our final evening in Nouméa, we were reunited with the talented Canadian-born sculptor Doug Hazelton, whom we had previously met a year ago while visiting Moorea in French Polynesia. During the last few months, Doug had sailed his boat westwards to Nouméa. Brigitte and I were invited for drinks on board MV *Sindbad*, which featured a built-in studio, where we also met Doug's wife Bethanne. Doug creates his sculptures using metal, and while looking round the studio, we discovered a magnificent metallic fish shoal artwork that we bought as a belated wedding gift for our friends Klaus and Alice Diederichs.

Aside from his creative endeavours, Doug is a passionate sailor and he regaled us with stories of his adventures at sea, many of which involved deep-sea diving in places such as the uninhabited Chesterfield Islands west of New Caledonia, and alongside Comte de La Pérouse enthusiasts on Vanikoro in the Solomon Islands. In 1788, the count and French explorer Jean-François de Galaup (known as La Pérouse) was on an exploratory mission in the Pacific with his two vessels *Boussole* and *Astrolabe*, and had just left Australia where he had encountered a British naval convoy known later as the 'First Fleet', which had arrived to establish the penal colony of New South Wales. Back in the tropics, he was caught in a cyclone and both his ships foundered on the reef at Vanikoro, drowning most of the crew. It was only after half a century had passed that a search party discovered telltale signs of the French fleet's demise, but not until 1964 that hard evidence was gathered which finally showed how the fate of the expedition had been sealed.

On Sunday 2nd August, we were ready to set sail for Australia and complete the final leg of our Pacific crossing. We made a brief stop at the fuel dock in Nouméa, where a modern-looking frigate from the French Navy was anchored nearby. Morgan said farewell to his family and we cast off the mooring lines, heading out of the harbour as we waved goodbye.

The 1,250-mile passage from Grande Terre, New Caledonia to Cairns, Queensland is generally pleasant in the winter months, with easterly trade winds to carry yachts travelling west. We were fortunate that, apart from a short interlude during the middle of the passage when we had to motor, we managed to sail all the way to Australia. Our progress was boosted by a westerly ocean current, caused by the persistent trade winds.

Throughout the journey, the presence of seabirds was almost constant. We often had visitations from boobies, who found their way to landing on the mast's spreaders, oblivious to the mess they were dropping onto the deck below. We also frequently saw frigate birds that would fly in circles around the boat. At one point a small tern joined us, perching on *Louise*'s dinghy davits at the stern, and accompanied us for a considerable period of time.

Two days of sailing out of Nouméa in the Coral Sea, we passed a few miles north of the Chesterfield Islands. The low-lying archipelago is around 75 miles long and 43.5 miles broad, made up of eleven uninhabited islets and many reefs, but none were visible from the boat. At this point we were now clear to steer a direct course for the Great Barrier Reef and our destination at Cairns.

Gradually, we noticed an increased presence of other vessels, a sign that we were getting closer to Australia. The Australian continental land mass is rich in minerals for which there is a great demand from China and other nations. The abundance of these mineral resources and their mining has led to a significant level of shipping in these waters as the bulk cargo is carried towards Asia.

On our fifth day at sea, we had a fly-by from an aircraft of the Australian Maritime Border Command, which went past the boat at low altitude. Over the radio, we were asked to report our crew roster. A little later, the aircrew radioed back to inform us that Brigitte didn't have a visa for Australia and legally could not enter the country without one. We had overlooked the fact that a visa was a mandatory requirement for Australia when arriving by sea. Fortunately, we were able to make the application online directly from the boat using our satellite connection. Relieved that our paperwork was all in order, we settled down to enjoy our last night at sea.

Approaching Queensland's vast Barrier Reef on Saturday 8th August, we sailed through Grafton Passage into the sheltered waters that lie between the reef and the mainland. We docked before breakfast in the well-appointed Cairns Marina, which became the boat's temporary home for a couple of months, and remained on board until the governmental authorities had checked the boat thoroughly. This included three separate visits from handlers and their dogs, each of which had been trained to detect a different illegal cargo. After the inspections, we received clearance to enter the country and soon after we went ashore. That evening we met my Harvard friend Ken Chapman and his wife Karen, who live in Cairns, and had dinner together.

The following day, we left *Louise* after seven weeks on board, full of fond memories of our recent leg sailing in the South Pacific. During the last fifteen months, we had zigzagged across the Pacific as part of the *Louise* Adventure and covered 12,500 nautical miles. Since departing Puerto Montt in Chile in May 2014, we had had the privilege of visiting seven Pacific nations. Dotted with beautiful tropical islands and blessed with trade winds that enable yachts to sail with ease from one stopover to another, these waters are arguably the ultimate destination for cruisers. Our experience on *Louise* had certainly lived up to expectations. With still so much out there that we had yet to see or discover, we would be sorely tempted to come back and explore these waters again.

Chapter 9 – The Spice Islands
Cairns, Australia to Indonesia and Phuket, Thailand

Wayag Island, Raja Ampat, Indonesia

In early October 2015, we rejoined the boat in Australia after a two-month break. We flew back to Cairns in Northern Queensland, where we met up with Scottish friends Gordon and Helen MacKenzie, who had emigrated to Australia and who would be accompanying us for the first week of the new leg. In fact, they had recently successfully completed their own world circumnavigation aboard their 57-foot yacht *Mantra*, sailing the entire distance as a couple without assistance. We were excited about the prospect of navigating through the Torres Strait and discovering parts of the Indonesian Archipelago that lay beyond.

On our return to *Louise*, we were delighted to learn that our captain Morgan had proposed marriage to Cheryl during the stopover. They had already decided that their wedding would take place in 2016 in the Seychelles, which we were planning to travel to along our path westwards. After leaving Australia, *Louise* was bound for South East Asia by way of the Indonesian Archipelago. Eventually, this itinerary would lead us through to the Indian Ocean beyond.

The following morning, on Friday 9th October 2015, the next stage of the Adventure got underway in the early hours when we slipped out of Cairns Marina, heading north to Lizard Island within the Great Barrier Reef. Our friend Ken Chapman had also joined us on board for the 140-mile sail. Named by Captain Cook when he discovered the presence of this species of reptile in 1770, today Lizard Island is home to a luxury resort and a centre for water sports, including diving. After about eighteen hours at sea, we reached the island and anchored at Mrs Watson's Bay.

On Saturday morning, Ken took Gordon and me on a snorkelling expedition with the dinghy. He pointed out sea cucumbers to us, which grow on the bottom of the seabed and are a popular delicacy in China. Gordon opted to stay on the dinghy and keep a watch from the surface, which may have been wise as we later learnt that two weeks after our visit to Lizard Island, a tourist was attacked by a crocodile and had to be flown to the mainland for surgery.

In the afternoon, we walked to Cook's Look at the summit of the island, the very spot from where the famous British captain sighted the Great Barrier Reef during his first circumnavigation. The explorer spotted an opening in the reef, later named Cook's Passage, which led out to open water and through which he was able to escape into the Coral Sea. Earlier in the expedition, his crew had been forced to conduct serious repairs to HMS *Endeavour*'s hull, as it had struck a coral reef a little south.

After our second night at anchor, on Sunday 11th October we said farewell to Ken, who left us to fly back home to Cairns, while we continued to voyage north on *Louise* with 330 miles to go to reach Thursday Island at the very north of Australia. With a following wind and good sea conditions, we spent much of Sunday under spinnaker, sailing close to the Queensland shore. In the middle of the day we gybed at Cape Melville, where we altered course to the west and then passed by some imposing sand dunes as we navigated the enclosed waters that lie between the Great Barrier Reef and the Australian coastline. A few of the yachts that sailed past us on the way were heading south, which was no mean feat in the face of the brisk prevailing south-east trade wind. Before sunset, we stopped to moor in Owen Channel, which is sheltered between the islands of Flinders and Stanley to the east of Princess Charlotte Bay.

After breakfast on Monday, we carried on northwards, aiming to reach Cape York, the most northerly point in Australia, by Tuesday afternoon. During the morning, staying close to the Outer Barrier Reef, we followed Lads Passage but were lacking wind, so we motored initially. By midday, the trade winds had picked up and we sailed the rest of the passage with the wind behind our beam. Cape York Peninsula, which faces the island of New Guinea, forms the north-easterly tip of Australia and is bordered by the Coral Sea to the east and the Gulf of Carpentaria to the west. The land, which was visible from the boat all the way from Cairns to the Torres Strait, is a low-lying wilderness full of eucalyptus, a large part of which is grazed with cattle. Cape York itself marks the entrance to the Torres Strait, which is approximately 80 nautical miles wide and separates the island of New Guinea and the southerly continent that we would soon be leaving behind.

The first recorded navigation of the strait by a European was by Luís Vaz de Torres, during a Spanish expedition from Peru travelling westwards in 1606. Realising the strategic importance of the discovery of a new route exiting the Pacific, the Spanish kept this knowledge a secret for many years. Over 150 years later, the Scottish geographer and the first Hydrographer of the British Admiralty Alexander Dalrymple found a record of Torres' passage in some Spanish documents that had been captured in Manila. Dalrymple subsequently published a book entitled *An Historical Collection of the Several Voyages and Discoveries in the South Pacific Ocean (1770–71)*, which at the time aroused interest in his claim of the existence of an unknown continent to the south.

The Torres Strait, which is shallow with multiple reefs and little islands scattered around, is now a busy thoroughfare for shipping. Our journey ended at Horn Island, when we anchored in the narrow stretch of water opposite Thursday Island, the principal settlement in the strait. Soon after, Morgan set about liaising with the Australian authorities to deal with the formalities involved in departing from Australia.

Stepping ashore, we found that the streets on Horn Island were empty and during the evening we were the only diners in the local Chinese restaurant where Gordon and Helen had invited us all to a farewell meal. On Wednesday morning, we rode on the dinghy to Thursday Island to explore the small township. After lunch onshore, we said cheerio to our friends, thanking them for their company before they left to catch a plane to Brisbane from Horn Island Airport.

With just Brigitte, Morgan, Cheryl and me now on board

Louise, after lunch on Thursday 15th October we were ready to leave Australia and set off for Indonesia. Pulling up the anchor, we headed out past Thursday Island exiting the Torres Strait, with the much bigger Prince of Wales Island to our south as we entered the area of water north of Australia known as the Arafura Sea. The last Australian territory we saw was Booby Island, so named by Captain Cook, which we left to our starboard.

Stretching far away to the south, off our port side, was the Gulf of Carpentaria, which makes a sizeable indent into northern Australia. This extensive shallow sea tends to be overlooked by passing sailors. Indeed, many who are making passage west will sail straight to Darwin, capital city of the Northern Territory, which is a convenient last staging post in Australia for yachts proceeding directly to the Indian Ocean. However, we had chosen to follow a more northerly route towards the eastern provinces of Indonesia in West Papua. Expecting that there would not be so much wind in Indonesia at this time of the year, we planned to head towards the equator, taking advantage of the season to do some scuba diving and visit some of the country's more remote areas.

Our sail across the Arafura Sea was assisted by the southeast trade winds, which continued to blow nicely for the first four days of our 1,000-mile passage to West Papua. A steady wind-driven current pushing us west helped to give our speed a welcome boost. Although shallow, the sea was initially a beautiful shade of light blue, but as we progressed further the sky became a little hazy during the day and the sea's colour changed to dark green. We passed the occasional cargo ship, as well as a few fishing boats, but generally there was nothing to disturb our view of the horizon.

Gradually, we began to detect the first signs that we were approaching the populated realms of South East Asia; during our night watches, the horizon was increasingly lit up by the lights of fishing boats. With over 250 million mouths to feed in Indonesia, the local fishermen were indeed kept very busy. This vast country, which lies at the intersection of the Pacific and Indian Oceans, is formed by just over 17,500 islands, making it the world's largest archipelago.

After three days' sailing, we had entered the Banda Sea and were now truly in Indonesian waters. There was a noticeable reduction in the strength of the wind from that point onwards and all of the last part of the passage was under engine. For the last few miles we navigated through the Sele Strait, which separates the island of Salawati from West Papua. Our destination was Sorong, a city in West Papua on the tip of the Bird's Head Peninsula, gateway to the Raja Ampat Islands. Anchoring *Louise* adjacent to Sorong's small harbour and town quay on Tuesday 20th October, this was the first time she had been moored in Asian waters.

Fortunately, Brigitte and I managed to find an excellent guide to facilitate our trip to Sorong. Named Alex, he drove us around the city, pointing out the main sights and recounting the history of West Papua, explaining how this region of New Guinea had become part of Indonesia. Following the retreat of the Dutch from Indonesia, Western New Guinea was taken over by Indonesia, but a promise to the local Papuan people to determine their future was never honoured. After showing us some of the significant places of interest, Alex took us to his home, where we met his wife and children, and then we had lunch in the restaurant within the local Catholic Diocese complex which looks out over the shorefront.

The next weekend, we were due to rendezvous in Sorong with my sister-in-law and her partner, which gave us some free days to explore the surroundings. So Brigitte and I decided to make a short plane trip east to Manokwari, the capital of the Indonesian province of West Papua, which lies on the Pacific Coast. Our flight was delayed due to bush fires in the provinces of Sumatra and Kalimantan, which were severely disturbing air traffic movement. On arrival, we checked into a well-appointed hotel just out of town and found that there were barely any other tourists about.

During our brief stay in Manokwari, one of the highlights was going for a walk in the rainforest above the town, where we admired the impressive canopy of trees high above as well as the dense and luscious foliage lower down, freshly watered by the torrential rain that had fallen overnight. Afterwards we had lunch in a restaurant close to the harbour and ate a simple meal of spicy local foods. We also took the opportunity to visit Mansinam Island in Manokwari Bay, which we reached by foot ferry. This was the original landing place for the first Christian missionaries who arrived in West Papua in the mid-nineteenth century.

On our return to *Louise* on Saturday 24th October, we welcomed Paul Brunskill (who preferred to be called Bob), who had joined us as dive master for our Indonesian cruise. Of English origin, he had worked for many years guiding and instructing people on diving in the rich waters of Indonesia.

The next day, we had been due to meet Brigitte's sister Isabelle and her partner Christoph, who were flying into Sorong from Switzerland via Singapore. Unfortunately, they were also held up by massive smoke clouds in the sky caused by the forest fires that had been burning for weeks in Borneo and Sulawesi, creating major flight disruption. The finger was pointed at unscrupulous business owners who, wanting to clear land to make way for oil palm plantations, were believed to have started the fires.

We were beginning to sense that environmental sustainability was an issue not yet regarded with great importance in Indonesia, and noticed different forms of damage that the local environment had suffered, which had been caused by society's voracious demand for consumer goods. For example, while motoring into Sorong Harbour on the dinghy, we saw huge amounts of plastic rubbish sloshing around the quayside. As we discovered during our cruise all around Indonesia and through the South China Sea, pollution from plastic was ever present and highly visible.

On Sunday morning, we enjoyed a short visit on the dinghy to Doom Island, which lies opposite Sorong's waterfront. In colonial times, the island was commandeered by the Dutch and built up as a settlement, as it offered a well-aired environment where the colonial masters were partially sheltered from any diseases that were present on the mainland. The Sunday service at the island's local church had just finished and in the grounds outside we had a friendly chat with the priest and some parishioners.

Early in the afternoon, our guide Alex collected Isabelle and Christoph, who had finally landed at the airport, and brought them down to the boat. We thanked him and bid him well, before lifting anchor and setting off for an overnight motoring passage to Wayag Island, where our exploration of the archipelago and its underwater wonders would soon begin.

The following morning, on Monday 26th October, we arrived at Wayag in the Raja Ampat Archipelago. The mooring ball at the principal anchorage in the middle of this extraordinary bay, which is surrounded by rocky limestone outcrops covered with vegetation, was free. So we tied *Louise* up to the buoy, thereby avoiding the need to drop our anchor in the deep water. After settling down, we made our first dive to check out the scuba equipment and conduct a safety drill. In the early evening, we climbed to the peak of one of the hills to survey the curved island. From the summit, we were treated to views overlooking the anchorage, where *Louise* was floating in the flat calm, and across the rest of the island. Below us the water was clear in the shallows, turning to dark green where the depth increased. We took photos of this picturesque scene in one of the most iconic anchorages in Asia.

On Tuesday morning we made a dinghy excursion, zigzagging between the maze of limestone outcrops. The sea had eroded the limestone over time and left the impression that many of the rocks were upside down. Later, *Louise* was visited by some local park rangers, who came over on a little boat to check our cruising permit.

Leaving Wayag behind before lunchtime on Tuesday, we headed out on a south-easterly course and soon arrived at a well-secluded anchorage on Uranie Island, which was hidden from any other boats. After successfully tying *Louise*'s stern to an overhanging rock hidden out of sight of any passing boats, we settled in and watched small kingfisher birds skitting about the place. During the afternoon, after a fifteen-minute dinghy ride, we experienced our second Indonesian dive on Magic Rock. Under the water we discovered an aquarium teeming with fish and coral. Our cameras clicked non-stop as we tried to capture as much of the sub-aqua scenery as possible.

The next day, we moved further south to Equator Island, where we snorkelled and then went ashore on the beach. An ugly looking monument had been erected to mark the point where the north and south hemispheres met.

As we motored around the islands of Raja Ampat, which translates as 'Four Kings', we made regular morning and afternoon dives in the warm sea. Raja Ampat forms part of the Coral Triangle, an area that includes the waters of Indonesia, Malaysia, the Philippines, Papua New Guinea, Timor-Leste and the Solomon Islands. Officially known to have the most biodiverse marine habitat on Earth, Raja Ampat itself covers approximately 15,500 square miles (40,000 square kilometres). Experts have counted well over 1,000 species of fish living among hundreds of types of hard coral. The waters provide the perfect breeding ground for coral larvae that feed the growth of coral reefs far afield. Around the islands in the north of Indonesia, the Pacific Ocean is home to reefs which teem with sea life. For the scuba diver venturing below the surface, each time the eyes are treated to a kaleidoscope of colours.

Our brief stay in the northern area of Raja Ampat was coming to a close and we headed south overnight, motoring all the way towards Misool Island, where we arrived on Thursday 29th October. To ensure we would have a variety of dives, over the following week we would move *Louise* to a different anchorage each day. With other boats around, finding mooring buoys was sometimes challenging, and when they weren't available we had to get the anchor to hold in the deep waters. After seven days spent in the Raja Ampat Archipelago, we had been on a dozen dives. Soft and hard corals lined the underwater reefs that burst with life and colour. Swarms of fish of all sizes milled about on the reefs close to the surface and in the surrounding waters. For Christoph and me, this was undoubtedly the most extraordinary scuba diving that we had ever experienced. To add to the fun, we all took underwater photographs, which we were able to share on board at the end of each day.

After spending our last night in Raja Ampat moored near Misool on Kalig Island, it was time to move on. Our next stop was on the historically famed Banda Islands within the Maluku province of Indonesia known as the Moluccas, south of the island of Seram in the Banda Sea. We were heading for

Banda Neira, the only settlement of significant size on any of the Banda Islands, which was the focus of attention in early colonial times as a prime source of valuable spices. In the Banda Massacre of 1621, the Dutch military conquest led to the local population being brutally overthrown, which resulted in a monopoly over the nutmeg trade for the invaders. The Dutch East India Company (VOC) pursued its commercial aims ruthlessly and secured access to lucrative spices, but at the cost of thousands of lives, approximating 90 per cent of the total population. Indeed, it was the VOC's Governor-General, Jan Pieterszoon Coen, who ordered the massacre and who conscripted Japanese Samurai to be brought to Indonesia for the purpose of assassinating the local leaders.

The short overnight passage took us close by the eastern tip of Seram, and after daylight, when the wind dropped, we sighted a couple of whales. On the morning of Monday 2nd November, we anchored near to the small town at Banda Neira. Later that day we visited Fort Nassau, a stronghold built by the Dutch in 1609, where we climbed on the ramparts. The area was quiet, although when the ferry from Ambon Island arrived, the streets came to life. In the evening we made our first night dive and observed a little colony of mandarin fish, which only come out of hiding at dusk. Moored nearby was another boat by the name of *Amandira*, a traditional Indonesian phinisi wooden sailing vessel. Taking the dinghy, we went over to introduce ourselves and met a group of Swiss doctors whom we invited for drinks on board *Louise*. The owner, a doctor from Geneva, was proud of his new acquisition that had only recently been launched. After dinner, we were asked aboard *Amandira* for a nightcap and found her to be very well appointed.

After all the motoring we had recently done our fuel reserves were now dwindling, so before leaving we took advantage of our time in Banda Neira to top *Louise* up with some diesel. The refuelling operation involved using a dinghy to ferry plastic diesel drums from the shore to the boat, which Morgan emptied one by one into the tanks. The procedure required a fair amount of toing and froing, but was successfully accomplished.

An unexpected surprise on leaving Banda Neira Harbour after our two-night stay was seeing traditional Moluccan kora-kora canoes as they passed close by. The rowers, who numbered about forty per vessel, were practising for an event, sitting one behind the other on opposite sides of the boat, each pulling a single oar.

Motoring the short distance to Banda Besar Island, we anchored in the bay at Lonthoir. In the afternoon, we went for a walk ashore and a local farmer, whom we had met at the main village, offered to escort us on a brief tour. We accompanied him up the hillside to his orchard, while he carried jerry cans of water for irrigation. On arrival, he gave us a passionate explanation about how his nutmeg and almond trees were husbanded, and we learnt how bats shook off the ripened almonds from the higher trees that provided canopy shelter to the smaller nutmeg trees below.

Drawing our Banda experience to a close, there were still another 1,000 nautical miles to cover in the fortnight ahead before we would reach our final destination of Bali. Our itinerary involved island-hopping in a south-westerly direction across the Banda Sea in the direction of the Flores Sea and then onwards west to Bali. By this point in the passage we had certainly begun to appreciate the sheer size and expanse of the Indonesian Archipelago.

Since our arrival in the Banda Sea, the weather had been really settled. The wind had dropped to virtually flat calm and the sea glimmered in the sunlight. The downside was the rising temperature, which ensured our cabins were hard to cool down and made it more difficult to get a good night's sleep. These conditions continued throughout the coming weeks. Moving from island to island now required us to motor and generally the sails were never raised.

After motoring overnight, our next stop on the morning of Thursday 5th November was Nila Island at Dusborgh Reef, 130 miles south of Banda Neira. Not long after our arrival, a local fisherman and his son came close to the boat and showed us their catch of moray eels and groupers. During our brief stay we managed to enjoy two dives, and in the afternoon I went beachcombing with Brigitte and Isabelle, where we found some beautiful shells. We moored there for just one night and that evening were unexpectedly entertained with a fireworks display ashore, which we watched from *Louise*'s cockpit.

Continuing west on Friday, following the chain of volcanic islands in the Banda Sea, we headed across glassy waters towards Gunung Api, or Snake Island. During daylight hours, in very calm conditions we were fortunate to encounter two blue whales, one of which was easily the size of *Louise*. Using our drone, Morgan filmed the whales gently swimming along the surface of the sea, seemingly oblivious to the presence of the boat. Unfortunately, Christoph began to show signs of fever, a result of an infection in one of his legs which had started to swell up. We spoke by satellite phone to Medaire, a medical support service to which we subscribe, whose adviser prescribed a course of antibiotics that we carry on board. Thankfully, the medication was effective and Christoph soon recovered, though he would miss out on a memorable dive at Snake Island.

Arriving at sunrise on Saturday morning, we anchored *Louise* off Gunung Api. After breakfast, we set off to dive with the sea snakes that breed on the island. They hunt ashore for birds' eggs but live in the water. While the snakes were curious and approached us during our dive, they were not threatening. Swimming in crystal-clear water, the bright colours of the corals showed vividly and Morgan captured the beautiful scene on video.

Moving on in the middle of the day, we motored all afternoon and into the night, taking advantage of the cooler hours after sunset. We marvelled that evening at the clear skies overhead, observing the stunning views of the stars and planets. Later that day, we received the happy news that we were going to be grandparents for the second time, as our daughter Valerie was expecting another child. Naturally, we celebrated that evening with a bottle of sparkling wine.

As we motored further west, the Banda Sea remained flat calm and we passed more whales and dolphins along the way. Making the most of the smooth conditions, we stopped the boat to snorkel with a pod of pygmy killer whales that were lazily enjoying themselves. Taking the dinghy when the whales were nearby, we got into the water and started swimming close to them, listening to their squeaking sounds. Meanwhile, the mammals didn't seem to notice our presence.

By now we were in close reach of Alor, about one day's passage to the south-west, and the first place that we would visit in East Nusa Tenggara province. This large island forms the eastern end of the long chain of Lesser Sunda Islands, which stretch towards Bali about 600 nautical miles further west. Alor lies north of Timor-Leste, where yachts arriving from Australia often make their first landfall. Sadly, on this occasion we wouldn't have time to go to Timor.

We arrived on Alor on the afternoon of Sunday 8th November, and had enough time for a dive in 'Clownfish Alley' on Pura Island. A highly colourful underwater experience, we clicked our cameras at the little clownfish that kept flitting around the coral, not staying still for a second. Late in the afternoon, we moved *Louise* into a well-protected bay close by the local community of Alu Kai, about 10 miles west of Alor's main township. On the shore, some boys were having a game of football. Many of the young men were playing barefoot on the gravel-surfaced pitch. They asked us which teams we supported and reeled off the names of famous soccer players who were their heroes. A van with ladies wearing headscarves stopped and they greeted us, wanting to know where we were from and curious to hear if we liked their country.

Walking back to the boat, we passed some houses where traditional wooden fishing boats were under construction. After dusk that evening, we attempted our first muck dive in the bay where *Louise* was anchored. We discovered a variety of creatures, such as cuttlefish, decorator crabs and nudibranchs, all of which take advantage of the cover of darkness to move around the sea floor.

On Monday morning, we went ashore and were met by a tour guide before setting off for Kalabahi, the main town and capital of Alor located at the head of the bay. After stopping briefly in Kalabahi to look for some fresh food, we continued to Takpala Village, about forty-five minutes from the town. While there we were entertained by Alorese villagers dressed in traditional costume, who marched down into the centre of their settlement carrying the head chieftain. There followed a performance of traditional 'lego-lego' dancing to the sound and rhythm of drums, while the chieftains also demonstrated their battle ceremonies. We were not allowed to leave the village until each of us had joined in with the dancing. All this offered a fascinating glimpse into the culture of the indigenous Alorese people.

On our way back to the boat, we visited the Panti Asuhan

Damian orphanage run by a German nun named Sister Gisela Borowka. Sister Borowka has dedicated her working life towards supporting children whose parents are either no longer alive or who have placed their offspring into foster care. We spoke to some of the children, who were all smiling and seemed happy.

We left Alor on Monday afternoon to begin the next leg to Komodo. All evening we motored towards Komba Island, about 60 nautical miles north-west of Alor, to observe the island's volcano. Stopping the boat on the flat, calm sea at two o'clock in the morning, we drifted and waited patiently for an eruption. Eventually, the volcano spat out three blows that lit up the night sky. This was evidence indeed that Indonesia, with all its volcanic activity, very much remains part of the 'Ring of Fire'.

With 240 more miles to cover, we continued our way west, motoring all of Tuesday in calm waters and warm temperatures. Shade on board was at a premium in our efforts to stay cool.

By mid-morning on Wednesday 11th November, we dropped anchor for the day at Sebayur Island, which is off the western tip of Flores Island, one of the largest of the Lesser Sunda Islands. Stopping here for the day, we took advantage of the clear waters to make a couple of dives and then relaxed in the afternoon. Before darkness fell, we moved the boat to Rinca Island. As we motored into the small anchorage, we accidentally came into contact with the sandy sea floor, which brought *Louise* to a standstill. However, as the bottom was soft and we were travelling at such low speed, no harm was done and we managed to extricate *Louise* from the situation. Soon after, we had settled down for the night in Crocodile Bay, next to the park rangers' jetty, in order to be ready to visit Komodo National Park early the following morning. Thankfully, there were no visible signs of crocodiles in the anchorage.

Before exploring the park we met our guide, whose main role would be to check on our safety. During our time there, we were fortunate to see nearly all of the animals on which the local dragons prey, including deer, wild pig, bush turkeys, monkeys and lizards. The highlight, however, was glimpsing the Komodo dragons themselves. For most of the time they are docile, but we did observe a younger dragon quickly climb up a tree to take shelter. The juveniles learn to avoid their elders, who sometimes cannibalise their offspring.

Later on Thursday morning, after moving *Louise* back out into the straits between the islands of Rinca and Komodo, we snorkelled with mantas. The rays glided underwater with seemingly little effort and dived down when we got too close to them.

After midday, Cheryl, Christoph, Bob and I prepared ourselves for a dive, moving *Louise* to stand off Batu Bolong, a pinnacle rock in the middle of the Lintah Strait, between the islands of Flores and Komodo. A local dive boat already had a group of scuba divers in the water. Currents flowing between the Java Sea and the Indian Ocean to the south can be powerful, and we could only dive safely on this site close to slack water when the tide switched direction and the current was minimal.

The first ten minutes of the dive went as expected, but coming around the northern side of the submerged pinnacle, we were suddenly dragged along by a strong current and I felt myself being pulled deeper and deeper. Yanking the toggle on my buoyancy vest to fill it with air stopped me from going down further and eventually I began to rise. Grabbing some coral with my fingers to steady myself, I could tell that Cheryl and Bob were visibly worried. Christoph, on the other hand, was nowhere to be seen. The three of us managed to congregate underwater in the shelter of a submerged outcrop. Glancing across at each other, we exchanged OK signs and Bob gave the thumbs-up signal to surface, still not knowing what had happened to Christoph. Once we were above the water, we could see *Louise* was fairly close by, and within minutes Morgan had driven over on the dinghy. He told us that Christoph was safely aboard *Louise* and each of us breathed a sigh of relief. We were clearly all shaken by this episode and, while the dive had ended safely, we reflected that it was a cautionary tale about the hazards of diving in tidal waters.

On Friday 13th November, our final day in the incredible area of East Nusa Tenggara was spent all alone anchored in the bay at Gili Lawalaut, off the north-eastern side of Komodo Island overlooking the Flores Sea. Our last dive in this part of the Indonesian voyage took place at Crystal Rock, where we swam with a school of giant trevally, a reminder of how spoilt we had been with regard to our underwater experiences.

In the afternoon, we walked on the deserted beach and climbed up to a promontory where we were rewarded with spectacular views to Flores Island in the east and the Lintah Strait in the south. A light breeze helped to cover the sea in ripples, which sparkled in the sunlight. After a quiet evening on board, delighting in the peaceful surroundings, we left our anchorage at first light on Saturday morning for the final passage to Bali, 215 miles further west.

The day began with another sighting of a huge blue whale, which appeared to tip its tail to *Louise* before diving. Later, we encountered a pod of dozens of pilot whales, and some time after that we were entertained by a school of spinner dolphins, who performed an acrobatics display. In the evening, we continued our path west, passing Sanggar Peninsula on Sumbawa Island, famed for Mount Tambora. The eruption of Mount Tambora in April 1815 was exceptionally powerful and is believed to be the most destructive volcanic event in recorded history, with 36 cubic miles of ash, pumice and rock dispersed around the world's atmosphere, lowering global temperatures and leading to harvest failures.

As we passed north of the Alas Strait, which leads south to the Indian Ocean between the islands of Sumbawa and Lombok, the wind caught up with us for the first time in weeks. This enabled a few hours of good sailing courtesy of the southerly wind.

On Sunday morning, we passed Lombok to the north of the island where we fell into its wind shadow. Sailing this route brought back memories of a cruise that Brigitte and I took in 1996 on *Cinderella II*, accompanied by our daughters and close friends the Abravanel family, when we visited Lombok and the Gili Islands. On that same trip we also spent time with Sherry and William Spurgin, and William and I did some excellent diving together at Nusa Lembongan, an island that we also cruised by on the last day of this passage.

Our approach to Bali was slowed down a little when leaving the Lombok Strait between Nusa Penida and Bali, while we bucked a strong tidal eddy. Fortunately, we managed to make it to Benoa Marina on Bali at 6 p.m. on Sunday 15th November just before sunset. Tying off our mooring lines brought our 1,500-mile Indonesian odyssey to a close.

We had been struck by the generosity of spirit of the people whom we had chanced to meet in Indonesia, and also by their rich culture. The natural beauty we had encountered throughout this vast archipelago was spectacular. Finally, we had been privileged enough to have seen an underwater world full of life and colour, and had more than made the most of it.

After saying goodbye to Isabelle and Christoph, who were

flying home to Switzerland, Brigitte and I boarded a plane to Singapore and arrived back in the UK the following day. We were laden with great memories, but there was so much more of Indonesia still to see and explore if the opportunity to return ever arose.

✻ ✻ ✻ ✻ ✻

In the next episode of the *Louise* Adventure, the aim was to reach Thailand in time for the New Year. Leaving Brigitte in London, I returned to Bali in early December together with my old Rugby classmate Andrew Speirs and my friend Alastair Whyte, who was also Andrew's cousin. Both of them had kindly offered to join the passage from Bali to the Singapore Strait and onwards to the Andaman Sea.

Unfortunately, Andrew's bags failed to arrive and nor could they be traced, so he had to do a little shopping to acquire a few essentials for his travels on board *Louise*. Taking advantage of our time in Bali, we also did some sightseeing, visiting a traditional theatre to watch a costume dance show and going to a local coffee plantation, where we enjoyed a product tasting.

Looking at the weather chart, calms were forecast all along our route and, disappointingly, there was no sign of the seasonal north-east monsoon winds kicking in. Much of Indonesia remained in the grip of a severe drought that experts advised was caused by an El Niño weather pattern in the Pacific Ocean, and as a result winds were still noticeably absent.

On Sunday 6th December 2015, with Morgan, Cheryl, Andrew, Alastair and me on board, we slipped our moorings and left the rather rundown marina in Bali. As we made our way out of the harbour through a narrow channel, we passed several pleasure craft full of people making the most of the end of the weekend. Once clear of the reef, we changed direction to head eastwards around Bali before setting a course west to Singapore, our next destination. We decided not to take the shorter western route between Bali and Java, as it would be dark while we navigated the straits and the presence of other boats could have been dangerous. Indeed, we expected there to be many hazards to deal with along the route, including unlit fishing boats, fish attraction devices and other types of shipping.

We would also discover that the Java Sea was very polluted, and now home to all kinds of floating rubbish. One morning while motoring along, Alastair was on watch when suddenly the boat lurched to a halt. Dashing onto the foredeck, he realised that we had run into a huge clump of rubbish made up of plastic bottles and tree trunks. Putting the engine into reverse, we were able to back *Louise* away from the floating mess. Morgan and I dived in to inspect the bottom of the boat, but found only a few scratches to the paintwork.

Without a puff of wind in the air, there was no possibility of our being able to sail and therefore no choice except to motor. Below deck, the heat was rather oppressive, with an average temperature of more than 30°C during the daytime. In the evening, when dinner was being prepared in the galley, we put on the air conditioning, which helped to cool down our cabins a little before night-time.

With nearly 100 million people living near the shoreline in Indonesia, coastal fishing is a major industry. No wonder then that we frequently encountered fishermen and their boats. Stocks of fish are under pressure and some fishing practices are non-sustainable, but attempts are being made to put matters right. This is a global challenge, but in South East Asia the battle to save their local fisheries is particularly acute. The Indonesian Government has initiated crackdowns on illegal fishing, similar to the combat against rainforests being burnt down and cleared for oil palm plantations.

Continuing on our way, we motored across a glassy ocean, heading continuously north-west towards the equator. Having left Java behind, off to our port side was Sumatra and to starboard lay Borneo Island and the Indonesian region of Kalimantan, neither of which would we visit during this passage. On Thursday 10th December, we celebrated Andrew's birthday with a cake that Cheryl had baked.

As we got steadily closer to the equator, we started to encounter tropical showers, which had the benefit of cooling the boat down. Our track crossed paths with the route taken on Louis-Antoine de Bougainville's expedition, which had sailed through the Java Sea in 1768 on its way to Batavia, capital of the Dutch East Indies and main colonial outpost in the region, now known as Jakarta.

As we emerged into the South China Sea the wind began to pick up, but it was still too light to sail. Just before midnight on our last night at sea, and with only 125 nautical miles left to run, we crossed the equator into the northern hemisphere. As expected, during the approach to Singapore there was noticeably more shipping, but most of the traffic was north of our path in deeper waters. The continuing presence of fishing craft meant that our watches required especially heightened attention. But this did not stop us from enjoying our daily games of backgammon or rounds of Bananagrams that we played on the deck at the stern of the boat. Everyone had their share of success, but Morgan won the backgammon tournament.

During the last morning at sea, we motored through some smaller channels close to Batam Island, which is one of the main Indonesian islands alongside Bintan Island bordering the Singapore Strait. Navigating in the main shipping lane was like driving along a busy motorway, with heavy seaborne traffic moving in both directions. Eventually, we had to commit to crossing the channel, turning the boat at a right angle to the oncoming traffic. Just as we changed course, heavy rain started to pour down, drastically reducing our visibility, but we continued to navigate a zigzagged course between vessels.

At one point, the boat's electronic plotter indicated that there were over 800 ships in the area, and the screen was completely cluttered with blue dots, each one representing a different vessel. One huge Chinese container ship passed close to *Louise*, travelling east at nearly 20 knots. There was no sign that any of the traffic was slowing down. But we eventually made it safely onto the north side of the Singapore Strait and headed to the immigration holding point. We were met there by a launch and had to drop our papers and passports into a basket held out on a pole by an immigration officer. Not long after, the launch returned with all the documents stamped, which allowed us to motor directly into the marina.

Crabbing our way sideways through the strong tidal flow, we entered Sentosa Marina and passed *Vertigo*, a 217-foot sailing yacht that made *Louise* look tiny. We found the marina to be spotlessly clean, just like the rest of this successful city-state in South East Asia, and we tied up *Louise* opposite the fuel dock at 5 p.m. on Friday 11th December, bringing our 1,000-mile passage to a close.

With three days to spend in Singapore before moving on, Andrew, Alastair and I took full advantage of our time there. Apart from going to museums, having dinners ashore and doing a little shopping, we stopped at the famous Raffles Hotel for a Singapore Sling cocktail. We all felt the drive and optimism that runs through the people in this multicultural place, with a population of nearly 6 million inhabitants. Our visit coincided with the fiftieth anniversary of the small island country, marking the day when it was expelled from Malaysia in 1965 and left to stand on its own. Lee Kuan Yew was Singapore's Prime Minister both before and after it became independent, and he successfully led the nation's emergence from the shadow of its neighbour. Viewed from the water outside the marina, Singapore's skyline stood out as a symbol of the country's prosperity.

On Tuesday 15th December, Morgan successfully completed the formalities for us to leave Singapore and mid-morning we made our way out of the marina to head north-west into the Malacca Strait. Motoring west, the shipping channel is fairly narrow and resembles a busy motorway with a separation zone that keeps westbound ships on the northern side of the channel adjacent to the Malaysian Peninsula. Unsurprisingly, there was a lot of traffic, so we tried to remain on the edge of the shipping lane. All the while, cargo ships travelling a lot faster than *Louise* kept overtaking us. There were also plenty of rain showers during the passage, which caused the visibility to drop, and so we had to be extra vigilant to avoid any hazards. With the global economic centre of gravity currently concentrated in Asia, it is no surprise that the Malacca Strait now closely rivals the Dover Strait for the title of the world's busiest shipping lane.

About 100 nautical miles north-west of Singapore, we passed by the old trading post of Malacca, after which the strait is named. Historically, the Sultanate of Malacca was the premier trading post in South Asia and in the sixteenth century it rivalled Venice in terms of the scale of its commerce. Cloth and glasswork from the Adriatic, perfumes from Arabia, nutmeg and mace from the Bandas, porcelain from China and many more goods were traded there. Muslim merchants from Java and Gujarat were responsible for most of the business conducted in the Sultanate.

In 1511, the Portuguese 'Capture of Malacca' took place under the command of Afonso de Albuquerque, which marked a milestone in the establishment of the first colonial empire by a European monarchy. The Western attackers were brutal, killing many of the local Muslim population. Around the time of the siege, legend has it that the Portuguese invaders chanced on discovering a Chinese chart that revealed sailing routes in the Pacific for the first time. By studying the stolen chart and using other information that he obtained from fellow Portuguese explorers, the ambitious navigator Ferdinand Magellan, who had also participated in the siege of Malacca, was able to deduce that it might be possible to sail around the world.

During this part of the journey, the environmental pollution was hard to ignore in both the sea and the air. On one occasion, we had to stop the boat to clear the propeller, around which some solid garbage had wrapped itself. As regards the airborne pollution, after some rain showers the roof of the cabin became blackened with a soot-like covering. Apparently, it was caused by the smoke from forest fires in Indonesia being blown high up into the atmosphere which then drifted westwards over Singapore and beyond.

Meanwhile, we continued our on-board routine with the daily ritual of board games. Our Malacca Strait backgammon champion was Alastair, who beat us all convincingly.

On Thursday 17th December, we emerged into the Andaman Sea where, for the first time in ages, we felt some wind as a land breeze emerged from the east and we were able to set the sails. A quick calculation revealed that *Louise* had endured the longest period of constant motoring in the

Adventure, covering a distance of 4,500 nautical miles from West Papua in Indonesia to Thailand. By midnight the calm conditions had returned and we decided to drop anchor off Ko Yao Yai. After a good night's sleep, we left early on Friday to motor the last few miles to the Yacht Haven Marina at the north end of Phuket Island.

Since leaving Singapore, we had travelled 500 nautical miles in just over two-and-a-half days, bringing to an end our passage. It was time to thank Andrew and Alastair for their great company and patience, after mostly motoring due to the almost total absence of wind. Happily, everyone was on good form and pleased to have arrived in Thailand as planned, ready to fly home to be back with our loved ones for the festive season.

* * * * *

Christmas brings together families from all over to reconnect and spend time with one another. The Gordon-Rebeaud family are no exception and in December 2015 we met to celebrate in Lausanne, Switzerland, with everyone's eyes on our grandson. We had fun playing games, while the array of delicious food and wines made it hard not to overindulge. Thus, with a few added pounds, Brigitte and I returned to *Louise* to celebrate the arrival of 2016 in Thailand.

The north-east monsoon arrives each year around December, lasting until March, and brings beautiful weather to Thailand's west coast as well as mainly clear skies. For pleasure-seekers, to which category the *Louise* Adventurers belonged, this area was a great destination during the British winter. On this short cruise, we were fortunate to be accompanied by two of our daughters, Juliette and Claire, plus Claire's boyfriend Dave.

We rejoined Morgan and Cheryl on Tuesday 29th December, and after our first night back on board *Louise*, we left Phuket's Yacht Haven Marina early on Wednesday morning to visit one of Thailand's most popular attractions, Khao Phing Kan. Popularly known as James Bond Island, it can be found in Phang Nga Bay, north-east of Phuket. The most distinctive feature of the island is its sheer limestone cliffs that jut out vertically from the water. It was made famous when it featured in the 1974 film *The Man with the Golden Gun* starring Roger Moore. We later moved on to moor at the island of Ko Roi, where we explored its many caves and mangroves before settling down for the evening.

For New Year's Eve, we stopped overnight at the anchorage at Koh Phi Phi Island, which had already filled up with other yachts whose crews were ready to participate in the revelry and partying ashore. And so we saw in 2016 on a crowded beach packed with other holidaymakers, and witnessed a spectacular fireworks display.

On New Year's Day, we motored further south to Koh Racha Yai, which we discovered was rather busy and full of day trippers from Phuket. In the afternoon, Juliette and I went paddle-boarding around the anchorage. I recognised a bright-yellow steel yacht named *Anfisa* with an oddly thin mast and Russian ensign, which was anchored not far from *Louise*. Approaching it on my board, I struck up a conversation with the owner, who introduced himself as Vladimir. I mentioned that we had already seen his boat in Savusavu, Fiji, back in April 2015. Vladimir said he was on his way around the world, heading home via the Mediterranean to his home port of Murmansk, and was about to leave for the Arabian Sea. I enquired if he was worried about pirates at sea and he responded with a shrug and a smile. By the evening, the bay had begun to quieten down as its visitors returned to Phuket, while on board *Louise* we played a few rounds of Bananagrams, which Claire and Dave won convincingly.

I celebrated my sixtieth birthday on Saturday 2nd January, marking the occasion with various fitness activities, including a swim, some gym exercises and a dive. The sporting theme continued throughout the day and later I did some paddle-boarding and had a jog on the beach.

In the afternoon, we sailed back to the main island of Phuket, anchoring next to the beach at Cape Panwa. The hotel of the same name faces the beach and is owned by Tirapongse Pangsrivongse. Tira and I first met at Rugby School in the early 1970s, and although there had been no contact between us for some years, we reconnected after starting our respective families. Before going ashore that evening, thanks to Tira's generosity we were treated to a fireworks display. An amazing dinner was then prepared for us by the hotel's chefs and served on the beach.

Just as the family, Cheryl, Morgan and Tira were about to tuck into the magnificent spread of food, we noticed that *Louise* appeared to be much closer to the beach. She was being pushed by the strengthening wind, and had moved from the place where we had originally anchored. The problem was that the mooring buoy that we had tied the boat to was too small for a large yacht. Alerted to the urgency of the situation, Morgan and Cheryl jumped out of their seats and ran to the dinghy, speeding out to *Louise*. After turning the engine on, together they managed to anchor the boat safely. Later on, after a great evening on the beach that had included the presentation of a birthday cake, we thanked Tira for his kindness and hospitality, as well as hotel manager Thomas Hain and his staff. We also said cheerio to Claire and Dave, who stayed ashore as they would be catching an early flight back to London to return to their jobs the following morning.

On Sunday, the rest of us motored round the southern tip of Phuket before heading north, hugging the coast and passing Khao Lak on mainland Thailand. *Panwa Princess*, which belonged to Tira, accompanied *Louise* all the way and we moored the two boats near each other in an open bay at Coconut Beach, north of Khao Lak. In the afternoon, we took cars to visit the market in the old town of Takua Pa which, a century earlier, had been the centre of the local tin-mining industry. Much of the original architecture in the main street remained well preserved. Tira insisted that we tasted some local sweet delicacies from the market stalls, so we bought some and ate them later.

On our way back to the boats, we drove further south to see the town of Khao Lak, a low-lying coastal resort facing the Andaman Sea. It was one of the places most devastated by the Boxing Day tsunami of 2004. On that terrible day, an earthquake in the Indian Ocean, centred off the west coast of Northern Sumatra, set off a series of tsunami waves that killed over 4,000 people in this area and caused more than 200,000 deaths across the wider region. A police patrol vessel was swept 1.5 miles inland by the tidal wave at Khao Lak and has been preserved as a monument to those who lost their lives.

The next morning, in convoy with the *Panwa Princess*, we left the anchorage and continued on our way, travelling west to the Similan Islands that lie 25 miles off the mainland coast. After a four-hour journey, we anchored late on Monday morning at Similan Island No. 9. Officially a Thai National Park, the islands are formed by smoothly curved granite rocks that protrude out of the sea and are mostly covered by vegetation. Once again we were the recipients of some great Thai hospitality, with a lunch that had been prepared by Tira's cook and which we ate on the fly deck of the *Panwa Princess*. In the afternoon, we took advantage of the clear waters to go diving and then spent the evening with Tira aboard *Louise*, enjoying more food, wine and conversation. After dinner, Tira bid us farewell and retreated to his boat, ready to return to Phuket and fly home to Bangkok on Tuesday morning.

We had decided to continue a little further north to the Surin Islands, a group of islets on the northerly limit of Thai waters. From the point at which we stopped, the Mergui Archipelago in Myanmar was clearly visible. On this trip, however, we had chosen not to go to Myanmar, having studied the restrictions for seaborne visitors, such as the requirement to have a local pilot on board at all times.

The views around the five islands that make up the Surin Islands National Park were spectacular. Forests run down into narrow sandy beaches with granite outcrops and distinctive rocks standing on the shoreline. Waking up on Wednesday morning, opposite the boat we noticed activity taking place in the little dwellings within the settlement behind the beach. Smoke was emanating from open fires that families had lit in order to prepare their breakfasts.

For two days we relaxed, chilling out in the water, scuba diving, paddle-boarding and making a few sightseeing trips by dinghy. We spent Thursday night at Ko Surin Nuea, the most northerly of the two main islands that make up the Surin Archipelago. This was the quietest spot of all the places we had been during our stay in Thailand. The air was still and the bay remained completely calm. After a simple meal at the island's campsite restaurant, we returned to *Louise* for a peaceful evening.

The next morning, on Friday 8th January, before leaving the islands we went to dive at the nearby Richelieu Rock. Entering the water from *Louise*, Juliette, Morgan and I swam through shoals of small fish that were swarming around the underwater pinnacles while being preyed upon by bigger species, hungry for a meal. We also found well-formed fan corals that had never been visible in any of the other places where we had dived in Thailand. After completely circling the iconic dive site under the water, Juliette and I got back into the dinghy, which Morgan had been pulling along while swimming in the water above us.

With our time in Thai waters almost at an end, we motored to the mainland and by late afternoon we had anchored *Louise* at Khuraburi Port, a busy fishing harbour just over 100 miles north of Phuket. Juliette, Brigitte and I were dropped ashore by Morgan and Cheryl, to whom we said cheerio before we travelled directly to Phuket Airport by car, a few hours' drive away. By late evening, we were on a plane waiting to fly back to London via Qatar.

The last few months spent on *Louise* had been exceptional, both in terms of the weather and our many experiences. We had really enjoyed visiting the nations of South East Asia, with their large populations of young people, generous hospitality and distinctive cultures, and were very much looking forward to the return trip, when the Andaman Sea would be our much-anticipated destination.

Chapter 10 – Monsoon Run
Phuket, Thailand to Sri Lanka and the Seychelles

Peros Banhos, Chagos Islands

Brigitte and I returned to Thailand in early February and joined *Louise* back in Phuket to prepare for the next stage in the Adventure – a visit to the Andaman Islands, an Indian archipelago of over 200 islands located close to Myanmar. Our destination was Port Blair on South Andaman Island, which was approximately 400 nautical miles, or two days' sailing, to the north-west of Phuket. During the northern hemisphere's winter weather in the Andaman Sea, the stretch of water to the west of Thailand and Myanmar is usually benign, attracting holidaymakers to the region. Cooler air temperatures mean that cyclones, which haunt these seas during the warm summers, do not appear, as the ability of warm tropical waters to brew up storms diminishes at this time of year.

We were delighted that our friend Ian Reid and his wife Pammy could accompany us on this short cruise. Unfortunately, Ian was recovering from a bout of flu, and so as soon as he arrived on board he went straight to lie down in his bunk. While Ian got some rest, Pammy, Brigitte and I set off to explore Phuket's old town and its Buddhist temple. *Louise* was moored in Nai Harn Bay at the southern end of the island, which was the home of the Phuket Yacht Club from where we would be checking out when we left Thailand.

On Friday 5th February 2016, we lifted anchor early to head to the Similan Islands, where we would have a brief stopover before embarking upon the open-sea passage to Port Blair. After motoring all the way, on arrival we found the main anchorage quite crowded compared to the last time we were there in January. We soon realised that our return trip coincided with Chinese New Year festivities, a time when a great many tourists come to spend the holiday. Overnight we moored at Similan's Island No. 4, known as Koh Miang, where we tied *Louise* to one of the mooring buoys and had a restful night's sleep.

The following day, we climbed a rock face behind the beach to reach a promontory that offered great views of the bay, and saw *Louise* swinging at her mooring. After lunch on Saturday, we tidied up and prepared to leave for Port Blair. We hoisted our mainsail before lifting the anchor and were able to sail away without the aid of the engine, setting course for the Andaman Islands. The journey westwards offered superb sailing, as the north-east monsoon, which blows in the winter, was in full swing and aft of the beam for the duration of the passage. Settling down into our watches, we enjoyed the simple pleasure of being back at sea. After sunset, with the moon absent it was quite dark outside but we made good speed through the night. The new moon showed its face before dawn at 5.30 a.m., and during the day, while *Louise* sailed along steadily, we were entertained by a large school of spinner dolphins.

As we were making excellent progress, during the middle of the second day of travelling on Sunday we slowed down to avoid making landfall in the hours of darkness. We timed it to perfection, passing the entrance at Port Blair after sunrise, and dropped anchor on Monday 8th February at 6 a.m. Indian Time. Surprisingly, India is unique among nations that have a vast geographic spread in that the whole country, from east to west, falls within the same time zone.

With one week to spend in the Andaman Islands, whose beautiful beaches have made them especially popular with young Indians and honeymooners, we had chosen to concentrate on exploring the lower end of South Andaman Island and its surrounding waters. Meanwhile, no stay in Port Blair would be complete without paying a visit to the Cellular Jail, which was built by British colonialists during the days of empire and used mainly as a place of exile for political prisoners on the remote archipelago. Known in Hindi as 'Kālā Pānī', meaning 'black waters', the jail that features a hangman's hut with gallows has also been called India's Bastille. It has become a monument to the fight for the country's independence.

On Tuesday morning, we left Port Blair under full sail bound for Havelock Island, 25 nautical miles to the north-east. As we departed, we overheard members of the harbour authorities talking excitedly about *Louise* over the radio.

While strolling on Radhanagar Beach early on Wednesday morning, we saw an elephant walking on the sand, swaying from side to side, being escorted by a couple of locals. After visiting Havelock's main village on the north of the island, we travelled further north through a narrow channel on the west side of Lawrence Island, which was low-lying and appeared to be uninhabited. It was a very tranquil scene, with no other boats or people in sight.

The next day, on Thursday 11th February, we reached North Button Island in the morning, where we went snorkelling and caught two lobsters using a simple wire trap that Morgan had rigged up. Once cooked, the fresh catch made for tasty pre-dinner canapés. Looking at the chart, we realised that we had reached 12 degrees north, the most northerly point in our exploration of the Andaman Islands, and observed that the Caribbean Islands were at approximately the same latitude.

Changing course to head back south, we stopped at Neil Island, which had an attractive village. On the southern side of the island, which we travelled to by taxi, there was an impressive overhanging rock formation called the Natural Bridge that faces the sea and has been gradually eroded over centuries. Tourists, including ourselves, stood under the rock and took pictures of the beautiful setting.

On Friday morning, we lifted the anchor early and motored to the Cinque Islands, which lie off the southern end of the Andamans. On the way we managed to hook a large marlin, which turned out to be far too big to bring on board. Consequently, we had to let it go, which was easier said than done. Lowering the dinghy into the water, Morgan and I got in and started to follow the fish, while Morgan hauled it in on the fishing line. As soon as the marlin was close enough to the dinghy, I grabbed its snout and Morgan immediately unhooked the lure. Having had a lucky escape, the fish plunged back into the deep.

We chose to moor in the attractive-looking bay between the islands of North Cinque and South Cinque. The area is a national park and has exceptionally clear water, with even some coral heads visible on the seabed. Our only neighbours were four fishermen aboard a little boat, who rested during the daytime after their hard work overnight. They told us that they were from Port Blair and each fishing expedition in their cabinless vessel lasted about four days.

In the time that we spent in the Cinque Islands, we went beachcombing, snorkelling and diving. Every morning we were treated to the spectacle of a school of cuttlefish swimming around the boat. Ashore, we discovered that North Cinque had a small population of deer. The beaches teemed with activity and had an abundance of hermit crabs.

On Sunday 14th February, we celebrated Morgan's birthday with a cake that Cheryl had baked. The next morning, we lifted anchor to sail north towards Port Blair, stopping en route near the southern tip of Andaman off the Chidiya Tapu nature reserve that faces Rutland Island. Famous for its sunset views, we went ashore to experience the vista as dusk descended, sitting on a bluff that overhangs the sea.

On Tuesday, we motored the short distance to Port Blair to drop off the Reids, who had flights booked to Chennai where they planned to do some more sightseeing until it was time to go home. We savoured our last Indian meal and taste of spice together, and then said farewell to Pammy and Ian before heading back to *Louise* and setting off for the return journey to Thailand.

The wind was moderate, and as it was coming from the north-east we sailed close-hauled, managing to keep up good speed. During the second night of the passage the wind veered to the east, which meant that we were sailing into it. So we started motor-sailing into the oncoming chop. This caused *Louise* to slam into the waves, which made it less comfortable on board, but fortunately the conditions did not last too long. As we drew closer to Phuket, the sea calmed down and we motored the final miles before anchoring in Nai Harn Bay at 9 p.m. on Thursday 18th February.

Our brief Andaman cruise had taken us over 900 nautical miles, during which we had discovered the beauty of this unspoilt and off-the-beaten-track archipelago, which is arguably one of India's best-kept secrets.

Back in Thailand, after completing the usual check-in formalities, we left *Louise* to fly home. In our absence, Morgan and Cheryl would be taking the boat to Langkawi, an archipelago off the north-west coast of mainland Malaysia, about 100 nautical miles south of Phuket. There, *Louise* would be lifted out of the water to have her bottom cleaned and painted, ready for the long trip home.

Ahead of us lay thousands of miles of sailing across both the Indian and Atlantic Oceans, giving organisms ample opportunity to grow under the boat. Anti-fouling paint is applied to vessels to stop marine life such as seaweed and barnacles from developing on the hull, because if they take hold they will slow any boat down. In olden times ships were 'careened', which meant hauling them onto their side at the water's edge to enable the sailors to scrape barnacles and other growths off the bottom. This was an arduous task, but necessary for keeping the ship in a seaworthy condition. So, a fortnight after arriving in Langkawi, *Louise* had been thoroughly checked over and was once again afloat in the water and bound for Phuket, ready to commence our journey across the Indian Ocean.

※ ※ ※ ※ ※

Over a month later, on Saturday 26th March 2016, Brigitte and I were back in Phuket and preparing to say farewell to Thailand and its kind people with their ever-welcoming smiles. We raised the anchor in Chalong Bay on a calm day destined for Galle, a small city at the southern end of Sri Lanka, just over 1,000 nautical miles west. Further ahead lay the rest of the Indian Ocean, and we planned to continue westwards, staying close to the equator until the Seychelles. From there we would turn south-west through the Mozambique Channel, passing down the east coast of South Africa and sailing onwards to the Cape of Good Hope and back into the South Atlantic.

We were joined for the second time by Errikos Abravanel, who was excited to be back on board for our crossing of the Indian Ocean. However, the expectation of our being able to do much sailing in the first part of the passage was low, as winds in the Bay of Bengal are generally light at this time of year. With spring approaching, the weather changes and the north-east monsoon dies away, to be replaced by the cyclone season that begins towards the end of May. During spring, which is also called the 'hot season', the sea heats up to produce moist air, which rises and forms clouds that fall as rain once they have reached the shores of the countries bordering the Bay of Bengal. From India in the west, Bangladesh in the north to Myanmar in the east, all these nations receive the monsoon rains. Rice paddies and field crops are watered, creating food and sustenance, but there is also the portent of flooding, which affects the low-lying communities on the shoreline and especially endangers the lives of people who live at or below sea level. Climate change is already exacerbating the situation through rising sea levels and increasing the risk of serious disasters.

Leaving the Thai coast behind us, we motored southwest towards Great Nicobar Island and the Bay of Bengal beyond. Although we initially passed a few fishing boats in Thai coastal waters, we were soon alone and during the first evening we continued our journey over a flat, calm sea with the night sky overhead shining bright. *Louise* was making good progress since receiving the fresh coat of paint under her waterline in Langkawi.

By the second night at sea we had drawn parallel to Nicobar Island, passing between it and the northern point of Sumatra. Commercial shipping is very busy in this area, with westbound cargoes leaving the Malacca Strait and heading towards the southern end of Sri Lanka and destinations beyond, including Suez.

In the days of sail, the movements of vessels crossing the Bay of Bengal and Arabian Sea were planned to coincide with the seasons. In the winter they travelled westbound, taking advantage of the north-east monsoon, and sailed eastwards during the summer in order to profit from the south-west monsoon. Cargo shipments were taken by sea from Africa and the Arabian Peninsula in the west to the coasts of the Indian subcontinent and eastwards, passing the Malacca Strait and into the South China Sea and East Asia beyond. The Silk Road, which was the land bridge from Asia to all places west, was complemented by seaborne connections established across the northern Indian Ocean, which allowed goods, people and ideas to journey in all directions. Sailors had long understood the annual cycle of the monsoons and by 100 BC they had managed to ride the winds between India and South East Asia. Notably, in the fifteenth century Chinese Admiral Zheng commanded expeditions from ports in China to South East Asia, South Asia and further afield to East Africa over a period of nearly thirty years. In the National Maritime

Museum in Galle, Sri Lanka, an engraving on a carved stone records the occasion of one of his fleet's visits.

Nowadays, the main shipping route across the northern Indian Ocean has become one of the world's busiest thoroughfares for trade. Day and night, we could see a line of vessels to our south, laden with goods and commodities. The sight of a procession of ships stretching to the horizon was a clear sign of how globalisation had truly taken hold.

Apart from experiencing the occasional shower, during the daytime it was hot, and we only cooled down courtesy of the speed of the boat and then later at sunset. On board *Louise* we relaxed, spending time reading and enjoying each other's company. The daily routine of post-lunch backgammon continued, and Errikos found his stride quickly.

While on watch, we kept a lookout for nearby fishing boats in particular, because on our approach to Sri Lanka we had begun to encounter more vessels. In fact, one fishing boat with a sizeable crew passed by at speed close to *Louise*'s stern. The fishermen, some of whom were standing on the roof of the boat's pilot house, perhaps thought that we would have a supply of cigarettes and offered to barter their fish in exchange. Not wishing to stop, we gave them a friendly wave of acknowledgement and continued on our way.

After five days at sea, we were nearing the low-lying Sri Lankan coastline, though it was still not yet visible. At one point we were overtaken by a convoy of ships from the Indian Navy, which was moving fast. During the last night at sea those on watch had a busy time of it, with numerous coastal fishing boats to avoid. We decided to slow down to ensure we made landfall during the following morning, after daybreak.

At breakfast time on Friday 1st April, 'Fools Day', we dropped anchor off the breakwater at Galle, an old walled citadel with a fort that was founded by Portuguese colonists in the sixteenth century. Known to Europeans since the time of the ancient Greeks, Sri Lanka lies at the crossroads of the Indian Ocean trade routes, at the intersection of the Arabian Sea and the Bay of Bengal. This land was known to Muslim traders as Serendib or the 'Island of Jewels' in Arabic. Serendipity, meaning the art of making happy discoveries, is derived from this name. Once *Louise* was safely moored alongside the quay in Galle's small harbour, we set off to explore the city.

Besides the Old Fort much of Galle is modern, in part as a result of the damage caused by the Indian Ocean tsunami on Boxing Day December 2004. Over 36,000 people lost their lives in Sri Lanka, including many local residents in Galle, when the powerful wave caused by the underwater tremor burst ashore in the low-lying coastal regions in the south and east of the country.

The streets of the Old Fort, which date back centuries to a time before Europeans first reached these shores, ooze with history. Traders from Muslim communities bordering the Indian Ocean, as well as the Chinese and others, used Galle as a trading post long before the first Western invaders landed. The colonial era itself began in 1505 with the arrival of the Portuguese, who originally stopped at Galle to take shelter from a storm and would go on to dominate the region for over 100 years on entering the lucrative spice trade. In 1498, Vasco da Gama's discovery of the sea route from the Atlantic to the Indian Ocean around the Cape of Good Hope enabled trade to be conducted on a trans-oceanic basis, bypassing historic land-based routes to compete with Venice. Galle (and Sri Lanka generally) was for centuries an important staging post where valuable commodities, including spices, passed through on their way to market. The Portuguese also left their mark on the region by giving the country its colonial name of 'Ceilão' or Ceylon.

However, Portuguese dominance did not last forever. The Dutch gradually displaced them and after the Portuguese lost a war between the two nations, they were expelled from Ceylon in 1656. The Dutch East India Company had gained the upper hand partly through their singular focus on capturing wealth, while the Portuguese had been distracted by a religious crusade against Islam, which had diverted their attention at times. Later, when the Netherlands were invaded by France during the Napoleonic Wars, the Dutch handed Ceylon over to England, who became the colonial masters of Sri Lanka at the onset of the nineteenth century. Galle's National Maritime Museum, which we visited, brings to life the constant ebb and flow of territorial control that had been a feature of this region over centuries.

On the day we arrived in Galle, with our bags packed and ready to commence a short tour around southern Sri Lanka, after lunch Brigitte, Errikos and I caught a train to the capital city of Colombo, which was about 80 miles north of Galle. The railway line is a relic from colonial times and travel was slow. The train was initially crowded with standing room only, but after the first stop, not far from Galle, a number of passengers got off and we all managed to find a seat.

A friendly man from Colombo, who was returning home after attending a funeral in Galle, introduced himself and we listened to his views on life in Sri Lanka. As we approached the capital, once again the train became more overcrowded and there were even people aboard who had grabbed hold of the train from the outside as it moved along. Others were also walking on the railway track, seemingly unworried about passing trains.

Upon alighting at Colombo's main station, our new

acquaintance handed us his business card before saying farewell and wishing us a good stay. We thanked him and hailed a taxi to take us to our hotel, which was one of the large international establishments facing the seafront. My first impression of Colombo was that it was more modern than I had imagined and featured a cosmopolitan aspect full of stylish eateries, galleries and shops. In older times, it was known as the 'garden city of the East', and the place still retains many open spaces and parks. It is also the commercial and political hub of the nation, with a vast seaport facing the Bay of Bengal. We only stayed for one night in the capital, preferring to set out for the interior the following morning, heading to Kandy.

On our way inland on Saturday 2nd April, we stopped to view the residents of the Pinnawala Elephant Orphanage. Every day the elephants, all of which have been found abandoned or injured, are led out of the orphanage for a bath in the nearby Maha Oya River, where they can play and cool themselves down in the water. Later in the afternoon we reached Kandy, finding our hotel at the top of a steep hill with a view over the city. Before evening, we visited the Temple of the Sacred Tooth Relic, one of the most revered places of worship in the Buddhist world. Kandy has always been a destination for pilgrims and was the last capital of the ancient line of kings of Sri Lanka. The temple and palace complex of buildings are beautiful and also featured a ladies' bathhouse where, housed within an imposing edifice on the lakeshore, the queen and her entourage could bathe in the lake without fear of being seen.

At the end of the day's sightseeing, an entrepreneurial young man persuaded us to come to his shop, offering to arrange transportation and a guide for the rest of our tour. We should have heeded the old adage 'caveat emptor' because on Sunday morning, when our driver arrived at the hotel, we were shocked to see the dilapidated state of his vehicle. Sticking to our plans, we told him that he could take us as far as Nuwara Eliya, but afterwards we would look for alternative transport.

We were driven into the Southern Uplands, passing some beautiful landscape along the way, and reached Nuwara Eliya during the evening. The following morning, we strolled through the well-tended Hakgala Botanical Gardens, imagining how in the colonial era families would have come here to escape the oppressive heat in Colombo. In modern times, many of the city's visitors travel from Saudi Arabia, especially during the summer, to take a break from the desert sun back home. A gardener whom we talked to at Hakgala told us about some of the shrubs and flowers that he tended, and kindly offered to post some seeds back to the UK for us.

Another highlight was driving through tea plantations and visiting a few of the factories. Of the tea estates that we went to, our favourite was Halpewatte Tea Factory near Ella, which we reached after a drive up a windy single-track road. Employing approximately 3,000 people, most of whom are pickers collecting leaves in the tea gardens, we enjoyed an informative tour and learnt that leaves are picked throughout the year, mainly by women who are paid by the bag. Nothing much has changed over the decades and the tea factories we went to were not modern, but they did the job required. For their picking staff, the plantations rely heavily on Tamils, who are not native to this part of the country but who move south to gain employment. One of the female pickers, perhaps in her sixties, offered to pose with some leaves for a picture, smiling warmly. Her heavily wrinkled skin was presumably a consequence of spending a lot of time in the sun.

Our last night on the road trip was spent in an unusual

hotel that had been built into the mountainside on a steep escarpment, adjacent to the main road. After seeing so many fascinating sights during our brief sojourn, the next morning it was time to head back to the coast and Galle. The car descended from the uplands, which rise to around 6,500 feet in this area, all the way back down to the coast. We stopped at a cave containing a Buddhist shrine that was decorated with brightly coloured murals. Further on, we went to the small Sinhagiri temple and seminary, home to young teenage monks who have been abandoned by their parents, mainly for reasons of poverty. We rejoined the coast at Hambantota, a new seaport which is being developed with the Chinese to create a magnet for commerce and business activity, though the development hasn't yet taken off. By late afternoon we were safely back in Galle, dusting ourselves off after the whistle-stop tour, which had opened our eyes to the beauty of Sri Lanka.

On our return to Galle, we were joined by Klaus Diederichs for the second stage of our passage to the Seychelles, thus reuniting the team that had sailed *Louise* through Patagonia. For some months we had been trying to obtain a permit to visit the Chagos Islands, but so far had not been successful. We were keen to go to the isolated archipelago located 800 nautical miles south-west of Sri Lanka, which is only accessible by sea and out of bounds for tourists, but didn't know if it would be possible. After dinner, I made a call and asked to speak to the director at the British Indian Ocean Territory (BIOT) office in London. I was surprised that he spoke to me, though he wasn't able to confirm whether our permit would be granted. I put it to him that if we proceeded to the Chagos, did he think that the permit application would be approved before we arrived, to which the response was 'I think so'. As a result, we decided to take a chance and set sail for the Chagos Islands the following day, keeping our fingers crossed for a positive outcome.

Casting off from Galle late on the afternoon of Thursday 7th April, we motored across a flat, calm sea in sweltering hot conditions. During the first evening and in the early hours of night, we crossed through the shipping lane that passes to the south of Sri Lanka. On the chart plotter we noticed how some ships, rather than indicating their destination, had instead posted the message 'Armed Guards on Board', presumably to discourage any pirates who might be lurking in the Arabian Sea. Indeed, on the dock in Galle we had previously observed launches either picking up or dropping off security guards. Fortunately, piracy has declined in these waters since Western navies had made a concerted effort to police them.

By midnight, we had motored about 40 nautical miles and were clear of the southern tip of Sri Lanka. The main shipping lanes were well behind us and the sea had started to look deserted, apart from the odd fishing boat.

At breakfast time on Sunday 10th April, *Louise* crossed the equator again, moving back into the southern hemisphere. It was still really hot on board, but the wind was picking up and we hoisted the sails while we passed the halfway mark on the passage. Klaus and Errikos were submitted to the customary 'crossing of the line' ceremony by Morgan in the role of Neptune and me as his assistant. The backgammon tournament was also in full swing and we were each drawn equal after four days of play. Errikos eventually pulled off victory in the tie-breaker round, with Klaus finishing as runner-up.

For the next two days we had the wind on the beam and, with a smooth sea state, *Louise* sailed along nicely in the trade winds. Temperature-wise it was thankfully cooling down a little, helped by the occasional tropical rain shower.

There was more excitement when we hooked a blue marlin after breakfast on the fourth day of the voyage. Once again, the fish proved too heavy to bring onto the boat, so we repeated our routine manoeuvre using the dinghy to get close to it. Morgan then reeled the marlin in and once the fish began to tire, we were able to bring it alongside the dinghy close enough for me to grip it by the snout while Morgan removed the lure to free it. At the very end of the trip, Klaus would present a ten-minute film called 'Fishing on *Louise*', capturing highlights of our struggle with the marlin, including underwater shots that I took of it fighting to escape.

On the morning of Tuesday 12th April, we sighted the Chagos Islands and the Salomon Atoll, the most northerly land in the archipelago, which are also part of the Great Chagos Bank, the world's largest coral atoll. As we were still waiting for a response from the British Government regarding the visitor permit, I called the BIOT office on the satphone again and managed to get straight through to the director, Mr Moody. He informed me that the permit had still not been issued, but went on to say, 'I am happy for you to proceed to the anchorage and you will receive the papers during the day.' After thanking him I hung up, feeling relieved, and shared the good news with the crew.

Passing through the cut at the entry to Salomon Atoll, we headed south to the main anchorage and discovered there wasn't a single boat in sight. *Louise* was all alone in this remote and abandoned atoll in the Indian Ocean, or at least we thought so. Not long after settling at anchor, a voice with an American accent came over the radio, enquiring if all was well on board. The caller announced himself as the captain of the USS *Page* and after looking on the screen we could see her on the plotter. A few minutes later a naval vessel that was presumably based at Diego Garcia, a heavily militarised island at the south of the Chagos Archipelago, came into sight outside the atoll. The captain enquired if we needed any assistance regarding our permit, which we declined, then a little later he wished us a good stay in the Chagos. Fortunately, in the afternoon we received an email from the British Government confirming that our permit had been granted – the document was stamped no. 5/2016. The fact that we had obtained the fifth permit in 2016 was an indication of how very few boats were allowed to visit the islands.

The Chagos Archipelago is formally a British overseas territory, but this is a controversial subject and has been the cause of a long-standing dispute with the Chagossian islanders. Between 1968 and 1973, Britain forcibly removed the local population, completely against their will, to make way for a US military base on Diego Garcia. Originally named in the sixteenth century by the Portuguese who discovered the atolls, the Chagos Islands lie about 300 nautical miles south of the Maldives, a short distance south of the equator. The French were the first to settle and established coconut plantations there. After the Napoleonic Wars, the islands were ceded to Britain and governed from Mauritius. Since their forced expulsion, the Chagossians have been fighting legal battles to gain the right to return to their homeland, but they have been constantly thwarted by the British Government's intransigence. The political temperature in these waters is still high, and sadly many Chagossians have died in poverty in the slums of Port Louis in Mauritius where they were relocated.

Our anchorage on Salomon Atoll was on Boddam Island, in front of the old village. Moored all alone, *Louise* swung around in the crystal-clear azure waters with a white sandy bottom. Over on the shoreline, a mass of coconut palm trees was gently swaying in the light tropical breeze. Taking the dinghy ashore, we fastened the painter (a rope used to tie up a dinghy) to a tree trunk that had fallen over and ended up in the lagoon. Someone had erected a swing and Morgan was soon sitting on it, suspended over the water.

Exploring the island, we waded through thick undergrowth and discovered the ruins of the abandoned village. Sailors had nailed various national flags to a board, a number of which represented Scandinavian countries. Generally, though, the place felt like a ghost town. The main signs of life on land were some coconut crabs that we found clinging to the palm trees. They looked tasty, but visiting rules forbid all forms of harvesting, including fishing and diving. That evening, we settled down in the calm of the anchorage to a quiet evening under the beauty of the southern hemisphere's sky.

When we got up on Wednesday morning, we were surprised to discover that we were no longer on our own, as Ernesto Bertarelli's motor yacht *VaVa II* was spotted moored outside the cut. Bertarelli's Swiss Team Alinghi had won the America's Cup twice, a great triumph for a team based in a landlocked country. After a while, one of *VaVa*'s ribs pulled up next to *Louise*, whereupon its occupants enquired if we were well and offered us a case of beer and a bag of assorted snack foods. After readily accepting the beer, we invited the rib's driver aboard. The young man introduced himself as Magnus, First Officer, and he explained that *VaVa* was engaged on a mission with fourteen scientists to track the local shark population and conduct a range of marine research. The Bertarelli Foundation has become a leading proponent in improving the health of the planet and promoting marine conservation and science. All day long we observed tenders coming and going, as well as the ship's helicopter making shark-spotting sorties.

Later that same morning, while snorkelling we discovered that much of the coral was bleached, a consequence of increasing water temperatures. On measuring the intake of the boat's watermaker (a desalinator unit), we found that the temperature reached an average of 31°C during the two days we spent there. Morgan also noticed a stranded turtle entangled in a fishing net, but after cutting away the net he was able to release the creature back into the lagoon.

On Wednesday afternoon we moved to Takamaka Island, the anchorage at the eastern side of the atoll opposite the cut. On the beach we saw the sad-looking wreck of a trimaran. Brigitte also found an empty triangular bottle of Grant's whisky among the flotsam washed up on the beach.

The next morning, we prepared to move further west to the Peros Banhos Atoll. Leaving the Salomon Atoll, we passed close by *VaVa II* and waved at some of her crew before heading on our way. Peros Banhos is a large atoll and once we had entered by the cut on the south side, we went to the old settlement at Île du Coin. The village now lies in ruin, like an abandoned film set, but the beach was beautiful and we all ended up swimming in the warm shallow water. For dinner that evening, we tasted some delicious yellowfin tuna that had been caught earlier that day during our passage between the islands.

After taking the dinghy out to go diving on Friday morning, we swam with a hawksbill turtle. On our way back to *Louise*, a school of dolphins came out to play with the dinghy and put on an acrobatics show. Our final stop before leaving the Chagos Archipelago was Fouquet Island, an idyllic spot to moor and take in the tropical surroundings. We strolled around the little island that had been seemingly colonised by crabs, which was bathed in the afternoon sun under a deep blue sky. Cheryl and Morgan went for an afternoon swim and snorkel on the reef close by *Louise*, when a black-tip reef shark came a bit too close for their liking.

Having experienced the pleasure of visiting one of the Indian Ocean's most extraordinary archipelagos, we were relaxed and ready to continue on our way westward.

On the afternoon of Friday 15th April, we left the Chagos Islands and set course for the Seychelles. Lifting the anchor, we slipped out through the cut in the reef, turning west. The sun was setting and the palm trees on the Île du Coin stood out against the horizon. Sunlight shone on the mist-like spray that rises from the reef as the ocean waves collide with land. During the evening, a few thunderstorms loomed in the distance, with their huge cumulus clouds rising miles into the sky. Meanwhile, we settled into our watch routines.

Ahead of us was the 1,000-mile westerly voyage to the Seychelles, following a line parallel with the equator. In the winter, the north-east monsoon is the dominant wind in the Arabian Sea. It was now spring and the weather was on the change, with the breeze becoming more variable as the inter-tropical zone moved north to cover the area through which we were sailing. Luckily for us, though, for most of the passage the wind blew from the southern quadrant, giving us excellent sailing conditions.

One feature in the tropics is the presence of showers, for which we were on the alert, as strong wind gusts can hide under the shadow of a rain cloud. Our weather map showed that a late-season cyclone was tracking parallel to our course about 500 nautical miles south. The tropical cyclone carried with it wind strengths of up to 100 knots, but being well to our south we were safely out of reach of its destructive forces. It would eventually pass over the Farquhar Islands in the Seychelles, a little north of Madagascar.

Most days we profited from the smooth conditions by doing some fishing and we landed some good catches, including mahi-mahi and another yellowfin tuna. For the third time, our lures unfortunately attracted a marlin whose size was too massive to be hauled safely on board. Once hooked, we responded with our well-tested dinghy routine, managing to release the lure from the fish before continuing on our way. Klaus, using his media talents, once again caught all of this on video for his 'Fishing on *Louise*' film, which also included a scene in the galley that captured Cheryl performing her culinary mastery.

Backgammon was also never far from our minds, and in the final of the Arabian Sea championship, Klaus emerged as winner in the run-off against Errikos. At night, the oppressive tropical heat ensured it was still very warm on the boat.

A sign that our destination would soon be in sight was the appearance of some sizeable fishing vessels. The Seychelles has an agreement with the European Union to develop a more sustainable fishery in its waters. Each year, a small number of large European tuna boats are permitted to fish in the country's rich territorial seas. The EU also provides resources for the Seychelles to police the vast oceanic area that the nation controls, to help ensure that illegal fishing does not occur. But controversy still surrounds the fishing practices of the tuna boats, as their nets, which are over 1.25 miles long, snare a lot of fish that is unintentionally caught – juvenile and undersized species, commonly known as bycatch. Later, when visiting the docks in the Seychelles capital Victoria, we saw containers in the Russian-owned fish market loaded with frozen fish ready for export to Asia and other markets. There are rich rewards attached to this industry and human demand for this form of protein is placing huge pressure on stocks.

On the morning of Thursday 21st April, we docked *Louise* in Port Eden, just over the water from Victoria on Mahé. The exceptionally well-developed marina, with modern apartment blocks and villas lining the seashore, is part of the Eden Island community that has been built on top of a reef. From our berth we had a great view over Mahé, the main island of the Seychelles Archipelago. The French claimed possession of the islands in 1756 and fourteen years later French settlers from Mauritius, accompanied by some African slaves, began to arrive. The islands were ultimately named after King Louis XV's finance minister, Jean Moreau de Séchelles. After the Napoleonic Wars, by the Treaty of Paris in 1814, the Seychelles were ceded by France to Britain, under whose control they remained until the country gained its independence in 1976.

Our arrival marked the end of our crossing of the northern side of the Indian Ocean, which had started in Thailand and totalled nearly 3,000 nautical miles. The closest city to the Seychelles on the African continent was Mogadishu in Somalia, about 800 nautical miles north-west. Although the risk of ocean piracy had greatly reduced, unfortunately we would not be visiting East Africa during the Adventure.

Before heading back home, we had set aside a few days to take in the surroundings. Fortuitously, we discovered that the upcoming weekend coincided with the Seychelles Annual Carnival. At our first dinner in the marina that evening, we were entertained by Brazilian dancers and ended up on the dancefloor ourselves.

With Morgan and Cheryl's wedding planned for May, there was the groom's stag night to attend to, so the next day we managed to find some suitable attire for Morgan in the shape of a dress purchased from a women's clothing shop, which Errikos had tried on for size. Morgan was very much up for some fun and had a full manicure in a local beauty parlour, later emerging dressed in drag. Following dinner in the main nightclub, we ran into the Brazilian dancers from the previous night, which added even more entertainment to the evening, especially when one of them, on noticing how Morgan was dressed, asked if he was marrying Errikos!

After a memorable night, on Saturday Errikos left us to head back home to Athens, while we remained behind to enjoy a couple more days with Klaus, whose wife Alice had joined him. Brigitte and I then flew home, leaving Klaus and Alice to stay for few nights on *Louise* and visit the nearby islands of Praslin and La Digue. They spent five days on board, but sadly there was no wind for sailing.

On our arrival back home, we were just in time to celebrate the birth of a granddaughter named Alba, the latest addition to our family.

Chapter 11 – African Shores
The Seychelles to Madagascar and Cape Town, South Africa

Outrigger fishing canoe, Madagascar

On Monday 13th June 2016, we left the UK to fly back to the Seychelles, and after a brief stopover in Abu Dhabi we were back on board *Louise* by Tuesday morning. Coincidentally, some of Abu Dhabi's riches have made their way to the

Seychelles, as its ruler Sheikh Khalifa has built a luxury mansion on Mahé.

Louise was still moored at Eden Island and we were greeted with broad smiles by our newly-wed crew, Morgan and Cheryl, who were overjoyed at being married and happily showed us their wedding photos. Both of their families had flown over for the occasion and made the most of their visit by staying on in the Seychelles for an extended period.

Although we were still close to the equator, the weather had noticeably changed with the onset of the southern hemisphere winter. Southerly winds were blowing and cooling down the atmosphere, making the conditions very pleasant. We were joined early on Wednesday 15th June by our friends Cherry Chau and Philippe René-Bazin for their second cruise on board *Louise*, and set off straightaway for Anse Lazio on Praslin Island, just a short sail from Mahé. In the quiet bay where we anchored, we went to the 'Honesty Bar' which seemed like the only place that had drinks for sale; apart from chairs and tables, the bar only had a fridge containing beers and a small box where you could leave some money.

But the main attraction on Praslin Island was the rainforest where the coco de mer fruit grows. This species of palm tree, whose fruit is shaped like two buttocks, is native to the Seychelles Archipelago and has bred countless stories about sailors and love. It is mainly found in the sheltered Vallée de Mai Nature Reserve on Praslin, which is an official UNESCO World Heritage Site and provides the ideal habitat for these huge trees that take twenty-five years to become fruit-bearing adults. We had an enjoyable walk through the tropical forest, wandering along the well-built paths and exploring the flora and fauna.

On Curieuse Island, close to the north coast of Praslin, we stopped to see the old turtle farm where, a century ago, there had been an attempt to grow these sea-going reptiles in captivity. The effort foundered when the turtles sadly died from disease. Ashore we took a walk along some paths and passed areas where the ground was a deep-red colour, which explained why the island's nickname was 'Île Rouge'.

After making our way to the island of La Digue, we hired some bicycles and headed to the famous Anse Source d'Argent beach, where the shoreline is dominated by imposing smooth granite boulders that are a feature of Mahé and neighbouring islands. The white sand looked magnificent against the backdrop of the enormous rocks and the shallow blue water of the narrow lagoon. As the waves hit the outer reef, spray was dramatically thrown up into the air.

On Saturday 18th June, back on the main island of Mahé at Beau Vallon, we picked up my old friend Hanjo Remy. Cherry, Hanjo and I had all met in Lausanne at Diavox Language School in 1974 and remained friends ever since. At the quayside, we watched locals playing dominoes and keeping well sheltered from the sun. There was great excitement surrounding the matches, probably because of the betting that accompanied them. We later enjoyed an aperitif at a hotel with a balcony, which offered great views over the Indian Ocean.

After dinner, we lifted anchor from our mooring and set sail for African Banks, the northernmost of the Amirante Islands. On arrival the next morning, following a brief overnight sail, we found a single fishing boat lying at anchor and chose a mooring spot nearby. Discovered by Vasco da Gama in 1503, the Amirantes are a group of coral islands and atolls that form part of the larger Seychelles Archipelago. African Banks, the little island where we had stopped, is less than half a mile long and is a sooty tern breeding colony. The greyish birds were absolutely everywhere and a strong smell of guano emanated from the rocks above the high-water line. By the time we had finished exploring, the solitary fishing boat had disappeared, presumably to continue working.

Moving south on Monday morning towards Remire, or Eagle Island, we anchored *Louise* in the lee of a long reef that provided shelter from the prevailing southerly wind. We managed to get a dive in and also did some snorkelling. With no other boats around and no signs of other human activity, we felt all alone in the Indian Ocean, though the sound of the waves breaking on the reef was soothing.

Early the following morning, we set off under sail towards D'Arros Island, a 25-mile hop south. We were close-hauled on the wind throughout, but the short sail went smoothly and by lunchtime we had found a spot to moor in the narrow channel between D'Arros Island and Resource Island. Across the water on Resource, there was a big house that appeared unoccupied. We later discovered that the entire island had once been owned by Liliane Bettencourt, the L'Oréal heiress and the wealthiest lady in France.

Lunch was a treat, with fresh ceviche and sashimi made from fish caught during our morning sail. Although there was some swell affecting our anchorage, which rocked the boat a bit, we would be fine for the night. We did some more scuba diving in the afternoon, drifting through the cut. The evening was spent playing more games of Bananagrams and generally relaxing.

Deciding not to distance ourselves too far from Mahé, on Wednesday morning we travelled to Desroches Island. Tacking all the way with the wind on our nose, it was another great day for sailing. Five hours later, we were passing under full sail through the wide entrance to the lagoon, which was about 6 miles in diameter. En route we had encountered just one sailing yacht heading the opposite way, which would be the only other pleasure boat we saw during our week in the Amirantes. Before lunch, we anchored off the beach in shallow water on a sandy bottom. We went for a walk ashore in the afternoon and met the local ranger, who had been alerted to our possible arrival and who presented us with our visitor permit. It transpired that the island's resort was temporarily closed and undergoing extensive building renovations using a workforce of 200 or so Indians.

Desroches is home to a number of giant tortoises and we saw up close a few of them strolling around; Brigitte even stroked one on the chin. The ranger ushered us in the direction of the vegetable garden, which had been neatly maintained by a small group of gardeners. The head gardener, who was of Indian descent, proudly told us about the variety of spices and vegetables they were growing and kindly offered us some chillies. The garden had a particularly important role in providing sustenance for the numerous Indian workers who were all vegetarians. Aside from exploring the island, we also swam in the lagoon's calm waters.

After breakfast the next morning, Morgan, who had been out in the dinghy looking at possible dive sites, came across yet another hawksbill turtle caught in a fishing net in the Indian Ocean. To free the animal, which is an endangered species, Morgan hauled it into the dinghy where he managed to cut off the net. The turtle's life was saved, although it had suffered some damage to its tail and fin. Meanwhile, Hanjo and Cherry decided to take advantage of the totally calm conditions and went off with the paddle-boards for a leisurely tour around the bay at the end of the lagoon, leaving the rest of us to have a lazy morning.

Not long after teatime on Thursday, we lifted the anchor, hoisted the sails and began our departure from the Desroches lagoon to return to Mahé. During the first few miles, the sea was very smooth. We were assisted by a southerly wind, which was ideal to speed us on our way. By early on Friday morning, we were well within sight of Mahé and at breakfast time we dropped anchor in Beau Vallon Bay.

Politics was not far from our minds during our time in the Seychelles and, being back in Mahé, after waking early on Friday 24th June we were able to tune into the news from home and find out the result of the UK's Brexit referendum. Brigitte and I had cast our postal votes before leaving for this trip and voted to remain in the EU. On discovering the outcome, I wrote in my diary about my feelings of sadness and how shocked I was by the result. Fellow Scots had mostly rejected leaving the EU and I wondered how we would be able to hold our 300-year partnership with England together.

To put the disappointing news out of our minds, we set off for a final dive on a sunken barge close by our anchorage. Then, moving on, we motored around to the eastern side of Mahé, stopping at Cerf Island for lunch, before finally tying up again in Eden Island Marina. Our tour of the northern Seychelles was complete. We had covered 450 nautical miles in just under a fortnight, cruising off the beaten track among unspoilt islands with great anchorages. That evening, we enjoyed a meal in a traditional Creole restaurant in Victoria.

Our last day on Saturday 25th June was spent ashore, when we hired a car to tour around the south of Mahé. We stopped to take photos at Anse Intendance beach, which is a popular wedding venue and where Morgan and Cheryl had got married. We also went to the Takamaka Rum Distillery, where we got to sample their spirits, though we couldn't see the distillery in production because the sugar cane harvest had not yet commenced.

The next morning, after spending a wonderful time

together, we said goodbye to Hanjo, Cherry and Philippe, and caught our respective planes home.

* * * * *

On Saturday 30th July 2016, we began our journey back to the Seychelles and landed in the evening at Abu Dhabi, where we met up with our old Swiss friends Paul and Monique Siegenthaler. As couples we shared one thing in common – we had all been classmates at Lausanne University HEC Business School. On top of that, Brigitte and Paul had studied together at high school, so had known each other for half a century. While we chatted, Paul told us that only two days earlier, the Swiss explorer Bertrand Piccard, together with André Borschberg, the son of our university marketing professor, had touched down at Abu Dhabi Airport on the Solar Impulse aircraft, completing the first-ever round-the-world solar flight and covering about 25,000 miles. Their aircraft was powered only by solar energy, demonstrating how humans can stretch the boundaries of the achievable.

We boarded our plane in Abu Dhabi in the early hours of Sunday morning and headed south to the Seychelles. By breakfast time we had landed in Mahé and were soon aboard *Louise* in Eden Island Marina, tucking into a late breakfast. We had decided to leave immediately for Praslin Island, where we planned to spend a couple of days settling back into life on board before sailing south towards Madagascar. In the first bay that we visited we noticed a shark net, which we imagined was meant to reassure tourists that it was safe to swim. The following morning, on the Swiss national holiday of 1st August, we returned to the Vallée de Mai to take Paul and Monique to see the coco de mer forest. On this occasion, we were in the company of an amusing young guide called Sean.

On Tuesday morning, with the sea calm, we set off to Albatross Rocks where we had an excellent dive with good visibility in the warm tropical water. Our day anchorage, surrounded by beautiful granite rocks, was most attractive and reminded us of the Lavezzi Islands off the southern end of Corsica. That evening, back in Eden Island Marina, Morgan and Cheryl began the final preparations for the next stage of our Adventure, heading towards Madagascar.

The following day, we rented a car and embarked upon our second tour of Mahé, this time in the company of the Siegenthalers. In the evening, we had dinner ashore in a restaurant owned by a friendly Swiss–Italian lady who had been in the Seychelles for many years.

Ready for our departure from Eden Island Marina on the morning of Thursday 4th August, we reflected on the relaxing time that we had spent on these beautiful islands in the Indian Ocean. The Seychelles were one of the most outstanding destinations that we had visited, with warm waters, wonderful scenery and a friendly population.

The voyage from Mahé Island to the northern tip of Madagascar is approximately 600 nautical miles, and we had decided to break up the journey south. The most convenient stopover was at the low-lying Alphonse Group, comprising two atolls located 240 nautical miles south-west of Mahé, which we reached on Friday after a smooth overnight sail. By the afternoon, we were safely moored in the lee of the reef at Bijoutier Island.

After initially anchoring just outside the reef, we managed to pass over the shallow sandbar with *Louise* and re-anchor for the night in a more sheltered spot. The water was quite murky with sandy sediment, caused by the reef being constantly pounded by the ocean waves. Inside the reef, which was completely visible at low tide, we relaxed while contemplating the vast Indian Ocean surrounding us on all sides. On the beach we found turtle nests and fallen palm trees that had probably been uprooted by a cyclone which hit the area in April.

Lifting anchor after breakfast on Saturday 6th August, we traced our way back out into the open water, hoisting sails in the lee of Bijoutier Island. Soon we were being carried along by the south-east trades that were well established and blowing at about Force 5, which was typical for the time of the year. Sailing fairly close-hauled, we headed off in a south-westerly direction. All day we made good progress towards Farquhar Island, one of the most southerly islands in the Seychelles and roughly the halfway point on our route to Madagascar. During the night, the wind strengthened a little and the sea was a bit bumpy, but we continued to move along at a steady pace.

On Sunday morning we altered course slightly, bearing away to pass in the lee of Farquhar Island, and for a while we got relief from the ocean swell. There was a further increase in the wind strength and we took in a second reef in the mainsail that morning. Sailing only with reefed main and storm jib, *Louise* remained nicely balanced. As we started to close in on northern Madagascar, as expected the wind rose further so that by dusk we had experienced a full gale, with gusts over 40 knots. This is common when passing Cap d'Ambre during the winter months from May to October.

As a consequence of the wind strength, the waves were noticeably higher and occasionally would give the decks a total rinsing. Just before dinner we were overtaken by a massive container ship that steamed close by. With the challenging downwind sailing conditions, the autopilot struggled to work properly, so Morgan and I took turns to steer at the helm.

An hour before midnight, the loom of the lighthouse

beam at the northern point of Madagascar became visible, an indication that we were nearing our destination. After midnight we began to feel some relief from the waves as we drew into the lee of Cap d'Ambre, the northerly tip of Madagascar. The huge island is over twice the size of the UK and stretches around 1,000 miles from north to south.

The Siegenthalers had taken the 650-nautical-mile passage, which was one of our bumpier rides, completely in their stride. During the sail, while *Louise* bounced along in the choppy seas, Monique didn't let up with her reading and Paul kept busy filming life on board; both remained cool, calm and collected throughout the three-day journey.

We found a good mooring spot in flat water at D'Andovo Honkou Bay, at the end of the small Orontani Peninsula in the far north-west of Madagascar, and were very happy to drop anchor late on the morning of Monday 8th August, seemingly all alone. After having lunch, we settled down to a restful siesta in our quiet surroundings. We later discovered that we were no longer on our own, having sighted a Swan 90 named *Alea* anchored in the adjacent bay.

In the afternoon we took a walk ashore, hiking up the hillside overlooking the water. The ground was brown-coloured and parched, a reminder of the eastern Atlantic coast in Argentina, and there were several baobab trees, which are found in arid regions of Madagascar. The evening was spent on board *Louise*, relaxing and catching up on any sleep lost during the passage down from the Seychelles. Above deck we stared at a clear night sky filled with glittering stars.

On Tuesday morning, we started heading south, making a lunchtime stop to enjoy our first dive in Madagascar. At our anchorage we were greeted by a soaring sea eagle. Continuing south we moved on to Nosy Mitsio, where we strolled on the beach late in the afternoon, watching the local fishermen prepare their dugout canoes before launching them. They explained that the evening was a good time to fish, and they normally stayed out for the night in their tiny outrigger-style boats. Aside from rowing, their main means of propulsion came from a single lateen sail.

As we walked along the beach, village children came rushing over to us. We shared some biscuits with them, which they swiftly consumed, all smiling happily. The fishing village we went to was cut off from the mainland without electricity, and life appeared to be very simple. Rows of fish that had been neatly filleted and cut open hung on lines to dry in the wind. We were struck by how friendly and approachable everyone was, all eager to engage in conversation.

On Wednesday, the last stop before our next destination of Nosy Be was Tsarabanjina Island. Morgan shared childhood memories with us of the time his family ran diving excursions for tourists visiting Nosy Be. Morgan had learnt to scuba dive on Tsarabanjina. Today it is home to a luxury resort and because we weren't able to book a table in the restaurant, which was reserved for residents, we settled for cocktails instead. Before relaxing for dinner on board *Louise*, we witnessed a perfect Indian Ocean sunset with the last rays of golden light glowing on the horizon.

The following morning, we covered the last few miles before reaching Nosy Be in the afternoon, marking our 'official' arrival into Madagascar on Thursday 11th August. Morgan went ashore to meet local officials to record our entrance to the country and get our passports stamped. The harbour at Hell-Ville was humming with activity, much of it related to the island's tourism.

Hell-Ville is named after a French admiral called Anne Chrétien Louis de Hell, who was governor of the Isle de Bourbon in the Indian Ocean – today called Réunion –

from May 1838 to October 1841. It wasn't until later in the nineteenth century that France invaded Madagascar and imposed colonial rule. Following the Second World War, the country was given partial freedom but this led to difficulties, and after aligning itself with the Eastern bloc and communism, it eventually slipped into bankruptcy. Madagascar remains one of the poorest countries in the developing world, with the majority of its inhabitants living on less than one dollar per day. This means that many Madagascans are among the world's 'bottom billion', a phrase coined by the British economist Professor Paul Collier.

We learnt that a local 'fixer', whom we had engaged for the duration of our stay, had found us a rental car for touring around Nosy Be. Stepping ashore at the landing pier on Friday morning, we met our guide who proudly revealed the car he had procured for us: a bright-yellow, decades-old Citroën 2CV. Brigitte and Monique quickly surmised that sitting in the back of a 2CV for hours while travelling on less-than-smooth roads would most likely be very uncomfortable. Though he was disappointed when we turned down the vehicle he was offering, the guide went off to secure some alternative transport and soon returned with a far more appropriate four-wheel-drive vehicle.

The first stop on our island tour was a nature reserve not far from Hell-Ville that was home to lemurs and other animals such as crocodiles, snakes and chameleons. The property included a well-maintained and attractive distillery that specialised in producing essence of ylang-ylang tree leaves, which is used for fragrances and aromatherapy products. Fresh leaves were neatly laid out on the floor to dry before being put into the brightly polished copper stills to be boiled with alcohol.

Passing nearby the airport, we deviated down a dusty

track to find the Manga Soa Lodge resort, which had been recommended by friends who had visited it earlier in the year. We stopped for a delicious lunch of spaghetti with shrimp sauce and refreshments. In the afternoon, we drove up to the island's highest peak and took in a beautiful pre-sunset view of the surrounds including the sea. Meanwhile, Morgan and Cheryl had moved *Louise* a few miles north and moored at Anse de Cratère, where we rejoined the boat.

On Saturday 13th August, in the morning we motored with *Louise* a short distance to a little island off Nosy Be called Nosy Tanikely, where we planned to dive with leopard or zebra sharks. We easily found the sharks and managed to swim with them, finding them to be quite docile. Morgan even tickled one of the shark's tails. Upon resurfacing, we discovered a yacht anchored to our stern, which we recognised as SV *Delos*. It was owned by two brothers who set sail from Seattle in 2009 and who have been at sea, circumnavigating the world, ever since. We invited the crew over to *Louise* before lunch, meeting skipper Brian Trautman and his brother Brady. The sailing team on board SV *Delos* have risen in fame through their popular video blog, with well over 500,000 YouTube subscribers.

After lunch they kindly welcomed me aboard their boat, and on stepping below I spied a small distilling apparatus in the saloon, which they employed to manufacture alcohol and make a range of spirits using flavour compounds for whisky, rum or gin spirit. The equipment had been acquired in Australia, after they had been shocked by the cost of spirits locally and had decided to make their own. I was invited to taste some of their products and found them quite palatable. When I was about to leave, they filled a bottle with a sample of their spirit, which I promised to send to Scotland for laboratory analysis. The test results later revealed that the spirit was well made and had no significant defects, and so I emailed Brian the good news. Some months later, I discovered that the story of the on-board tasting had featured in a YouTube video, and I had thus earned a minor role in the SV *Delos* saga, making praise of their home-made spirit.

On Saturday evening we moved further south to Russian Bay, which is so called because of its role as anchorage for the Russian naval fleet during the Russo-Japanese War of 1904–05, when its ships coming from the Baltic sailed around the Cape of Good Hope en route to the theatre of war in the Pacific, attracting worldwide attention. Most of the Russian vessels that stopped over in Madagascar were sunk by the Japanese Navy in the Battle of Tsushima Strait in May 1905, the first major naval battle fought between modern, steel battleship fleets.

Over the course of the following week we continued south, covering small distances each day and taking in some islands along the way. The weather was excellent and everyone felt relaxed taking in the lovely coastal scenery. Every day we went ashore to stretch our legs and also did some diving, although the sea life and underwater scenery was less impressive compared to many other places where we had dived.

The village on Nosy Berafia was a particular highlight, with local residents and children welcoming us on the beach en masse. The children had toy-size model outrigger canoes, which they demonstrated in the water. Meanwhile, the village ladies were busily pounding rice with mallets to separate the grain from the husk. With the permission of the chief, we strolled around the village, wandering between the straw huts erected on stilts that mainly only have one room. On our last morning at Nosy Berafia, just next to *Louise* a mother humpback whale and her calf played together, which Brigitte and Monique were able to watch close up.

Before leaving our final island stop at Nosy Iranja, we went for a walk on the long sand spit that extends into the sea from the island. We ran along the white sandy beach, with the waves splashing at our heels, while Morgan caught the scene on film with the drone.

On Friday 19th August, back in Nosy Be we began making preparations for the journey back home. Our flights were booked via Mayotte, the French overseas department close to north-west Madagascar and part of the Comoros Archipelago, which stayed French when independence was declared in Comoros in 1974. The short flight from Nosy Be got us to Mayotte's airport at Dzaoudzi on Petite-Terre Island late in the afternoon.

With only limited time to take in some of Mayotte's culture before catching our onward connections, on Saturday morning we left our hotel and took a foot ferry from Petite-Terre over to Mamoudzou, the capital of Mayotte's largest island, Grande-Terre. The streets bustled with residents going about their daily activities and we managed to find a few gifts in the market to take home.

The next day, when Brigitte, Paul and Monique boarded their plane for Paris, they were most surprised to discover that their flight wasn't direct but had been routed via Madagascar's capital, Antananarivo, resulting in a detour back south. I was travelling to London via Nairobi alone, and as I waited at the gate to board my plane, a group of elderly pilgrims dressed neatly in white were getting ready to join the same flight and start their journey to Mecca. Sitting on the plane bound for the Kenyan capital, I reflected on how Islam has held sway as the main religion in many parts of East Africa for centuries, dating back to when Arabs dominated trading on the Swahili coast, also known as the Zanj. A century before the Portuguese first arrived in 1500, Chinese fleets had exchanged goods with local Muslim traders. The European colonisers who followed were often highly zealous, seeing themselves as crusaders and not hesitating to promulgate war around the shores of the Indian Ocean.

* * * * *

For the rest of August and most of September 2016, *Louise* remained in Madagascar, while back at home Brigitte and I celebrated our sixtieth birthdays with family and friends. Cheryl and Morgan had stayed in Madagascar with *Louise*, readying the boat for the trip south to the Cape of Good Hope. They met up with their old friends Toya and Steven Louw from Walvis Bay in Namibia, who had offered to join *Louise* for our passage to Cape Town. The crew of four duly set off from Nosy Be to travel the brief distance to Mayotte, where we had agreed to rendezvous.

Leaving Brigitte behind in London, my journey to Mayotte involved a connecting flight to and an overnight stopover in the bustling capital of Kenya. Alastair Whyte, who had already sailed on *Louise* during our trip from Bali to Phuket in 2015, had agreed to join us as we resumed our travels through the Indian Ocean, and we met at the gate to board the Kenya Airways plane to Mayotte. On a day with very clear skies, while airborne we had an exceptional view of the coast of Tanzania as well as Pemba Island, and then, further south, the bigger island of Unguja, or Zanzibar as it is commonly referred to, which was surrounded by a beautifully coloured coral reef.

In ancient times, Zanzibar was one of the most prominent trading posts in East Africa, forming a central role in Swahili coastal trade. Vasco da Gama visited the island in 1499, which led to Portuguese rule that lasted for two centuries before Zanzibar fell under the control of the Sultanate of Oman. Independence finally arrived in 1964, after a revolution that killed thousands of people and resulted in both Pemba and Zanzibar joining the new state of Tanzania.

Sadly, we would not be stopping on this part of the African coast, which is laden with history, as we were keen to push on south to take advantage of the changing season and return to the Atlantic on our way homewards. We were well into spring, but as we sailed down the eastern coast of South Africa we would need to keep a watchful eye out for south-westerly 'busters' – a term used to describe southerly blows created by depressions sweeping through from the South Atlantic that can come in quick succession.

Arriving in Mayotte on Sunday 25th September, as we looked out from the plane before landing we could see *Louise* moored at Dzaoudzi on Petite-Terre Island, next to the airport. With the full complement of six crew all gathered, we had our first meal together in a local restaurant called Le Fare, where we tucked into some delicious steaks.

The following morning, we took a minibus to the airport to clear immigration and check out of Mayotte. Early on Monday afternoon, with the safety briefing completed, and the dinghy and davits packed away in our stern locker, we were ready to leave. Lifting anchor, we motored south towards a cut in the reef that led out into the waters of the Mozambique Channel. Later that afternoon, we enjoyed great views of the slopes of Grande-Terre covered with green vegetation and rising to almost 2,000 feet above sea level. It took a long time before Mayotte had faded from sight.

Out in the open sea, my thoughts turned to our destination at the southern tip of Africa, 2,000 nautical miles away. Morgan had been studying the weather forecast and we speculated on the chances of making a non-stop passage. The long-range forecast looked good, with settled weather in the Mozambique Channel and no sign at this stage of depressions on our track south. But forecasts were always changeable and we would have to be patient and monitor the weather outlook on a daily basis.

The sea was flat calm for the first twenty-four hours of the passage. When the south-east trade winds are well established across the southern Indian Ocean, Madagascar's high mountain creates a vast wind shadow to the east of the island, across a large part of the Mozambique Channel. On our first night at sea, we had a clear sky accompanied by the galaxies shining bright through the Earth's atmosphere.

After breakfast on Tuesday morning, Morgan discovered a mechanical hitch with our motor, as well as water in the engine room. The problem was traced to a broken pipe in the engine's heat exchanger, which Morgan and Steven worked all morning to fix, enabling us to restart the engine.

Now into our second day at sea, we had distanced ourselves from Madagascar's shoreline, moving out of its wind shadow, and the breeze had started to pick up. With a steadily increasing easterly, we were able to set the spinnaker in the afternoon. Leaving the autopilot to steer for a while, I was distracted and didn't notice that we had borne away too much downwind. The change of course took the wind out of the sail, which caused the spinnaker to wrap around the forestay. It took a good hour to untangle the sail and get it back down on deck, but with patience we succeeded.

Meanwhile, we kept a watchful lookout for fishing boats and other vessels, which we saw regularly. During the early hours of Wednesday morning, a fishing vessel radioed *Louise* to enquire about our draught, seemingly worried that our keel might get caught in their huge net. Fortunately, the boat's net was floating almost 30 feet below the surface and so we were safe to pass over it. Later that afternoon, we hooked a substantial tuna, which Steven fought hard to haul in, building up a full sweat in the process. After a long struggle, the fish was next to the boat and we were at our stations, ready to hook it with the gaff, when the line broke and the lucky fish swam away.

After dark on Wednesday evening, concerned about another fishing boat on our path, we radioed it to ask what the master's intentions were. A curt response came back over the radio – 'Fishing business'. The vessel then turned on its spotlight and *Louise* was briefly lit up by the powerful beam. The number and size of similar vessels that we encountered in this area was an indicator of the importance of the Mozambique Channel as a fishing ground.

Life on board *Louise* was relaxed and our daily activities aside from fishing included baking, reading and playing board games. We were making good progress south, and by the early hours of Thursday 29th September we had picked up the Mozambique Current, a strong current in the Indian Ocean that flows south along the east coast of Africa in the Mozambique Channel, between Mozambique and Madagascar.

At dawn, while Alastair was taking over the watch, he heard a faint screeching that was audible inside the saloon. Back up in the cockpit, he noticed a school of dolphins swimming close by *Louise*. Some of them were jumping out of the water, while others played at the bow. The adult mammals were quite big, around 10 feet long, and there were also a few juveniles in the school. We identified them as Risso's dolphins, distinguished by their bulbous heads without a beak.

During Thursday morning, favourable winds enabled us

to do more downwind sailing with the spinnaker. But then the wind started to drop and so around midday Morgan flew the drone to take some aerial shots. Initially, it circled above the boat successfully, but the second time round the control panel indicated that contact with the drone had been lost and it gradually disappeared out of sight and was gone, together with the film footage, which was disappointing.

With the spinnaker packed away but the wind still well behind the beam, we hoisted our other downwind sail, the Code 0 reacher. The sailing was exceptionally smooth and we continued to move at good speed for the whole day and through the night. It also helped that the Mozambique Current was still giving us a good push. At dinner time on Friday, we spotted that a tear had emerged on one of the reacher's seams, so we furled it to avoid further damage.

The night of Friday 30th September, our fifth at sea, began with a pitch-black sky and the stars in splendid view. But during the early hours of 1st October, as we passed the southern end of the Mozambique Channel where it opens out into the Indian Ocean, the sky clouded over, signalling a change to the weather. The day before, we had spotted on the long-range weather chart that a low-pressure weather system was emerging from the South Atlantic and eventually would make its way towards our position, with an accompanying front bringing strong southerly winds and waves. With the safety of the boat and crew as our first priority, our hopes of making a non-stop passage to Cape Town were definitively dashed. The question now was, where we would go to on the coast to shelter from the oncoming gale?

At breakfast time on Saturday 1st October, a front passed over and the wind picked up, shifting to the south-east. In these conditions we were sailing swiftly and we altered course westerly to head towards the African coast. We debated the pros and cons of going to Richards Bay, the most northerly harbour in South Africa, over a distance of around 300 nautical miles, or to Maputo Bay in Mozambique, about 200 nautical miles further north. Based on the shorter distance involved, and the fact that our arrival in Richards Bay might coincide with the passing front and the associated high winds, a decision was made to divert west to Maputo Bay. The next twenty-four hours consisted of a high-speed dash to the shelter of Mozambique's shores.

Louise moved along boldly, reaching on the building seas as we closed in fast on the African coast. The wind speed rose above 40 knots at times, but the boat handled the conditions really well. Approaching Maputo Bay from the sea requires a lengthy detour northwards around a long sandbank that extends from the Machangulo Peninsula Nature Reserve at the eastern side of the huge bay. The last 15 nautical miles were hard going, as we motor-sailed in the choppy waves created by the gale.

We dropped anchor in a narrow channel under the low cliffs off the north of Inhaca Island, but a strong flood tide was running, pushing *Louise* into the wind, and the boat started to ride over the anchor. Hemmed in by the beach on one side and a sandbank on the other, we felt very unsafe. Struggling with the high winds, we managed to lift anchor and avoid drifting any closer to the shallow water. Breathing a sigh of relief, we motored off to find a safer spot to moor *Louise*, eventually settling for an area of shallow waters in the southern part of Maputo Bay, but quite far from land. The only other boats visible were Chinese dredgers that were working to keep the shipping channel deep enough for cargo vessels to pass through.

At 7 p.m. on Sunday evening, the anchor was safely down with the full length of the boat's chain paid out, so we sat down to eat a nice hot dinner. There was no question of going ashore, with the wind still blowing strong from the south. Any journey in the dinghy across the 10 miles of the bay would be hazardous. Meanwhile, I had alerted our insurers that we were planning to make a stop in Mozambique waters, which was excluded under our policy, to shelter from the strong weather conditions. We received a quick response, presumably after they had conducted some research to verify the circumstances and consulted with the underwriter, assenting to our plan.

After breakfast the next day, we took stock of the situation and checked *Louise* for any damage that the wind had inflicted upon her. Armed with needle and thread, Alastair, Toya and Morgan set about making some repairs to the sails and the cockpit cover, while the rest of us completed other chores on the boat. By Monday evening, after a hard day's work we were all ready to contemplate leaving as soon as there was a break in the rough weather.

From where we swung at anchor in Maputo Bay, the city skyline was clearly visible in the distance behind *Louise*'s stern. During the colonial era, Maputo was known as Lourenço Marques, the name given to the city by the Portuguese, the country's former colonial masters. From 1976, it was renamed after Chief Maputsu I of the Tembe clan.

On the second day at anchor, the wind began to die down and the bay started to come back to life with the odd boat passing. Just after dawn on Wednesday 5th October, following three nights spent patiently waiting, we set off to sail down the coast to Richards Bay in South Africa. Leaving Maputo Bay, we were obliged to make a detour of 40 nautical miles, initially heading north to avoid the dangers of the long sandbank that borders the sea. We had considered going through the narrow Canal do Sul at Inhaca Island, but when checking the gap with the binoculars there were breaking waves visible, which made it too dangerous to risk.

Despite the wind having dropped, the sea swell made running under engine slow, with the boat slamming uncomfortably into the waves. At one point, we were entertained by the antics of a humpback whale performing some aerobatics, which involved leaping out of the water a number of times with a huge splash to follow. The afternoon concluded with a beautiful sunset over the African shoreline. By midnight we had entered South African waters and were making better progress, though still motoring. The sky was very clear, creating a bright starry night.

By breakfast the next morning, the wind was starting to build as another upcoming weather system approached from the south. We were now assisted by a northerly wind and reached Richards Bay around midday. Passing between the breakwaters, we made our way into the harbour, which was tucked in north of the main channel adjacent to Naval Island, where we dropped anchor on Thursday 6th October.

We were welcomed by Alice and Alfredo, a retired couple who were also on their way south and who rowed over to *Louise* from their sailing boat *On Vera*. Morgan had known the couple for some years, having met them during their respective travels. Alfredo, a retired Italian businessman, and his wife Alice, from the USA, had first become acquainted in the Chagos Islands. It was there, about ten years earlier, that Alice had quite literally jumped ship, leaving her first husband on board their yacht after deciding to join Alfredo, who was sailing single-handed at that time.

In the small ships' harbour there was not much room for *Louise* to swing, and while we were having drinks before dinner, a powerful gust struck and we felt the boat heel. Pushed by the sudden blast of wind, *Louise* swung 90 degrees and began to move astern, which was a sign that we were dragging our anchor and were out of control, drifting rapidly towards the nearby shore. Leaping into action, we turned on the engine and managed to stop the boat with the depth gauge reading 2 metres, just before we ran out of depth. After re-anchoring, we settled down for the night, ready to push further south again the following day.

The Richards Bay Coal Terminal was once the largest such export facility in the world, but in spite of climate change it is still busy exporting fossil minerals to Asia and elsewhere. Once the wind had picked up, coal dust blew across the harbour and started to lightly cover the deck. We remained on board all day to avoid formally checking into South Africa, which we would do on our arrival in Durban. On Friday evening, we motored out of Richards Bay to continue on our journey and make the brief hop to Durban.

The wind was initially south-easterly, and after sailing a short way out to sea we tacked onto port to head south. Early in the journey, we passed through the fleet of empty-bottom ships waiting to collect their cargo of minerals. We counted over forty vessels at anchor, rocking from side to side in the swell. During the night we motor-sailed slowly down the coast, which was well lit and quite visible in spite of some drizzle falling. By 7 a.m. the following morning, we had cleared the Durban breakwater and entered the compact but busy commercial docks in South Africa's third most populous city and the largest conurbation on the Indian Ocean coast.

On Saturday 8th October, we tied up on the Royal Natal Yacht Club's rickety pontoon, which was badly in need of repair, and went ashore to visit the marina office, to enquire about finding a safer berth for the night when the next big blow was expected to hit. The marina's manager didn't seem to share our worry that *Louise* might not be securely moored, given the poor state of the marina. Overhearing our discussion, the receptionist suggested that we call the yacht club's commodore, whom she thought would be more helpful. When I eventually managed to reach Gordon Rose, who was not at the club that morning, he was very apologetic about the condition of the pontoon moorings. For our safety, he recommended that we moved *Louise* to a fishing dock at Bluff in the city's inner harbour.

Taking his advice, we left the marina and moved to the suggested location. On finding a fishing boat tied up to the dock, we moored alongside it. Two friendly faces greeted us from the deck of the vessel. They were from Dar Es Salaam in Tanzania and staying on board as skeleton crew while the boat was laid up for servicing. We couldn't help but notice that, hanging from a clothes line that had been put up behind the vessel's bridge, a number of plucked chickens were drying in the wind.

Once *Louise* was safely secured, we jumped into a taxi to head to the immigration office in order to officially check into South Africa. After completing the formalities in the cavernous Customs House building, which was almost empty except for a couple of Filipino sailors who looked eager to spend their Saturday leave visiting the city, we went to a restaurant for lunch. Later that afternoon, Steven, Toya, Alastair and I attended a rugby union test match at the Kings Park Stadium between South Africa and New Zealand. The atmosphere in the ground was naturally hyped up and the sell-out crowd mostly cheered for the home team. The game, however, ended in a humiliating 57–15 defeat for the Springboks, with the All Blacks comprehensively outclassing the hosts.

In the evening, we had some cocktails in a smart lounge in the suburb of Musgrave where, attired in T-shirts that we had worn to the rugby game, we felt rather underdressed. We finished the night in a nearby Indian restaurant and had an excellent curry. On Sunday morning, Alastair and I set off to explore more of Durban, starting with brunch in a small bakery. Emerging from the cafe, we burst out laughing when we walked straight into Steven and Toya who had been breakfasting in an adjacent cafe. The rest of the day was spent walking around the city, whose centre was very quiet but there was a crowd having fun on the boardwalk.

The following morning the weather was settled, and at 6 a.m. on Monday 10th October we cast off, leaving our hideaway in Bluff, and motored the full length of Durban Harbour and out through the breakwater into the open sea. The city skyline, including the downtown office towers and apartments, stood out magnificently in the early morning sunlight. The impression left behind was of a friendly city, but one that had experienced more prosperous times.

Before the next weather front arrived we were hoping to reach East London, which would be our third stopover in South Africa in quick succession. There were 250 nautical miles to go to reach the city's harbour, which is formed by the Buffalo River that runs into the Indian Ocean. Heading south, the coastline remained visible most of the time. Known as the Wild Coast, the stretch between Durban and East London is a popular destination for holidaymakers. We managed to pick up some of the powerful Agulhas Current, which flows down the coast towards the Southern Ocean at about 2 knots. On the way we were treated to regular sightings of whales that were travelling in the same direction as us, taking advantage of the southerly current to migrate from their tropical breeding grounds. The whales were easy to spot, as each time they exhaled they would send a spray of water into the air.

The wind remained favourable for the leg and we sailed

through the night, so that by breakfast on Tuesday morning we had luckily found a berth on the visitors' pontoon at the Buffalo River Yacht Club, where we tied up. There was little sign of life in the club, and during our stay no one asked for any mooring fees, so before departing we put some cash in an envelope and dropped it through the clubhouse's letterbox.

Alastair and I set off into town for a stroll to find a shorefront restaurant. From our chosen eatery, sitting on the balcony enjoying a salad, we could see the imposing sand dunes to the north that were set behind a long, white, sandy beach facing the Indian Ocean. The sea was also still rough as whitecaps were plainly visible on the waves. After we paid the bill, the restaurant owner warned us not to walk on the promenade for the sake of our personal safety. It was disappointing not to wander along the beachfront, but we heeded his advice and returned in a taxi to the boat.

Our stay in East London was brief, and by evening on Wednesday 12th October we were back out at sea. We hoped that this leg would be the final one of our stop-start passage around the south-eastern coast of Africa. By erring on the side of caution, and sheltering in harbours to avoid each of the successive southerly busters, we had saved *Louise* from potential damage and also kept ourselves safe. And by taking the extra time, we had been able to visit places that we would otherwise not have seen.

Although we still had just over 500 nautical miles to run to Cape Town, the weather had settled down with high pressure becoming re-established. Over the next three days at sea we saw even more whales, including one minke that passed close by our stern, as well as penguins and seals. The temperature started to drop noticeably as we pushed further south. Passing Port Elizabeth, we altered course west and were helped along by a good following wind.

Later on Thursday evening, while dozing in my bunk, I was roused from my sleep by raised voices. Everyone down below was woken up and we were all asked to come on deck as soon as possible. During a gybe, which had just been made, the mainsail had developed a huge tear and ripped apart. We managed to drop the sail and fold it on the boom. It had been on our mind that it might not last much longer, so the situation hadn't come as a complete surprise.

With Cape Town about 300 nautical miles ahead, without the mainsail it was now a case of motoring to our destination. Thus, we spent our last day in the Indian Ocean during the Adventure. It struck me that the time it had taken to cross this ocean seemed to have gone by very quickly.

On Saturday 15th October at 1 p.m., we passed Cape Agulhas, the most southerly point of Africa. After sailing over 40,000 nautical miles, *Louise* was back in the Atlantic Ocean heading home and we toasted the occasion with shots of vodka and lemon. For Morgan, this was his fourth rounding of Cape Agulhas, the first of which had been in 1986 when he was only eight years old. Just before midday we rounded the Cape of Good Hope, the most famous of the southern capes in Africa. Shortly afterwards, as if saluting our arrival into Atlantic waters, a humpback whale flipped up his tail close to the boat, just managing to avoid the bow.

Arriving in Cape Town later in the afternoon, on our approach we had a great view of the Twelve Apostles and Table Mountain, a sight which sailors dream of experiencing. By teatime, we were tied up safely in the Victoria & Alfred Waterfront Marina, on the pontoon at the Cape Grace Hotel. That evening we all went out for a celebratory meal together and later discovered a great bar where we had some drinks.

The next day we said our farewells, thanking in particular our newfound Namibian friends Steven and Toya for being great crew-mates during the successful completion of the passage to Cape Town, and also expressing my appreciation for Cheryl and Morgan. Alastair, to whom I was particularly grateful, had decided to prolong his stay for a few extra days to explore the area. Most kindly, before his departure he left us with a case of excellent local red wine, which we would certainly make the most of in November, when Brigitte and I returned for the final leg of the *Louise* Adventure.

Chapter 12 – South Atlantic High
Cape Town, South Africa to St Helena and Grenada, Lesser Antilles

Goose-winged, Eastern Cape, South Africa

It was approaching summer in Cape Town in early November 2016 as our thoughts turned to our return to the northern hemisphere. The Adventure had so far taken *Louise* over 40,000 nautical miles, but now she was back in the Atlantic Ocean, our home waters, having passed the Cape of Good Hope in mid-October.

Portuguese explorer Bartolomeu Dias first reached the southern tip of Africa in 1488, giving it its original name of 'Cape of Storms', and was followed by Vasco da Gama almost a decade later. The landmark was renamed the Cape of Good Hope, reflecting the optimism of the Portuguese colonialists as they dreamt about the riches that they hoped to find in the Orient. However, it was the Dutch who established Table Bay and the settlement at Cape Town a few miles north of the Cape, as their trading firm, the Dutch East India Company, had sought and found a staging post for ships that were passing between the Atlantic and Indian Oceans. Our stopover was planned much in the same vein and, with barely three weeks of time available to spend in port, there was a lot to do in preparation for the transatlantic crossing that lay ahead. Aside from the mainsail repair, new batteries had to be installed and other routine maintenance checks were necessary to make sure *Louise* was properly equipped and primed for the long trip north through the Atlantic. Cheryl and Morgan worked particularly hard to get the boat ready to ensure we would reach the Caribbean before the year end.

On Friday 4th November 2016, Brigitte and I flew back to Cape Town together with Ian Reid, all keen to set sail. The next morning, when we attended the Customs House to check out, everything seemed to be going smoothly until the clerk noticed a minor anomaly in our paperwork. The error resulted in the boat being fined the equivalent of twenty-five dollars. We offered to pay on the spot but were told that we would have to wait until Monday, which delayed our intended departure time by forty-eight hours. The silver lining of the forced extension to our stay was the opportunity to explore the area further.

On Sunday we drove to the False Bay Yacht Club in Simon's Town, where we met Stuart Kirk and his charming wife Charlie. I had briefly met the couple at the Cape Town International Boat Show, which was running at the V&A Waterfront in mid-October when *Louise* arrived in Cape Town. They had just launched their new boat named *Urchin*, a good-looking, 56-foot exploration yacht that was designed by Chuck Paine and built locally by Jacobs Bros. The proud couple revealed they were planning their inaugural cruise in the Indian Ocean. We also recognised another boat in the marina, *Lady of the Lowlands* from Holland, which we had seen in Durban. A lady popped her head out of the hatch, keen to have a chat, and she shared her story of sailing around the world for the past eight years with her husband.

Later, we had a walk to the Cape of Good Hope at the end of the Cape Peninsula, which overlooked an exceptionally settled sea, before returning to the marina in Cape Town.

After breakfast on the morning of Monday 7th November, we slipped our moorings bound for the Caribbean. On our way there, we planned to stop at both St Helena and Ascension Island. The harbour's pedestrian bridge had been raised to let us through and some onlookers waved at us as we passed by. Heading out beyond the breakwater, we hoisted full sail and once we had cleared the wind shadow of Table Mountain, the sails filled in the breeze.

While heating up lunch in the galley, Cheryl noticed that the oven had switched itself off and so she called Morgan for help. On opening the hatch of the cockpit floor to inspect the main electric-circuit breaker, Morgan found that the lazarette (or stern compartment) had filled up with water. Reacting to the emergency, I immediately grabbed the helm and we tacked, turning the boat 180 degrees to point back towards the shoreline. Morgan soon discovered that, for some unknown reason, the stern door seal was not working as it had allowed seawater to flood into *Louise*. Our first priority was to empty the water from the locker and, with help from Ian, we used our portable petrol-driven pump and cleared out most of the water fairly quickly. By slowing the boat down, we also managed to limit the intake of seawater through the stern door to just a trickle.

Within a couple of hours of leaving, we found ourselves back in Cape Town's marina at the same berth that we had only recently vacated. Without any delay, we set about resolving the problem, beginning with emptying the lazarette and washing all its contents in fresh water. Particular attention was paid to checking the electrical systems, which we also rinsed using distilled water to protect them from corrosion. Fortunately, we were able to sort everything out and by Tuesday had successfully restored the stern door's seal system to normal working order. With all the problems fixed, we felt confident that the journey could resume.

A happy consolation of the unexpected stopover was that I had the time to visit Paarl in the Western Cape that same evening and have dinner with my friend Lambert Retief, who had been suffering from cancer, and also his wife Carole. While we chatted over the meal in their dining room, Lambert's natural sense of humour shone through and it was obvious to me how pleased he was to be surrounded by his family. As he said farewell, he handed me two very fine bottles of South African red wine from his cellar, which I stored in *Louise*'s wine locker later that evening.

By working hard, within forty-eight hours we had turned the boat around and, on Wednesday 9th November, a beautiful sunny morning, once again we went under the bridges leading out from the Victoria & Alfred Waterfront Marina. Table Mountain was magnificently silhouetted in the background. We soon passed Robben Island, heading out into the rolling seas of the South Atlantic. The weather forecast for the coming days was ideal for beginning our 1,700-nautical-mile passage to St Helena. A strong southerly wind, which was already well established, would swiftly carry *Louise* north. With a steady 25–30-knot wind on our stern, in the first twenty-four hours we managed to cover 250 miles. On one of Brigitte's watches, she broke the boat's cruising speed record with a peak of 19 knots surfing down a wave. These favourable sailing conditions stayed with us for several days, helping us to record some excellent daily runs. When up on deck everyone enjoyed the sailing, and in the times off watch we mainly caught up on sleep or read books.

The underwater Walvis Ridge mountain range stretches out into the South Atlantic from Namibia. It was while navigating a shallow patch on the ridge that, late on Saturday afternoon, we witnessed the spectacle of a full-size humpback whale breaching the surface not far from *Louise*. It made a huge splash as it fell back into the ocean. A little later on, a pod of three other humpbacks started to rollick about, flapping their fins and entertaining us before exhaling and submerging out of sight.

Just after midday on Sunday, we crossed over the tropic of Capricorn, an invisible line in the ocean and a marker that warmer weather and more sunshine could be expected. Shortly afterwards, a quick check of the log revealed that we had clocked up 1,000 nautical miles since leaving Cape Town.

Our progress was being assisted by the presence of high pressure to our west, with good southerlies blowing to the east of the anticyclone. The South Atlantic High, or St Helena High, is a semi-permanent feature of the weather in this region of the Atlantic Ocean. Clear blue skies accompanied by fresh winds brought smiles to all on board. But the wind was forecast to fade as we progressed further north. As expected, the last three days of the run to St Helena were completed under motor, as the sea gradually became becalmed.

During the evening of Monday 14th November, we experienced a supermoon, when the moon was at its closest to Earth in over sixty-eight years. Using the binoculars, we were able to observe the features of the moon's surface, which stood out really clearly. This was a rare opportunity, as the next time that the moon is due to be as near to Earth again is not until 2034. Just before midnight we crossed the Greenwich meridian at 0 degrees longitude, marking the point at which *Louise* had travelled 360 degrees from west to east around the world.

My watch in the early hours of Tuesday morning was going very smoothly when a blue icon appeared on the chart plotter, indicating that a ship was nearby. The name of the vessel, RMS *St Helena*, soon popped up. This was the island's mail ship, also on her way from Cape Town to St Helena. As she passed close by *Louise*, overtaking us, I radioed the vessel and spoke to the duty officer. Overhearing my conversation, Cheryl got up and I handed her the radio so she could speak to the officer herself and exchange news. We discovered that the *St Helena* had been delayed in departing from South Africa because the day after we left Cape Town, a powerful gale had led to a temporary ban on all movements in and out of the harbour.

The same morning, the conditions for sailing were excellent and we ran under spinnaker all day. In the afternoon we passed sailing yacht *Maggie*, owned by Rob and Carol Harvey. She was one of only three boats participating in Jimmy Cornell's Blue Planet Odyssey, a round-the-world sailing event that started in 2014 and is aimed at raising awareness of the global effects of climate change. The other two boats in the rally were ahead of us and had already reached St Helena. Speaking on the radio to *Maggie*, we learnt that they had made a stopover in Namibia en route from Cape Town.

On Wednesday 16th November, while getting dressed for my morning watch, I was surprised by a fish that came hurtling unexpectedly through my cabin's hatch and landed beside me with a thud. Outside, *Louise*'s deck was covered with flying fish, which was a sign of the warmer weather. We collected the unfortunate creatures and Morgan filleted them before frying them and preparing a tasty lunch.

During the evening, we drew into full sight of the towering island of St Helena, which appeared like a shadow in the dark. By midnight we had passed the eastern shore, before swinging around onto the northern side to anchor in the shelter of the cliffs by the island's capital, Jamestown. St Helena-born Cheryl filled out the log with the simple phrase, 'My Island, My Home'.

First thing the following morning, we were picked up by a water taxi and taken ashore. Cheryl hadn't been to her home for some years and there was great excitement as we stepped onto St Helena. We parted company with Morgan and Cheryl on the docks as they had lots of catching up to do with family and friends. Meanwhile, Ian, Brigitte and I set off to explore this iconic South Atlantic island.

St Helena covers around 47 square miles of land and at the time of our stay its population was approximately 4,500, making it far from crowded. During our visit, we decided to use a small B&B on the main street in Jamestown, the Town House, as our base for exploring the island and its culture over the next three days. The town has retained much of its Georgian colonial features and charm. In the bank, shops, restaurants and bars, the locals we spoke to, who are known as 'Saints', were usually keen to converse and friendly. Aaron Legg, our tour guide on Saturday, was optimistic about the future of St Helena, since tourism was expected to get a shot in the arm with the opening of its new airport. He earned a living from a combination of two jobs: running a little farm and offering island tours.

Known as the 'Secret of the South Atlantic', St Helena was discovered by the Portuguese in 1502, but since 1659 has been under British governance. Historically, the island was used as a victualling and watering station for sailing ships returning from the East Indies via the Cape of Good Hope. But it is arguably best known for its role as a prison. In October 1815, its most famous visitor arrived on a British naval ship along with an entourage of twenty-eight people. Napoleon Bonaparte, the defeated Emperor of France, lived the last few years of his life on St Helena, dying in May 1821 at the age of fifty-one. Just over nineteen years after his death, his remains were repatriated to France and eventually laid to rest at Les Invalides in 1861. During Napoleon's exile, the island was under strict military control and maintained as a stronghold. Soldiers conducted round-the-clock patrols to prevent any opportunity for the renowned prisoner to escape.

Our visit in 2016 coincided with St Helena's first and long-awaited airport undergoing some teething problems. Although this huge building project, commissioned by the UK's Department for International Development, was complete, safety concerns had been discovered with regard to landing planes in potentially strong winds. As a consequence, the new airport had not yet been allowed to open for scheduled flights. The media blamed the British Government and their appointed contractors for this fiasco.

One of the last stops on our island tour was the Governor

of St Helena's official home, Plantation House. The property is best known for Jonathan, its resident tortoise, and the world's oldest living land animal. Believed to have been born around 1832 in the Seychelles, it is known that he was left on the island in 1882 but the circumstances of his arrival are unclear. The Governor's attractive two-storey home stands in contrast to Longwood House, where Napoleon lived during his exile. The latter is a modest, single-storey, T-shaped building and was chosen as the Emperor's residence mainly due to its location, as it was far enough away from the populated area of Jamestown. On the day we visited Napoleon's final home, which is preserved with its original furniture, the weather was overcast but the hills to the north were visible. The Emperor's bedroom featured the military-style camp bed that he slept in, but had few decorations and seemed modest.

On the evening of Saturday 19th November, *Louise*'s crew reconvened to continue the passage onwards to the Caribbean via the island of Ascension, a further 700 nautical miles north-west of St Helena. The two South Atlantic islands form a pair that remain under British sovereignty together with Tristan da Cunha. The latter is the most isolated of the three, lying 1,200 nautical miles south of St Helena in the remote South Atlantic Ocean, on the same latitude as the Cape of Good Hope. As we got on our way again, the lights on St Helena gradually faded astern. North of St Helena we passed close by the underwater Grattan Seamount, which at its highest reaches a depth of only 230 feet from the ocean's surface. In earlier days, Morgan made fishing trips there with his family, to catch tuna using long lines.

On our second night, and during my watch, we were motoring on a very glassy sea when navigation lights became visible on a ship heading straight for us. Once again we had run into the path of RMS *St Helena*, who this time was returning south after her trip to Ascension. Aware of our presence, she altered course to port, passing *Louise* with her starboard side facing us. Through radio contact I learnt that Cheryl's cousin was the Second Officer on board, and he soon came to the deckhouse to speak with her. At that time, the ship's deck lights were lit up and we could make out the colours on her funnel. We responded by switching our spreader lights on and off. As the *St Helena* disappeared over the horizon, we continued on our way.

On the morning of Wednesday 23rd November, we sighted Ascension Island, which is dominated by a large hill and visible from far away, and entered Clarence Bay at breakfast time in pleasant conditions. Three-and-a-half days after leaving St Helena, we were anchored at our next destination. Before securing *Louise* at her mooring and going ashore on the dinghy, we tied up to a floating refuelling barge to top up our tanks with diesel. This was a precautionary measure, in case we had to rely heavily on the engine during the remaining 3,000 nautical miles to the Caribbean.

Our day-long pit stop gave us the chance for a brief trip to Ascension, the most northerly of the South Atlantic islands, which lies approximately halfway between north-east Brazil and Africa. It was named by the Portuguese navigator and explorer João de Nova, who sighted the island on 21st May 1501, which was Ascension Day. Another famous visitor was Charles Darwin on his second voyage aboard HMS *Beagle* in 1836, when he described the place as an 'arid treeless island'. Not much has changed since his passage; Ascension's topography is mostly dominated by its volcanic terrain. In olden days, sailing vessels used the island as a stopover for victualling. Turtles, caught locally, were among the foods traded. Ascension remains a breeding ground for turtles that migrate across the Atlantic from Brazil to lay their eggs on the protected beaches.

Maximising our opportunity for sightseeing, we toured the island all day. This included driving up a steep and windy road leading to Green Mountain, the highest point on Ascension with an elevation of just over 2,800 feet. The lower level terrain has something of a lunar appearance, courtesy of the volcanic rock formations. A large military airfield is shared by British and US forces, and as we drove past the runway we observed a British Army drone taking off.

Supporting the presence of defence troops and other workers on the island is a small hospital. Cheryl's mother Eileen had been the senior nurse there for a number of years, and our arrival coincided with her final days living on Ascension before taking retirement at the end of 2016.

In the evening, we were invited to dinner at Eileen's house, where we also met Pete, Cheryl's stepfather. They made us most welcome and after a delicious meal we drove back down to the pier in their car. A group of fishermen were busy gutting their catch of the day, throwing scraps of fish into the water. These discarded morsels had attracted sharks, which milled around in the shallow water. The biggest was over 9 feet long, which we identified as a Galapagos shark. This species, often found around oceanic islands, is a ferocious predator.

Morgan went down the ladder to fetch the dinghy, which we had earlier left moored to a buoy tied by a line to the quayside. One by one we stepped into the dinghy, while holding onto the supporting ropes with great caution to avoid falling into the quay. As we were pulling away from the dock, a shark poked its head out of the water at the stern, startling us. Everyone quickly leant inwards, fearing that it would reappear. Needless to say, we were all very glad to get back onto *Louise*'s deck and feel safe once more.

A little later, at 10 p.m. on Wednesday evening, we lifted the anchor and motored quietly away from Ascension. Now bound directly for the Caribbean and our return to the northern hemisphere, we settled back into our regular watch routine. That night the sky was totally clear and the stars shone brightly over *Louise*.

Our plan was to head north-west initially and approach the equator before changing course to the west towards north-east Brazil. With the forecast for the coming few days promising very little wind, we wanted to get out of the area of calm and find the trade winds, even if they were weak, further north.

Meanwhile, we had plenty of free time on our hands. In terms of pastimes, Ian was focused on honing his astro-navigation knowledge, taking sights with his sextant and plotting our position, partly in preparation for the 2018 Golden Globe Race which he had formally entered. The event would coincide with the fiftieth anniversary of the first round-the-world, single-handed, non-stop race in 1968, which was won by Sir Robin Knox-Johnston. At this point in November 2016, Ian was still keen to take part and had already secured a boat, but the following year he chose to withdraw his entry. It turned out to be a wise and prescient decision: of the eighteen yachts that crossed the start line, just five completed the race, and of those that retired from or abandoned the competition, five were dismasted. Many suffered capsizings too, and one injured sailor had to be rescued from his damaged boat in the Southern Ocean.

As our forecast had predicted, about 250 nautical miles north-west of Ascension we began to pick up the trade winds. Waking up to a bright morning in the tropics, on Friday 25th November we pulled up the spinnaker and enjoyed a good day's run. Saturday was spent similarly under spinnaker, steering by hand mostly, with *Louise* gliding along in the smooth conditions. The only other company in the vast ocean was an occasional fishing vessel.

At teatime on Monday 28th November, 1,000 miles since departing Ascension, *Louise* crossed the outbound track of our maiden Atlantic crossing to Brazil in 2013 at 1.52° South and 30.18° West. Three years and two months earlier, we had sailed past this very point in the ocean, approximately 170 nautical miles north-east of the Brazilian archipelago of Fernando de Noronha. This was a cause for celebration and a bottle of champagne was opened. Before drinking any of it, we poured some onto the deck, toasting *Louise* who had carried us safely across the oceans. Checking the log revealed that, to reach this point, we had covered over 47,000 nautical miles in our circumnavigation. It was a moment to savour. The atmosphere on board *Louise* was calm, no doubt in part due to the constant south-easterly trade winds pushing us gently on.

In a sign that land wasn't too far distant, a number of boobies began to appear overhead. The course we were sailing ran almost parallel to the north-eastern coast of Brazil, passing offshore Fortaleza before continuing west towards Belém and then just beyond the mouth of the Amazon. One of the advantages of this route across the Atlantic is to profit from the westerly equatorial current that flows parallel to the coast of South America, which helped to carry us along the entire north coast of Brazil until we reached the waters of French Guiana.

While sailing off the Brazilian coast, we managed to pick up one particular booby that took a liking to perching on *Louise*'s bowsprit. The black plumage on its head looked like a judge's wig. From its vantage point, the bird could survey the waters ahead of the boat and keep an eye out for prey. We watched the booby take off regularly to catch flying fish, but it was never successful. Each time the bird missed his target he circled back around the boat, landing on the bowsprit to wait for the next opportunity. We, on the other hand, were lucky and caught a wahoo weighing over 15 pounds, which brought smiles in anticipation of another meal of fresh fish. During most nights our watches were uneventful, which afforded us the time to contemplate the constellations in the starry universe above at our leisure.

On Friday 2nd December at 5 a.m., we passed the equator at 42.50° West. As is customary, we performed the ceremony of initiation for crossing the line on the aft deck. 'Scallywag' was the derogatory name that was given to less experienced sailors who had not yet crossed the equator. Our Scallywag Ian submitted with good humour to the time-old ceremony, which included dunking his head in a bucket full of galley waste.

When passing the mouth of the Amazon, we were expecting the colour of the sea to change to brown, caused by sedimentary deposits from the world's largest river. But 200 miles from land we were too far offshore to encounter any sign of sediment in the ocean. After leaving Brazilian waters we paralleled the Guyanas, at which point our progress slowed down a little as the trade winds softened. The sea turned slightly brown as we sailed into the shallower waters on the continental shelf for a short period of time.

The days continued to pass by quickly, and there were more frequent sightings of freight ships and fishing boats. With regard to on-board recreation, our backgammon tournament reached a crescendo and in the closing round Morgan won convincingly to be crowned Champion of the Atlantic.

In the final few days of our approach to the Caribbean, the trade winds picked up again and we achieved excellent average daily runs. On Wednesday 7th December, during Brigitte's breakfast time watch, we passed by Tobago sailing full speed. Then, less than two weeks since leaving Ascension, we spotted Grenada just before lunch. Helped along by wind and current, we had managed to average over 10 knots during the passage. Once the mainsail had been dropped and neatly folded, and we had got out our fenders and mooring lines, we motored into the Port Louis Marina at St George's, Grenada's capital.

As we approached the dock, we were surprised to see my friend Andrew McIrvine with his wife Deborah waving to us from the pontoon. We soon discovered that our arrival had coincided with the Royal Ocean Racing Club (RORC) Transatlantic Race from Lanzarote, which was scheduled to finish around the same time. Andrew was on duty as the RORC Admiral to officially welcome the finishing teams.

Our emotions were buoyed by the realisation of having sailed 3,000 nautical miles from Ascension on top of the prior leg from Cape Town, via St Helena, thus completing the longest passage of the Adventure. We also began to acknowledge the fact that we had, in effect, completed our world circumnavigation. On safely reaching our destination once again, we shared a quiet feeling of accomplishment with Morgan and Cheryl, who had been our fellow travellers all the way. For their part they had decided that, upon arrival in the Caribbean, it was time for them to bid us farewell and set off to pursue their own dreams. Reflecting on the years that had passed since we first met the couple in early 2013, it had been our great fortune to share their company during the journey to this point. We snapped a final picture of the four of us on the foredeck of *Louise*, before wishing them happiness on their own boat.

After exchanging good wishes with Ian we said goodbye, thanking him for his friendship and company during the long Atlantic crossing.

As I sat on the plane as it took off from Grenada to bring

Brigitte and me home for Christmas, my mind wandered back over the many miles that had led all the way from Jersey to Grenada, via the Atlantic, Pacific and Indian Oceans. Stopping in the Caribbean Islands was a detour on the way home, but a great place to visit as we approached the end of our Adventure.

Chapter 13 – Treasure Islands
Grenada, Lesser Antilles to Bermuda and Halifax, Canada

Francois Bay, Newfoundland, Canada

Just over three weeks later, on Friday 30th December 2016, Brigitte and I returned to *Louise* in Grenada along with our old friends Enrico and Marcela Bombieri. The boat was still lying in Port Louis Marina, where we were met by her new crew, Richard Boutet and Elena Aloisio. It was their first role together crewing as a couple and they were obviously keen to get going. Morgan and Cheryl had given them a comprehensive briefing and induction to ensure a smooth handover, although it is hard to pass on tacit knowledge and so makes the start for any first-time crew a challenge.

Richard took us to see *G Force*, the 100-foot catamaran that he had skippered for the previous five years, which was moored a few berths away from *Louise*. Originally named *Gitana 13*, in her heyday this vessel had won the Jules Verne Trophy for the fastest round-the-world sailing record in 2002, completing the voyage in a little over sixty-four days. It was difficult to imagine that she was used by the present owner for cruising.

During our visit to Grenada with the Bombieris, we made an island tour with a local guide named Dave and stopped at the River Antoine Rum Distillery. The buildings dated back to the colonial era and the equipment was mostly antiquated. The distillery's charming guide, Patsy, offered us a tasting of their finest rum. On inspecting the label, we discovered that the product was a stiff 85 per cent alcohol by volume.

Another agricultural feature on Grenada and the West Indies generally are breadfruit trees, whose fruit was originally imported by the British Navy from Polynesia in the eighteenth century in order to improve the diet of the slaves who worked on the sugar plantations. The first expedition to transport seedlings from the Pacific was under the command of Captain Bligh and was interrupted by the mutiny on HMS *Bounty*, which Bligh commanded. The ship's cargo of plants was completely destroyed, but this did not stop breadfruit from eventually reaching the Caribbean.

We spent our first night on board at anchor, leaving early

on New Year's Eve for Union Island, part of St Vincent and the Grenadines and a quick sail north in the easterly trade wind. The boat gently heeled over in the reaching conditions with the wind on our beam and we sailed along nicely. Making a pit stop at Union to conduct customs formalities, we continued later to Saline Bay on Mayreau, the smallest inhabited island in the Grenadines, to anchor for the last night of 2016. Ashore that evening we ate alone in a little family restaurant named Island Paradise, where friendly staff served us a great meal. As we walked back to the beach, we saw that a crowd of locals had gathered in the main street, with Caribbean sounds blaring from loudspeakers celebrating the final hours of 2016. Back on *Louise*, we brought in the New Year with a toast at midnight. The Bombieris had commandeered the cockpit as their night quarters, preferring to sleep outside under the open sky.

On New Year's Day 2017 we motored the short distance around to Tobago Cays, one of the most iconic anchorages in the Grenadines. Although already quite crowded with visiting yachts, we found a good spot to anchor in the shelter of the reef. The next morning, we took the dinghy to explore the nearby uninhabited island of Petit Tabac, where Marcela, Enrico and I went for a stroll, admiring coral sculptures that had been erected on the beach. We also enjoyed a swim in the transparent blue water of the island's lagoon. To mark my sixty-first birthday that same day, Brigitte gave me a copy of Wouter Verbraak's book *Beyond the Break*, about the grounding of *Team Vestas Wind* during the 2014/15 Volvo Ocean Race on the Cargados Carajos reef at St Brandon, an archipelago in the Indian Ocean north-east of Mauritius. Wouter, whom I have always admired, would join *Louise* the following month as our navigator for the RORC Caribbean 600 race.

Returning to Mayreau that evening, we had arranged

for a beach barbecue to be organised by a local fisherman named Patrick. With his quirky entrepreneurial streak, Patrick asked to be called Mr Handsome and his young assistant, who cooked us fresh lobster on the grill, was introduced as Mr Spliff. The names seemed to capture their respective characters quite well.

Moving further north on Tuesday 3rd January, we later arrived at Canouan, which we found rather non-descript. The northern part is off limits to visitors and has a chequered history of failed real-estate projects, one of which involved Donald Trump. On the southern end of the island, private jets land at the airstrip, ferrying well-to-do tourists in and out. Canouan's brand-new Glossy Bay Marina was deserted and there wasn't a boat in sight. Continuing our tour on an old golf cart, we noted that the locals were always smiling.

On Wednesday morning, we sailed a short way north to Mustique, made famous by Princess Margaret and Mick Jagger. We were met on the dock by a German acquaintance who drove us up to his family's house, perched on the hilltop in the middle of the island. From the verandah there were beautiful views east over the Atlantic and west to the Caribbean on the leeward side of Mustique. On the journey back to the boat after lunch, we made a brief tour of the north of the island, passing elegant villas hidden from the gaze of passers-by. Mustique's population is made up of owners who come to relax and make the most of the exclusive surroundings, and locals who mainly help to run the small tropical island. We had dinner in Basil's Bar that evening and were entertained with some live music.

Our next stop on Bequia, the most populated island in the Grenadines, was not far away. After being dropped ashore in Friendship Bay, we found a taxi and went to do some sightseeing. During the drive, we took the opportunity to visit a local turtle farm, an initiative that was started to protect the species from the ravages of illegal fishing.

Much of the history of Bequia relates to the past struggles between France and Great Britain. Both nations set great store on mastering the seas to manage these faraway islands in order to control the proceeds from trade. The Treaty of Paris in 1763 produced a significant realignment in the map of the Caribbean: the former French colonies of St Vincent and the Grenadine islands, including Bequia, as well as Grenada were given to the British in exchange for Guadeloupe, Martinique and St Lucia.

Richard and Elena moved *Louise* on Thursday afternoon, anchoring for the night in Admiralty Bay, which was named after Lord Nelson who had been to the Caribbean as a naval commander. Tied up adjacent to *Louise* was a Southern Wind 82 yacht named *Ammonite*. Owned by Marcus and Caroline Blackmore from Sydney, whom we had last seen in Fiji almost two years previously, they invited us on board their new vessel for drinks. The sleek-looking boat was only a year old and had just completed her first transatlantic crossing. Marcus is an accomplished skipper and winner of multiple trophies, racing TP52s and other boats, including Dragons.

Moving off early on Friday 6th January, we bid farewell to our Aussie friends, hoisting our sails for the 60-mile passage north to St Lucia. By mid-afternoon, after a fast day's sailing, we had docked in Marigot Bay. This harbour on the leeward side of St Lucia was a convenient place for Enrico and Marcela to leave us. We celebrated the end of our cruise with the Bombieris that evening at the Rainforest Hideaway restaurant, catching a foot ferry back to the boat after dinner.

On Saturday morning, we completed the departure papers, albeit with some delay, and waved goodbye to our friends as we sailed out of the harbour. Next up was a short passage to

St Maarten, 275 nautical miles to the north. As expected, the sailing was stop and go due to long wind shadows in the lee of the islands of Martinique, Dominica and Guadeloupe. Arriving at St Maarten on Sunday afternoon, we managed to miss the opening of the bridge into the lagoon by just ten minutes. After a night spent rolling slightly while anchored at Simpson Bay, we found our berth mooring on Monday morning alongside some quite large yachts, which made *Louise* look small by comparison. The following day, on Tuesday 10th January, Brigitte and I set off back home, leaving *Louise* in her new temporary island home in the Caribbean.

* * * * *

In February 2017, we decided to take some time out from our cruising on *Louise* to compete in the ninth edition of the Royal Ocean Racing Club's Caribbean 600 race. The event, which had become a popular addition to the offshore sailor's bucket list, takes competitors on a 600-mile tour around the West Indies' Leeward Islands, starting and finishing at Antigua. At its most northerly, the race passes around St Maarten before heading south to round Guadeloupe, and en route it sails by Barbuda, St Kitts and Nevis, St Barths, Montserrat and the tiny island of Redonda, which is the final racecourse mark prior to returning to Antigua. By the time the yachts have crossed the finishing line, contenders have sailed twelve legs past eleven islands, most often in strong winds, putting both boats and crew under pressure.

While we were away, Richard and Elena had stayed on in St Maarten to prepare *Louise* by putting her into race mode. Mirroring the adjustments made for the Sydney Hobart Race, furniture had been removed, non-essential gear offloaded and the tanks emptied, so the slimmed-down boat now weighed about 5 tons less than usual. Once everything was ready, the crew sailed her down to Antigua a week before the start of the race.

When Brigitte and I landed in Antigua on Friday 17th February, we found *Louise* moored in the marina at Falmouth Harbour. The rest of the crew also started to arrive, including our friends Klaus Diederichs and Jens Rathsack, who came with their wives, as well as Dwayne Lysaght and Andrew McIrvine. We were joined by a further nine sailors, most of whom we had raced with before, and the boat's regular crew, Richard and Elena. Our former skipper Morgan Morice had also flown in specially, excited to rejoin Team *Louise* for the event, and was accompanied by his wife Cheryl.

On Sunday we took *Louise* out sailing, with race tactician Ruairidh Scott and crew boss Maurice O'Connell, aka 'Prof', taking charge while we practised manoeuvres. We went through some drills, including checking the boat's set-up and running through the safety procedures. Back onshore, gathered in front of the whole team, our navigator Wouter Verbraak provided a comprehensive weather briefing. His forecast predicted that the trade winds would be interrupted by a winter front moving through the race area from north to south. Unfortunately, such unstable conditions would lead to the regular easterly trade winds temporarily shutting down and the wind dying for a period. As expected, Wouter's predictions proved to be accurate.

On Monday 20th February, the day of the race, we said goodbye to our wives as we left the dock. The weather was perfect, with classic warm Caribbean conditions including a fresh easterly wind. Soon after exiting the marina, we hoisted our sails and then gathered around the start line at Fort Charlotte outside English Harbour, along with seventy-six other competing yachts. We were grouped together with the biggest boats in the race, and although many were faster than *Louise* we picked a good lane in which to get going after the gun. It took us around an hour sailing close-hauled before we could bear away onto a spinnaker reach to head north towards Barbuda, where there was a turning mark.

During the first night, we rounded south of St Kitts and Nevis, changing course to head north. The next day, morale on board was excellent and we kept up good speed right into the second night, when we ran south past Montserrat in the fading breeze. By the third day of the race, however, as predicted *Louise* became totally becalmed as we passed by the south of Guadeloupe. It was barely possible to keep the boat moving and we sat on board frustrated by the inaction. For much of the day the sea was flat calm, glistening mirror-like in the sun. Some competitors began to give up hope of finishing and abandoned the race, but we remained patient in the knowledge that the wind would return, which it did on the Thursday afternoon. In the end we completed the 600-mile course in just under four days, crossing the finishing line off English Harbour, Antigua, in the early hours of Friday 24th February. We docked *Louise* just before sunrise and were greeted by our wives, who had got up at dawn to welcome us back.

That afternoon we were invited, together with our race crew, to a champagne lunch in the beachside restaurant at Pigeon Point. Naturally, I responded with a brief speech, thanking everyone for their efforts and saying our farewells. *Louise* had done us proud in the Caribbean 600 race, but it was time for the boat to revert to her normal life as a blue-water cruising yacht.

* * * * *

Our final opportunity to sail in the Caribbean came up during the Easter holidays, and we arrived in the British Virgin Islands (BVI) on Friday 14th April 2017. During the upcoming nine-day voyage there, we only sailed 80 miles, which included a full tour of the archipelago. It would turn out to be the shortest leg of the entire Adventure.

This area of the Caribbean has long been a favourite haunt for sailors. In the seventeenth century, with the growth of trade with the New World, pirates appeared in search of riches that they could steal. The islands and inlets that make up the Virgin Islands offered the perfect hideaway for these lawless buccaneers. One famous character associated with the Virgin Islands and the Caribbean more generally is Sir Francis Drake, a privateer whose ship sailed under a 'letter of marque', which was a form of licence granted by the reigning monarch. These letters sanctioned individuals to wage war, capture prisoners and take prizes, such as enemy vessels. Any valuables were usually sold and the proceeds shared among the ship's owners, the captain and crew, together with a reward for the king or queen. The pirates and privateers are long gone, but the Virgin Islands remain a popular destination where sailors can enjoy sheltered waters and well-protected anchorages.

Brigitte and I landed at Beef Island Airport together with our eldest daughter Juliette, where we were met by our captain Richard. Before our arrival, the crew had sailed *Louise* over from St Maarten, where she had been based since the Caribbean 600 race. We walked to the dinghy dock, which is conveniently located next to the airport car park, and found *Louise* anchored close by. Brigitte's sister Isabelle and her partner Christoph were already on board, along with our other crew member, Elena. Everyone was naturally happy at the prospect of a short family reunion in this beautiful part of the tropics.

On Saturday morning, we woke up early to start exploring and motored a little way to the other side of the Sir Francis Drake Channel. We stopped at The Baths in the south of Virgin Gorda Island, a popular attraction for visitors. The shoreline is strewn with big granite boulders, some balancing one on top of another, which create sheltered sea pools on the edge of the beach. Tying the dinghy on a buoy close to the beach, we swam ashore and began crawling through the paths under the rocks. Just behind the shore we could see lizards and snakes moving around in the dry undergrowth. We climbed up some boulders from where we could admire the transparent blue water lapping on the small beaches and inlets below. Reaching the southern tip of Virgin Gorda, we were rewarded with an uninterrupted view of the expanse of the Caribbean Sea stretching out over the horizon. The rocky scene reminded us of similar shorelines in the Seychelles in the Indian Ocean. In both cases, over millennia granite rocks had been shaped and smoothed by the pounding of ocean waves.

A short afternoon sail took us further along Virgin Gorda Sound, where we anchored at Leverick Bay not far from the Bitter End, beyond which the Atlantic Ocean lies. We had arranged to rendezvous here with our Scottish friends and fellow Ocean Cruising Club members, the MacKenzies. Gordon and Helen were moored in the bay on board their yacht *Mantra*, a Sundeer 56 on which they had successfully completed a full circumnavigation.

During the evening, we were all generously invited to dinner at the Leverick Bay Hotel as the guests of David and Mary Tydeman, where we joined an Oyster Yachts prize-giving dinner. We chatted with some of the Oyster owners, who had just finished their regatta and, notwithstanding any rivalries, were clearly enjoying each other's company.

On Sunday morning, we set off on a brief sail to Anegada Island, just 15 miles north of Virgin Gorda. The MacKenzies had already charged on ahead under full sail and were proceeding nicely in the steady easterly wind. We put a reef into our mainsail and eventually caught up with *Mantra*, and not long after both yachts were anchored in the lee of Anegada at Pomato Point. We went ashore to make an exploratory visit of the sparsely populated island by car.

Whereas the Virgin Islands are mostly mountainous, Anegada is low and flat, formed by coral and limestone. We passed by some ponds where pink flamingos breed and so we stopped to observe these elegant birds. The highlight of the island tour was swimming in clear blue water inside the ocean reef at Loblolly Bay on Anegada's north shore. Our dip in the sea was followed by a delicious lobster lunch, which the MacKenzies treated us to at a laid-back beachside restaurant.

For dinner that evening, which we ate on board *Louise* with Gordon and Helen, Elena had prepared a lamb dish, the traditional meal served at Easter in Italy. It was accompanied by some Groot Constantia red wine that we had brought with us from Cape Town. This particular wine was Napoleon's favourite and it is known that he drank it with his meals during his exile in St Helena.

After dinner we said farewell to the MacKenzies. Before departing, they left us with a bag of warm clothing that they had packed in readiness for the North Atlantic crossing back to Europe, as they would be rejoining us later in the year.

On the morning of Monday 17th April, we set sail, heading south to return to sheltered waters where we could relax for the rest of our short stay in this Caribbean idyll. Unfortunately, with quite a swell running in the Sir Frances Drake Channel, it wasn't going to be comfortable to stop at the day anchorage at the Dog Islands as we'd intended, so we continued further west, also bypassing Ginger Island before finally setting anchor at Manchioneel Bay on Cooper Island. In the afternoon, Juliette, Christoph and I managed to dive at Red Bluff Point, where the visibility underwater was good. Later in the evening, we watched the sunset from the beachside terrace at the Cooper Island resort.

Eager to do more diving, the following day after breakfast we set off to explore the wreck of the RMS *Rhone*, which had foundered off the coast of Salt Island in October 1867 and was remarkably well preserved. Her entire iron hull is encrusted with coral and overrun by fishes, and although the wooden decks have rotted away, she still provides an excellent swim-through for divers. Entering the water from our dinghy, this was an easy dive for amateur scuba enthusiasts such as ourselves and we all had a great experience.

Peter Island, our next stop, offered scenic walks ashore, and then on Wednesday we went to nearby Norman Island and donned our diving gear once again. This beautiful location is one among many that is said to have been the inspiration for Robert Louis Stevenson's *Treasure Island*.

Later in the afternoon, we took the dinghy to the William Thornton, a floating drinking establishment where yachties gather for a fun end to the day. Richard was celebrating his birthday and, after observing other patrons jumping off their boats into the water, it was not too long before he joined in and leapt off *Louise*'s stern, plunging into the sea. The day ended on the boat with Richard cutting a birthday cake that Elena had baked for him.

Early on Thursday morning, Christoph and I managed a pre-breakfast dive on Angelfish Reef off Norman Island. Underwater the light was beginning to penetrate the depths and we saw lobsters scurrying about along the seabed, before probably going into hiding for the day.

Moving further on the following day, we sailed close by St John Island, which is the easterly of the two main US Virgin Islands that border BVI territory and is home to the Virgin Islands National Park. The national park encompasses most of the island, which has a beautiful landscape and is covered from shore to peak in green vegetation. St John's coastline, which we observed as we passed by, is dissected by various bays, many of which have attractive beaches. Unfortunately, cruisers sailing on yachts like *Louise* can only set foot on these islands if they possess a full USA visa. As none of us had one, our only option was to remain in the BVI, and so we rounded the western tip of Tortola Island to continue a short way north to Jost Van Dyke Island.

We aimed straight for the most easterly anchorage in the lee of Green Cay. To the south of Green Cay, the land extends to form Sandy Spit, which offers good shelter for visiting yachts. We took the dinghy to explore the spit and saw a couple of kite surfers making the most of the windy conditions. After a relaxing lunch on board *Louise*, we moved back west to the bay at Great Harbour. Late in the afternoon, together with Juliette, Isabelle and Christoph, we drank sweet 'Painkiller' cocktails – made with pineapple juice, orange juice and rum – at Foxy's, one of the BVI's most famous drinking establishments. The spirit measures must have been generous, as after the second round of drinks we all felt quite tipsy.

On Saturday morning, after abandoning the idea of attempting a final dive due to the murkiness of the water, we decided to make one last onshore trip to Jost Van Dyke and walked to Bubbly Pool. Standing on the edge of the water, we were doused by waves as they surged through a narrow gap in the rocks leading out to the sea. A friendly group of American travellers from California chatted with us while they also enjoyed the waves in the pool.

After lunch, we put up the sails and headed towards Cane Garden Bay on the northern side of Tortola. Pulling the sheets in tight, we sailed close to the wind, reaching Cane Garden after a couple of tacks. The bay has a narrow entrance through a gap in the reef, which we approached cautiously. After successfully negotiating the reef, we then dropped anchor at a good spot close by the beach. Visiting the village, we discovered Callwood Distillery, which is the oldest rum still in the Eastern Caribbean but looked more like a museum. This was perhaps not surprising as the Callwood family had been distilling Arundel rum here for more than 300 years. We bought a few product samples for savouring back on board *Louise*.

Later in the day, Juliette and I paddle-boarded around Cane Garden Bay and discovered a large shoal of tiny fish on which some birds were hungrily feeding. To celebrate the end of our cruise around the Virgin Islands, we ate our final dinner in the village and then went dancing at the bay's Paradise Club.

The next morning, on Sunday 23rd April, we said farewell to Isabelle and Christoph, dropping them ashore on Tortola so they could start their journey back home to Switzerland. Once they had departed, we motored further east, passing Tortola's north shore to reach Beef Island, where we anchored close to the spot where we had commenced this cruise nine days earlier. In the afternoon, Juliette, Brigitte and I flew back to Antigua where we would pick up a connecting flight onwards to London. As we took off in the early evening, our plane climbed up through the clouds, leaving behind the BVI and the Caribbean where we had created many more good memories.

✵ ✵ ✵ ✵ ✵

Following our visit to the BVI, *Louise* returned to St Maarten briefly before travelling north to Bermuda to complete the first stage of our homebound North Atlantic crossing. This short leg was the only one during the entire *Louise* Adventure that I decided not to sail, and instead remained at home while Richard and Elena took the boat north along with two other crew. On Wednesday 17th May, they arrived in Bermuda after successfully completing the 800-mile passage from St Maarten, journeying along the eastern side of the mythical Bermuda Triangle in just under five days.

Bermuda is a popular destination for European yachts heading eastbound. Our stop in Bermuda in late June coincided with the staging of the 35th America's Cup finals at Great Sound, whose entrants compete for the oldest international sporting trophy, also known as the Auld Mug. Under the rules, the challenger – in this case Emirates Team New Zealand, representing the Royal New Zealand Yacht Squadron – was competing against the defender, which in 2017 was Oracle Team USA, representing the Golden Gate Yacht Club. The first team to attain seven points would be crowned 'Defender of the America's Cup'.

Earlier in the competition, during the challenger series (officially known as the Louis Vuitton Challenger's Trophy), five teams had competed for the right to take on the defender. Team New Zealand had convincingly outperformed four other teams representing Great Britain, France, Japan and Sweden. According to the rules, the Americans had won the qualifying round in early June, earning Oracle Team USA a bonus point. The challenger from the southern hemisphere would therefore begin the finals a point behind, a deficit that they were doubtless keen to overturn.

Having recorded four wins out of four on the opening weekend, 17th and 18th June, Team New Zealand had already established a strong lead and so to hold onto the Auld Mug, the USA would have to make a big comeback. But tension was still high at the start of the concluding round of races, evoking memories of the 2013 competition in San Francisco, when Oracle overturned a similar lead by Team New Zealand to retain the Cup.

I had arrived alone in Bermuda on Thursday 22nd June, just in time to witness the climax of the America's Cup before continuing with the next leg of the Adventure, bound for Canada. Joining me for both events were my friends Michael Barlow – a keen sailor whom I had met at Harvard Business School – and his partner Clélia Gueguen. Yolanda Williamson, a Canadian friend, would also be accompanying us on the passage to Halifax, Nova Scotia. Yolanda had previously lived in Bermuda and kindly introduced us to her friend and local Bermudian Albey DeSilva. Albey's help with the local authorities was most useful in securing a berth for *Louise* at the Royal Naval Dockyard, which was conveniently located right by the America's Cup Village.

The following day, I took a foot ferry across the harbour to do some sightseeing in Hamilton. Bermuda was full of visiting yachts of all descriptions, in particular the magnificent J Class fleet, most of which were moored together at the Royal Hamilton Yacht Club. These classic yachts, which range from about 120 to 140 feet in length, are considered the peak racers of the era when the Universal Rule determined whether a yacht was eligible to race in the America's Cup between 1914 and 1937.

On Saturday 24th June, I went for a brief morning stroll along the road overlooking the America's Cup Village and watched the boats being prepared for racing. Prior to launching, the wing masts are lifted into place on the catamaran before the vessel is craned into the water. Other onlookers were also observing the preparations for the day's racing. The GBR Land Rover BAR Team camp was deserted after their decisive elimination from the challenger series, and of the other challenger syndicate sheds, only Japan's Soft Bank Team base showed any sign of life, with a huge Rising Sun flag fluttering from a crane.

To watch the races, we planned to use *Louise* as a spectator boat and so we left the dock with Michael, Clélia, Yolanda and Albey plus three guests. Dan Gribble, an American friend of my brother Lloyd, had sailed his boat to Bermuda from New England together with fellow sailing buddy Steve Wimsatt, and they joined us along with Dana Timmer, who himself had competed in four America's Cups with US teams. Choosing a good spot in the spectators' area, we anchored close to the leeward mark. From our vantage point we could see the 45-foot catamarans close up as they charged downwind before rounding the mark onto the next leg. As the start for each race approached, tension began to build, with helicopters buzzing overhead adding to the atmosphere.

In the first race of the second weekend, Oracle got the best start, but Team New Zealand had an edge in terms of speed that the defender was lacking and soon overtook Oracle, moving into a commanding position. Losing the fifth race in a row, by that point the Americans had their backs to the wall. So it was good to see Oracle win the second race and keep their chances alive going into Sunday.

Also visiting Bermuda to watch the America's Cup finals was fellow Dragon racer and friend Ferenc Kis-Szölgyémi and his wife Johanna, who had chartered a sailing boat in Bermuda on which they could watch the finals. After the races on Saturday, the couple joined us on board *Louise* for drinks.

On Sunday, we returned with *Louise* to another spot on the course, this time without Dan and his friends, to follow the action on the water. After Oracle lost the first race, a sporting miracle was needed to save the USA's chances of retaining the America's Cup. When the eighth race ended with Team New Zealand pulling off a decisive victory, the Kiwi challengers had an almost unassailable five-point lead and needed to win just once more to triumph in the America's Cup.

After the day's sailing was over, we moved *Louise* to a bay where we could have a swim in the warm water. In the evening, we met Ferenc and Johanna for a dinner in the town overlooking Hamilton Harbour. They introduced us to their guest, the Hungarian sailing legend Nándor Fa, who had successfully completed two Vendée Globe round-the-world races, and with whom we enjoyed a fascinating evening of conversation.

On Monday morning, we passed Dan Gribble on his boat *Brigadoon* outside the Royal Naval Dockyard as *Louise* was leaving the marina. It had been prearranged that *Brigadoon*, an attractive, 55-foot cafe-racer-style yacht designed by Bill Tripp, would take over *Louise*'s berth. Coming over in the dinghy, Dan and his crew gave each of us the gift of a cap, before bidding us farewell.

By late morning, we had motored round to the eastern end of the island at St George's, which had a lovely harbour where pleasure craft check in and out through Customs and Immigration. Ashore we went to St Peter's Church, one of the oldest places of worship in the Americas, and strolled around the town's small and pretty-looking streets. At lunchtime, we congregated in a pub in the harbour to watch the ninth Cup race on TV. From the beginning, it was clear that the USA team had still not found the speed required to overcome the Kiwi challenger. Crossing the line to secure a seven points to one victory, the tiny nation of just under five million people could celebrate winning the America's Cup for the third time.

For the Bermudians, who had successfully hosted sailing's most prestigious trophy, the moment was tinged with sadness as the next competition would move on to Auckland.

As soon as the Immigration Office reopened after the final race, we completed our checkout and prepared to leave. Late on the afternoon of Monday 26th June, we lifted anchor and left St George's on our way to Nova Scotia, Canada. As we exited the harbour, the crew gave Michael, Clélia and Yolanda the customary safety briefing. Motoring out, we passed the reef that surrounds Bermuda and provides the island with some much-needed protection against the ocean swell beyond.

Halifax, the capital of Canada's Nova Scotia province, lies 750 nautical miles due north of Bermuda. At this time of the year, the weather is usually good and we expected the passage to take approximately four days. During our first night we encountered some thunder and lightning, but it was a long way off. However, the following twenty-four hours brought rain, hail and some windy squalls. Taking it all in our stride we continued north, savouring the peace and tranquillity of being at sea again. We passed by a group of pilot whales, who paid absolutely no attention to the boat.

During the passage we crossed the Gulf Stream, which flows in an easterly direction towards the mid-Atlantic. Although this warm ocean current is not visible to the naked eye, satellites monitor sea temperature to allow real-time charts to be produced that show its location, direction and speed. Reaching approximately 36 degrees north, although we hadn't altered *Louise*'s compass heading, the boat's course changed dramatically as we were pushed east by the current. The Gulf Stream, which was up to 3 knots at its most powerful, drove *Louise* sideways as we sailed through it. As we approached Halifax, a steady south-westerly wind picked up, which made our journey easier. However, it had also become noticeably colder on board and during the last night of the journey some fog was visible on the horizon.

Arriving in Halifax, which is home to one of eastern Canada's most well-sheltered harbours, on Friday 30th June we dropped our sails and motored to our berth downtown at the Maritime Museum pier. Coincidentally, we were just in time for Canada Day on 1st July, and this year's celebration would mark the 150th anniversary of the country's independence. Large crowds had already gathered in the city for the special occasion, and the pavements were thronged with smiling, friendly people. We also received a wonderful welcome from the pleasant local yacht agent, Anne-Louise. Once the immigration formalities were completed, we stepped ashore to visit Halifax and its bustling shorefront.

On Saturday, after some more daytime sightseeing mainly along the city's attractive waterfront, we walked up to the main park overlooking the town to watch the Canada Day fireworks in the evening. There were masses of people and all around there was a happy and celebratory atmosphere.

The following day, after saying cheerio to Michael, Clélia, Yolanda and the crew, I set off to catch a plane back to London. The flight only took five hours, a sure sign that *Louise* was getting closer to home.

Chapter 14 – Home Waters
Nova Scotia, Canada to St Pierre & Miquelon and Jersey, Channel Islands

Homebound, North Atlantic

On Sunday 16th July 2017, after shutting the door of our London flat, Brigitte and I flew back to Canada accompanied by our friends Alastair Whyte and his lovely wife Kathy. Alastair was joining us for the third time on *Louise*, but this would be Kathy's first experience. During the flight over from Heathrow, the plane skirted Ireland's southern coast, and from my seat window I managed to see very clearly the famous landmark of Fastnet Rock. On our return to Canada, the plan was to explore the Atlantic coast of the country's Maritime Provinces before heading home by crossing the North Atlantic.

Outside of Halifax and a few other larger towns, eastern Canada is sparsely populated. The indented nature of the coastline means that visiting sailors are spoilt for choice in terms of anchorages and shelter from the winds and tides. There were many decisions to be made regarding the best places for stopovers and sightseeing during our upcoming cruise.

Before we arrived back in Canada, Richard and Elena had moved *Louise* a little further along the coast from Halifax to the old town of Lunenburg, a UNESCO World Heritage Site, where we would begin the final chapter of the Adventure. Steeped in history, this pretty-looking port offered us a great introduction to the heritage and culture of Nova Scotia.

Lunenburg is one of the earliest settlements that Europeans had established on the Canadian seaboard and the town's name is closely associated with fishing. Commercial fishing took hold shortly after the discovery of North America in 1492, once it became known that the cold waters in these latitudes had plentiful stocks of fish. For centuries, boats crossed the Atlantic on a seasonal basis to fish for cod. Once caught, dried and salted, the fish was exported to Europe and other regions, becoming a staple part of ordinary people's diet. Though fishing was a dangerous business, with harsh working conditions and frequent loss of life, the rewards were substantial. The Grand Banks of Canada were the richest fishing grounds in the North Atlantic, until overfishing during the twentieth century drove them to the edge of extinction. Man's greed and short-sightedness succeeded in killing off an entire industry, putting tens of thousands out of work and driving many communities to breaking point. Though fishing had always been at the heart of Canada's soul, in recent times society had been forced to adapt to new circumstances.

The town seemed a good place to start our Canadian cruise and begin exploring the rich history of this part of the Atlantic coastline. To settle in properly, we decided to spend two nights there and take full advantage of the opportunity to see the local sights and enjoy some meals ashore.

Lunenburg's quayside is lined with colourfully painted houses and old commercial premises that are associated with age-old fishing activities. During a guided tour around the town, we learnt how the Acadian settlers were expelled in 1760 after France's defeat in the Seven Years' War. In the Treaty of Paris, which settled scores after the war, France ceded control of Canada to England. Lunenburg became a base for fishing Atlantic cod and rode the wave of the export boom in salt cod. The bustling town, with its well-protected inner harbour, flourished and attracted a large fleet of boats, reaching a high point in the age of the *Bluenose* schooner. This magnificent sailing boat, which we visited, still floats and has been well maintained, capturing the spirit of a bygone industry and historic way of life in Canada's Maritime Provinces.

At anchor we spotted *Ticonderoga*, the iconic Herreshoff 72-foot ketch built in 1936 at the Quincy Adams Yacht Yard in Massachusetts. We had first seen her in Bermuda the previous month. She would pass close by *Louise* the next morning when leaving Lunenburg, and we managed to exchange a few words with her skipper, who revealed that they were returning to her home waters in New England.

On the morning of Tuesday 18th July, Brigitte and the Whytes set off in a rented car to head back to Halifax by road in order to explore the scenic coastline, including the fishing village of Peggy's Cove with its famous lighthouse. Meanwhile, Richard, Elena and I cast off *Louise*'s moorings to take the boat to Halifax. We motored all the way and spent much of the time driving through dense fog, though on the land it was a clear day with blue skies. Fog is common off these Atlantic shores. It's caused by warm air from the south passing over cool seawater, which is then chilled by the Labrador Current.

That evening, we all met up at the dock in downtown Halifax close to where we had stayed on our initial visit to Canada back in late June. Prior to our arrival, we had spoken on the phone with the Ocean Cruising Club Port Officer John van Schalkwyk, who later met us on board *Louise*. Over a cup of coffee, he shared information about the coastline and recommended a number of stopping places.

Being in no rush to leave, over the next two days we spent time sightseeing in Nova Scotia's capital, riding bikes through its parks, going to the Canadian Museum of Immigration, where more than a million immigrants had landed during the twentieth century, and sampling the cuisine in local eateries. On our second evening, Dan Gribble, with whom we had parted company in Bermuda in late June, coincidentally arrived on his boat *Brigadoon* from Maine. He and his wife invited us for dinner that evening and we ate a superb meal at a nearby seafood restaurant.

On Friday 21st July, we left behind this memorable Nova Scotian city and started to make our way further along the coast. First stop was Owls Head Harbour, a good anchorage

40 nautical miles east of Halifax, where we secured *Louise* by the small breakwater and dock. We took an afternoon stroll in bright sunshine over the peninsula, walking a couple of miles to the old fishing village. It was eerily empty, with the fishing boats all tied up and seemingly inactive. We later learnt that the lobster season had closed at the end of June, when the entire fleet stops work to give the fishery a rest.

The following day, we set off towards Sheet Harbour, and finding ourselves with a little time to spare we decided to explore further up the river towards the town, where we had a brief walk ashore. We had planned an overnight stop at Sober Island so as to meet up with my friend and former business colleague Peter Mielzynski Jr, a larger-than-life character who had accepted our invitation to stay with us on *Louise* on Saturday night. Entering the anchorage, which we discovered was very well sheltered, we gave Peter a call and agreed whereabouts we could pick him up, then took the dinghy to fetch him.

In the afternoon, we went on a pre-arranged outing to Sober Island Oyster Farm, which Richard had organised for us, and were later greeted at the pontoon by the owner, Trevor Munroe. After becoming acquainted with his family over a welcome beer on the Munroes' patio, we climbed onto the back of their pick-up trucks and were driven over to the oyster farm. Then, we were all invited to get into an open boat, on which we motored through the farm, going by rows of oyster beds until we reached a spot where the water flows in from the sea. After anchoring, Michelle Munroe and her daughter started to shuck open some pre-harvested oysters, passing them around for everyone to taste. Their son had brought his fishing line and soon began hauling in some small mackerel. We opened a bottle of locally produced white wine to accompany the oysters, which everyone agreed tasted delicious. Back ashore, and joined by other members of the Munroe family, we ate barbecued oysters topped with cheese, which were also really tasty. Once all the food was consumed, we went back to *Louise* and had a late dinner.

On Sunday morning, we invited the Munroes on board for some coffee, and they arrived laden with pastries that they had freshly baked. We sat out in the cockpit, chatting over coffee, and thanked them for their hospitality during the previous afternoon. After the Munroes had left the boat, we decided to explore the bay at Sheet Harbour Passage, taking a ride on the dinghy around Westhaver Island, which was very pretty. Back on *Louise* we ate lunch in the cockpit before saying goodbye to Peter, whom we dropped ashore so that he could head home to Toronto.

In the afternoon, we motored further east to the Liscomb River, discovering another quiet and well-sheltered anchorage. Close by *Louise* we spotted our first bald eagle, sitting high atop a tree overlooking the anchorage. The weather was forecast to change and a strongish easterly wind was expected, so we decided to spend the next two days in West Liscomb and make the most of this peaceful corner of Nova Scotia. Shore activities included hiking up the river along a forest trail and passing beautiful waterfalls, which we did on Monday morning, before sea kayaking in the afternoon with the Whytes in one canoe and me alone in the other. The Whytes treated us to dinner that evening in the Riverside Lodge, where we enjoyed grilled salmon cooked on a cedarwood plank over an open fire.

On Tuesday 25th July the sky was grey and overcast, but although this did not put us off from wanting to explore the historic village of Sherbrooke, we couldn't find any transportation for the 20-mile journey. When the marina manager, Chester, overheard our predicament, he offered to lend us his car for the day, a gesture that clearly demonstrated how generous and hospitable Canadians can be. After arriving at Sherbrooke, we found the open-air museum that depicts village life in the late nineteenth century. We looked inside some of the original old buildings, including a working blacksmith's, a pottery shop and several animal barns, before having a good lunch in Beanie's Bistro. Back on board *Louise* in the surroundings of the secluded anchorage at Liscomb, with no other boats in sight we were treated to a beautiful sunset.

The next morning, we set off at sunrise for the short passage across the Canso Strait to Cape Breton Island. The sea was mirror-like as *Louise* made her way out of the inlet where we had been tucked away. Just before reaching the open sea, we discovered that the engine was overheating, so we dropped anchor to stop and examine what the problem was. Richard found that the seawater intake impeller had broken, starving the engine of any cooling, but after he installed the spare part we were on our way again.

With little wind we motored all day, heading for Louisbourg, and at lunchtime passed Cape Canso, which lies at the easternmost point of Nova Scotia. At one point in the journey, we came close by the three-masted brigantine *Guayas* of the Ecuadorean Navy under full sail. Later, we also saw the German sail training ship *Alexander von Humboldt II*. Both vessels were participants in the Tall Ships Transatlantic Race and had most probably just left the Gulf of St Lawrence and were navigating the Canso Strait before starting their Atlantic crossing towards Europe. The other highlight of the day was sighting a leatherback sea turtle.

During Wednesday evening, we arrived at our destination on Cape Breton Island, passing the imposing buildings of the old French settlement of Louisbourg near the entrance to the bay. The seaport, named after King Louis XIV of France, was settled by the French in 1713 and was an important centre for commerce and trade with Canada until 1758. Following the first Siege of Louisbourg in 1745, during which a British fleet and a New England colonial force overcame the town, and a second siege in 1758 that led to a definitive victory for the British Royal Navy, the French colonial era in Canada was brought to an end.

On the morning of Thursday 27th July, while standing on the Louisbourg pier we watched a boat being unloaded and the fish being weighed. One huge halibut was hoisted by its tail high above the dock and the person at the weighing-machine shouted '185 kilos'. Everyone let out a loud cheer for what we assumed was a record catch. Some fishermen kindly offered Elena a selection of locally caught fish for free, which she gratefully accepted. We then set off to the Louisbourg visitor centre, catching a bus that took us the short distance around the bay to where the old settlement formerly stood. The fortress, which was built in the imposing French neoclassical style, had already been designated a National Historic Site of Canada in 1920, and in 1961 the Canadian Government began a $25 million project to reconstruct about a quarter of the original town and fortifications, 200 years after their destruction at the hands of the British. Throughout the fortress site there were guides dressed in period costume, either acting the part of an historic character or providing information.

That evening we enjoyed a costume dinner at the Beggar's Banquet, an eighteenth-century-style themed restaurant, where we dressed up as sailors. Food was soon served and we joined in the fun with dancing led by the owner of the restaurant, Linda Kennedy, whom we would later meet.

The next day, we set off to round the eastern tip of Cape Breton at Scatarie Island, taking a shortcut through the Mainà-Dieu passage. Later we passed by Sydney, the main town on the island, before continuing further north towards the entrance to the Bras d'Or Lake, south of Cape Dauphin. While we waited at anchor for the tide to turn, we spotted an eagle soaring high above Scatarie, before entering the narrows that lead into the lake. A road bridge with a 118-foot clearance crosses the lake near the entrance, leaving just enough for *Louise* and her 105-foot-high mast to navigate through.

By early evening, we were moored at the lovely village of Baddeck, a brief journey by dinghy from its yacht club. We were greeted by a local couple, Paul and Donna Jamieson, who had been visiting a Swiss yacht named *Whimsy*, which was anchored adjacent to *Louise* and owned by the Racamier family. The late Henry Racamier, who built *Whimsy*, was a non-executive board member at Laurent-Perrier Champagne like me, and best known in sailing circles for helping to establish the Louis Vuitton America's Cup challenger series with Bruno Troublé in the early 1980s. During a conversation with Paul, he enquired what our plans were and then offered to lend us a car the following day, so we could drive around the Cabot Trail.

At 9.30 a.m. on Saturday 29th July, we met Paul in the car park next to the yacht club and then set off on the 185-mile drive to take in the magnificent scenery on the western side of Cape Breton, overlooking the Gulf of St Lawrence. In the distance, the Magdalen Islands were now discernible. We made a number of stops on the way to take in the views and to eat lunch. The end of the tour took us over a narrow stretch of water on a chain ferry and we were back in Baddeck by teatime. After going to see Paul and Donna at their house, which overlooks the Bras d'Or Lake, we thanked them by inviting them out for dinner that evening.

On Sunday morning before leaving Baddeck, we went to the Alexander Graham Bell National Historic Site, which is just across the water from Beinn Bhreagh, the home where the Scottish-born inventor of the telephone spent much of his time during the summer months, mainly to escape the heat in Washington DC where he was based. His love for Canada dated back to when his parents emigrated to the country from Edinburgh in 1870, when he was a young man. Baddeck would become Bell's spiritual home.

Prior to our departure from the Bras d'Or Lake, that afternoon we stopped for lunch in a quiet bay and then had a pleasant swim in the warm waters. Afterwards, we continued on our way to Sydney, leaving the lake via the main easterly entrance through which we had originally passed, and docking adjacent to the cruise ship terminal in the evening. Later on, Kathy presented us with some lovely drawings and sketches that she had made over the last two weeks.

On Monday morning, we had another visit from Paul Jamieson, whose office was in Sydney. He offered to introduce us to Andrew Prossin, the Managing Director of One Ocean Expeditions which operates polar adventure cruises. A little later, we went aboard one of the company's chartered ships, the *Akademik Ioffe*, which was moored at the cruise dock next to *Louise*, where we met the captain and some of the officers. Back in 2014, we had passed the *Akademik Ioffe*'s sister ship, the *Akademik Sergey Vavilov*, in Antarctica.

At lunchtime Gordon and Helen MacKenzie arrived as planned, having driven all the way up from Halifax Airport. They handed over the keys of their rental car to the Whytes, who would be returning it to Halifax Airport before catching their flight home. After lunch we said cheerio to Alastair and Kathy, wishing them a safe trip back to London.

In the early evening, we ate outside on the verandah at a

tavern overlooking the harbour, basking in the warm sunshine. Back on board *Louise*, after a safety briefing we cast off our moorings from the tidy pontoon in Sydney at 9 p.m., leaving the small river estuary and setting course for the island of Newfoundland.

We were happy to be sailing again with the MacKenzies, who had first been on *Louise* in Australia, two years previously, during our trip to the Torres Strait. We were also excited about crossing the Atlantic together, and had planned some exploration ashore once we reached our destination. From Cape Breton we headed north-east towards Newfoundland's south coast, much of which is deserted. Newfoundland is a large island that lies off the north-east coast of Canada. Aside from the Avalon Peninsula, where half the population lives, the rest of the island is sparsely inhabited. The provincial capital, St John's, faces the Atlantic on Newfoundland's east coast.

For the 175-nautical-mile crossing from Cape Breton, we had decent conditions and made landfall close to Aviron Bay during late afternoon on Tuesday 1st August. As we motored into the fjord that cuts about 4 miles into the south coast, passing dolphins and seals on the way, eagles glided around the hilltops that towered over the fjord. At the head of the inlet, beyond a narrows in the bay with a sandbar, was a cove where we found ourselves alone and surrounded by steep slopes.

The next morning, we went on a hike and climbed up a hill adjacent to a mountain stream that ran down into the cove. The air was still, and looking down over the bay we surveyed the wilderness around us, but could see no obvious signs of life.

After returning to *Louise*, we lifted anchor and motored back out into the open sea, following the coast a short way further east. By lunchtime we were moored at a pontoon in the picturesque tiny settlement of Francois, which is pronounced Fran-sway. The sun was shining and the village, with about seventy inhabitants, could not have looked prettier, except possibly on a crisp and frozen winter's day. Isolated from civilisation, except for a daily ferry service, there are no roads to Francois and so in the afternoon we set off on foot to explore the surroundings. A chat with a fisherman revealed that the local accent was similar to Cornish. He explained that the fishing season was closed, so he had time on his hands to relax and exercise by walking.

Our visit included a brief hike to the lookout high above the bay, from where the island territory of St Pierre & Miquelon was clearly visible in the distance. In the evening, we experienced one of the finest sunsets we had seen in Canada, against the backdrop of the bay with the mountain shadow reflected on the water.

On Thursday morning, once again we motored further east to the Bay d'Espoir, where we encountered a spouting whale. Moving the boat closer, we were able to identify it as a fin whale. Often around 80 feet long, this species of whale rarely displays its flukes. Our whale gracefully gave out three bellows of air before disappearing underwater.

As we made our way along the north of Long Island, the shoreline reminded us of the approach to the Firth of Clyde near Glasgow, where Gordon, Helen and I had all seen the sea for the first time as toddlers. We found a secluded bay to stop for lunch, but the holding ground was poor so we continued on our way westwards around Long Island and through Little Passage, where the occupants of a little fishing boat were busy collecting scallops. In the narrow cut, some eagles were in flight and we spotted one land on a rocky outcrop overhanging the sea below.

Further south we motored into Gaultois, a small fishing harbour on Long Island, but again couldn't find stable holding ground that was fit for anchoring. However, we eventually located a good shelter for the night in the cove at Piccaire, a bit further west.

Our final day's sailing in Newfoundland, on Friday 4th August, involved an easy passage 45 miles south to Fortune, on the Burin Peninsula, which is a long stretch of land pointing out into the North Atlantic. Anchoring in front of Fortune's harbour, we went ashore to do some reconnaissance and have a walk around the little fishing community.

The harbour, from where the ferry to the French island of St Pierre departs, was crowded with fishing boats that were mainly tied up to sheds, some of which were built on stilts and stood over the mud. We managed to find a car to rent and, that evening, Brigitte, Gordon, Helen and I each packed an overnight bag and left the boat to explore part of Newfoundland by land. In our absence, Richard and Elena motored with *Louise* the short distance to St Pierre, to begin preparations for our transatlantic crossing.

After an overnight stop on the way north, on Saturday the four of us drove towards Bonavista, over 180 miles north of Fortune. We wanted to explore where John Cabot had landed on Newfoundland in 1497, five years after Christopher Columbus had discovered the Americas. Both these great navigators were Italian, working for the monarchies of England and Spain respectively. Cabot, born Giovanni Caboto, was believed to be from the region of Genoa and gained Venetian citizenship before being commissioned by King Henry VII to 'find, discover and investigate whatsoever islands or countries, regions or provinces'.

Walking on the cliffs overlooking a calm sea near the Cape Bonavista lighthouse, we could clearly see a number of whales basking in the sea below, while a few puffins perched on the rocks. In Bonavista itself we visited a reproduction of Cabot's ship, the *Matthew*. Inside a specially constructed building, we found the replica of the wooden caravel that Cabot had sailed on with a crew of eighteen seamen, after leaving Ireland and making landfall in the vicinity of Bonavista on 24th June 1497 following a six-week crossing.

Driving on a further 220 miles westwards, on Saturday evening we reached Twillingate, a quaint village that looks out over sea stretching north to Labrador. It was too late in the season to see any icebergs, as all had melted by this point in the summer, but during our brief stay we enjoyed eating fresh snow crab for dinner.

Early on Sunday we set out for Fogo Island, which we reached by car ferry. Stopping at a roadside shop with a sign that read 'Flat Earth Society', we learnt why this island is believed to be one of the corners of the Earth. I bought a small drawing, which had caught my eye, of an ancient sailing vessel falling off the edge of the ocean. Exiting the road at the iconic Fogo Island Inn, a stark modern edifice built on rocks, we were only able to glimpse at the lobby as other parts of the famous hotel were off limits to non-residents.

At this point it was time to start heading back south to rejoin the boat. Looking at the map, we realised that we had only visited a corner of the vast island of Newfoundland. Sadly, we didn't get close to seeing L'Anse aux Meadows in the far north of Newfoundland opposite Labrador. It was there in the early eleventh century that Vikings became the first Europeans to step onto North American land, crossing on their longboats from Greenland. The courage the Vikings had to venture forth and explore was without limit; these early Nordic seafarers were truly made of hardy stock.

Back in Fortune, after our three-day round trip that

took us over 1,000 miles on the road, we returned the rental car to Don, the owner of the local garage. Reflecting on our Newfoundland experience, the people whom we met were friendly but generally a little reserved. Indeed, Newfoundlanders are well known for their introspection, a character trait that is captured exceptionally well in *The Shipping News*, a book by E. Annie Proulx which is set in this unique Canadian province.

While waiting in Fortune for the ferry to St Pierre Island on Monday 7th August, we had a lunch of simple fare in the local cafe that we discovered was another of Don's businesses. Boarding the foot ferry, we noticed French police were keeping a beady eye on the passengers, but they were friendly when they asked us why we were visiting.

On our arrival in St Pierre after the one-hour crossing, we could see *Louise* moored on the pier next to the yacht club alongside a few other boats. One of them, a beautiful classic Alden design, was on its way back to the USA after a summer cruise. While chatting later to the friendly Seattle-based crew, they kindly offered us their help if we ever sailed to America's west coast. *Midnight Summer Dream*, an elegant French-owned Sparkman & Stephens yacht, was moored stern to stern with *Louise*. She had competed in the Royal Western Yacht Club's Two-Handed Transatlantic Race in May 2017 and had encountered some extremely rough conditions. The boat had been knocked down twice, with the mast touching the water, but had still managed to finish the race successfully and its crew was now preparing to sail home to France.

We had been encouraged by Paul and Donna Jamieson, the Canadian couple whom we had met in Cape Breton, to introduce ourselves to a friend of theirs named Marcel Dagort, who was the owner of the largest supermarket on the island. Late on Tuesday afternoon, Brigitte and I met him in his office above his family's retail premises, and then invited him for a drink on *Louise*. After driving us back to the dock, Marcel came aboard and we listened to him talk about the history of St Pierre, particularly that of the twentieth century. We learnt that the first major setback to the island's economy was when the ban on alcohol sales in the US was repealed in December 1933. This marked the end of the lucrative 'rum running' trade, which duly collapsed. St Pierre had been at the heart of this operation and Al Capone was one of the island's most famous visitors during Prohibition. We had previously noticed that on a few of the streets in town, some of the houses had wood-panelled walls made from the sides of old shipping crates, mainly from Scotch whisky brands.

Marcel also told us that, more recently, the moratorium that the Canadian Government declared on the northern cod fishery along the east coast in 1992 caused many local fishing businesses to go bankrupt, and with heavy job losses the island's population dropped. As a consequence of extreme ignorance, people had simply not understood that fish couldn't be heavily fished and then swiftly reproduce in such a way as to be permanently sustainable. St Pierre's past mirrored these historic events.

On Wednesday we went to L'Île-aux-Marins, which still has a few inhabitants but is also a living museum to St Pierre & Miquelon's maritime heritage. Walking around the island stirred up images of its culture and history of fishing, which stretches all the way back to the first settlement of the Acadians on these shores, arriving as immigrants from France, to the collapse of the Atlantic cod fishery.

Meanwhile, Richard and Elena were making final preparations for our departure and we kept periodically examining the weather predictions to check for the ideal moment to set off home. Before leaving, we took the opportunity to go for a short hike on the highest part of St Pierre, which led along a path that took us down to the west side of the island, where there were good views over Langlade, the southerly part of Miquelon. The sun shone brightly on the channel between the two islands, making the sea sparkle. All in all, this small French outpost off Canada's Atlantic coast is unspoilt, but at times can be a very windswept place.

Looking back on the three-and-a-half weeks we had spent in Nova Scotia, Cape Breton and the southern coast of Newfoundland, it had been an exceptional experience. During our stay, we had been kindly welcomed by the people, seen some charming sights, learnt about the history of the region and discovered some great anchorages and night stopovers along this attractive coastline. Thanks to many warm and sunny days, the weather had also treated us well and never hampered our progress. It no doubt helped that we had timed our visit to coincide with the height of the summer.

On Thursday 10th August, all was set for the final leg of our round-the-world adventure, which was now nearing the end of its fourth year. Choosing St Pierre & Miquelon as the point of departure meant that a comparatively brief voyage of 2,200 nautical miles lay ahead, which was considerably shorter than our two earlier Atlantic crossings. Apparently, luck was on our side in the form of a reasonable forecast for the coming few days. At 8.15 a.m. we let go our lines and motored slowly out of St Pierre Harbour. By mid-morning the breeze had filled in and we set full sail. For the first two days of the passage, *Louise* slid along really smoothly over the Grand Banks, making the most of the settled weather conditions. Apart from a few fog patches the going was good, all the time on a flat sea. This was not the scene that we had imagined, but we were grateful to accept the mercy shown us by the wind gods.

East of the Avalon Peninsula there had been some reports of ice drifting south in the Labrador Current, which runs parallel to the eastern shore of Newfoundland. To avoid any close encounters with ice, we sailed south-east to stay away from danger. By tracking *Louise* in this direction, it had the additional benefit of positioning the boat to the south of any passing low-pressure weather systems crossing the Atlantic from west to east. So by keeping south of any such lows, when a front arrived we would benefit from a following westerly wind.

Brigitte and I stood our first night watch from 11 p.m. to 2 a.m., and with mist persisting over a perfectly smooth sea, it was very quiet on board and felt like *Louise* was sailing in stealth mode. Lying in my bunk when I was off watch, I could hear the water glide by the hull and the waves lapping on the boat's side. On our second day, we continued to sail under bright-blue sunshine, passing a couple of fishing boats. In centuries past, these waters would have been full of fishermen in their dories jigging all day long for cod, then filling up the hold of the mother ship before returning to port in Newfoundland or to harbours further west.

Later, a ship that was invisible on the chart plotter began to draw close. As it came nearer we could clearly tell that it was a warship. Passing by *Louise* the Canadian Navy vessel acknowledged us, in a friendly gesture, with a blow of its horn.

By sundown on Friday evening, we had left the continental shelf and the shallow waters of the Grand Banks. Heading out into the North Atlantic, there were just under 2,000 nautical miles to run. Meanwhile, we had entered an area of high pressure and the wind duly dropped, so we motored onwards. The sea was mirror-like, not what you would normally expect in this part of the North Atlantic so far away from land.

Throughout Saturday there was still no sign of any wind.

On Sunday morning, there was a beautiful sunrise over a flat, calm sea and just before lunch a couple of whales were spotted. By the end of the day we were lucky enough to have rediscovered some steady breeze and set the sails again. During the evening it became a little squally, with the wind picking up to a steady Force 6 to 7, and so we reefed the main. The night sky was very clear, with Venus's reflection visible on the water.

Louise moved along nicely over the next few days, with the wind always aft of the beam and surfing along at up to 15 knots. The boat took the pleasant sailing conditions in her stride and it was a comfortable ride for everyone on board. We only encountered a limited amount of shipping traffic, being overtaken one night by a freighter, whose AIS signal indicated that she was bound for Antwerp on the River Scheldt. At one point a lone turtle swam by *Louise*, which was unusual considering how far distant we were from any land. The odd tern also fluttered past; these seabirds are known for travelling long distances across water, migrating to and from the polar regions.

On Tuesday 15th August, we gybed onto port tack to run further north in search of better wind. The harbour master in St Pierre had advised us that locals regard mid-August as the time when the weather begins to turn. The windier autumn season usually starts to show its face around then and Atlantic depressions appear more frequently. As if on cue, on downloading the forecast we observed a deep depression that had swept up from the Caribbean, tracking northwards parallel to North America's eastern seaboard, and was now off Newfoundland bringing gusts of over 80 knots. Talking over dinner that evening, we remarked that we were fortunate to have left Canada when we did, timing our departure well.

Thankfully, we had established plenty of distance between *Louise* and the big blow to our north.

From first light on Wednesday, we were entertained by shearwaters carving their flight path close to the water and showing off their white underbellies. On a few occasions they were accompanied by pods of dolphins that played with the boat's bow wave. There was more to celebrate as we reached the halfway mark of the journey and were treated to a tea party complete with a delicious apple and haskap berry cake baked by Elena. The midpoint in the crossing also coincided with our passing the same longitude as the Azores, a group of Portuguese islands that are part of the mid-Atlantic Ridge, and which we sailed over that day. Richard had spent some time living in the Azores and highly recommended visiting the archipelago.

With the wind holding up from the west, our destination was now less than a week's sailing over the horizon to the east. At this stage, I was running out of reading material, so Gordon and Helen offered a book from the selection of novels they had brought and I dug into *Monsoon* by Wilbur Smith. The story reminded me of when we were sailing in the Mozambique Channel, where much of the hero's swashbuckling adventures take place. I finished the last few pages one evening while on watch, when sailing under a clear sky with only the stars and the Milky Way resplendent above, and occasional flashes from aircraft lights.

On Friday 18th August, excellent news reached us via email that our daughter Valerie was expecting our third grandchild, a baby girl. Meanwhile, the wind had begun to drop again, so more motoring was in prospect. During the day, we realised that our AIS ship identification system was not functioning when a huge container ship overtook *Louise* at speed but wasn't visible on the plotter. Consequently, extra care was needed when looking out for other vessels, although we would still use our radar to plot the speed and direction of any boat within close proximity to *Louise*. That same day we were regularly accompanied by larger birds that circled the boat, which we identified as petrels. They frequently landed on the water and then dipped their heads into the ocean, presumably to fish.

With approximately 600 more nautical miles to go to reach Land's End in England, we started to encounter quite a lot of whales, which were easy to spot each time they spouted. Now that it was late summer, we could tell by studying the chart that they were migrating from the feeding grounds of Greenland, Iceland and other polar waters, and heading to warmer seas further south. Our guidebook indicated that many would be on their way to the Cape Verde Islands, a popular summer breeding location for the whales, about 2,000 miles south of our current position. A few of these mammals passed close enough to *Louise* to enable us to identify them as humpbacks.

As we began to approach the European continental shelf and the Celtic Sea, fulmars and gannets appeared in fairly sizeable numbers. One solitary gannet flew below our stern, gliding away effortlessly, while the fulmars circled around *Louise* for what seemed like an eternity. The constant sight of seabirds was a sign that land was no longer too far away. On the penultimate night at sea, our spirits were raised further by Richard cooking us roast lamb, which we thoroughly enjoyed, accompanied by a full-bodied red wine.

During the last full day at sea on Sunday 20th August, we had a great run under sail. There were considerably more ships to contend with and on a couple of occasions we furled our headsail, slowing down to keep our distance from cargo ships passing close by. Not wishing to be outdone by Richard, Elena prepared a delicious three-course meal for the final dinner of the passage that featured Canadian scallops and various Italian-inspired delicacies on the menu. There was no doubt that we had certainly been well fed for the duration of the crossing.

At eight o'clock after dinner, with the wind dropping we lowered the sails. As dusk descended, we began motoring the final few miles towards the English Channel. The sea was busy with fishing boats and as we approached the shipping lanes, cargo ships appeared to be heading in all directions. Gordon and Helen's final night watch coincided with crossing the main shipping lane off Ushant, with freight vessels passing the western tip of France to be avoided in particular. Navigating was not made any easier by the dense fog that came down during the night as we motored parallel to the French coast. These conditions off Brittany are quite common during the summer. Using our radar at night we kept track of passing fishing boats, and during daylight hours, when we were close enough to read their bow numbers, we noticed that most of the fishing boats were from Roscoff in north-west France.

On Monday 21st August 2017, the date of my late father's birthday, the fog had finally cleared by mid-morning on our final day at sea. At 11.30 a.m., we sighted the Roches-Douvres lighthouse and by teatime we had reached the Channel Islands, and moored *Louise* securely at Jersey's Elizabeth Marina.

The round-the-world *Louise* Adventure thus drew to a quiet end, just as it had begun in August 2013. We thanked our friends Gordon and Helen, as well as the crew Richard and Elena, for their help in steering *Louise* back to home waters. But most of all, I thanked Brigitte for her support and for being my soulmate in achieving our goal of circumnavigating the globe.

Crossing the Atlantic for the third time during this expedition had taken eleven days over the final leg, and had shown once again how capable *Louise* was in bringing us successfully to port. The end-of-passage celebration that evening naturally concluded with a dram of whisky to toast our safe arrival.

Our circumnavigation had landed us on the shores of thirty-five countries with over 55,000 nautical miles passing under *Louise*'s keel. During her four-year-long Adventure, the Blue Lady had passed Cape Horn, the Cape of Good Hope and navigated each of the world's three great oceans, opening our spirits and stretching our minds. We had visited old friends and met new ones along the way, and gathered some unforgettable memories. For all this and our other many blessings, we could only be thankful.

Acknowledgements

I wish to begin by thanking everyone who sailed with me during the *Louise* Adventure, beginning with my wife Brigitte. Together we planned the construction of *Louise* and she accompanied me on board for most of the expedition, missing only a few passages. We also were very fortunate to have our daughters Juliette, Valerie and Claire, along with our son-in-law Luka, Ivo our eldest grandson and Claire's partner Dave, join *Louise* at different points in the journey. My brother Lloyd, sister-in-law Isabelle and her partner Christoph were all wonderful companions, too.

To all our friends who travelled with us for parts of the Adventure, whose names are mentioned in the book, an enormous thank you for standing watch, helping out above and below deck in various different ways, playing multiple rounds of backgammon and spending time together during explorations ashore. Most of all, thanks to each of you for your loyal friendship and trust. Our fellow Ocean Cruising Club members, whom we met during the voyage and who offered us their camaraderie and support, also brought us inspiration.

To other friends and racing crews who joined *Louise* for limited periods, including during the Sydney Hobart and Caribbean 600 races, you all did such a great job. There are others, too many to mention, whom we met along the road, for whose generosity and hospitality we are also most thankful.

For anyone who followed the *Louise* Adventure blog from their armchair, I hope that you will find the content of this book consistent with my posts. I much appreciate your interest in my passion for all things related to the sea.

Our professional crew deserve particular thanks for making the expedition possible and keeping the show on the road, especially in the face of the inevitable challenges that arose along the way. Morgan Morice stands out as the best all-round sailor who I've had the privilege to be on a boat with. His passion, knowledge, seamanship and dedication are truly outstanding character traits, and his advice was always sound and hugely appreciated. Cheryl, his wife, was ever at his side and worked hard to keep the boat in good condition and ensure that everyone on board felt welcome and was well fed. In the closing stages of the Adventure, Morgan and Cheryl's shoes were ably filled by Richard Boutet and Elena Aloisio, who together picked up the baton and ensured that we continued to make safe landings, for which we are very grateful.

The team that helped to design and build *Louise* were acknowledged in the Prologue, and once again we are thankful for their craftsmanship and dedication. I wish, however, to express a special word of appreciation to our naval architect, Olivier Racoupeau. *Louise* exceeded all our expectations and was the perfect yacht with which to enjoy this round-the-world challenge; we certainly owe Olivier our sincere thanks for that.

Finally, I would also like to thank Helen Cumberbatch, who has diligently edited the manuscript, pointing out many inaccuracies and errors, which I hope have been corrected. But where the facts are not entirely true or there are other mistakes, I take full responsibility, and I hope that you will excuse me accordingly.

Grant Gordon
Kensington
July 2020